PROGRESSIVE PUNISHMENT

T0341360

Progressive Punishment

Job Loss, Jail Growth, and the Neoliberal Logic of Carceral Expansion

Judah Schept

NEW YORK UNIVERSITY PRESS

New York and London

NEW YORK UNIVERSITY PRESS
New York and London
www.nyupress.org

© 2015 by New York University
All rights reserved

Library of Congress Cataloging-in-Publication Data
Schept, Judah Nathan.
Progressive punishment : job loss, jail growth, and the neoliberal logic
of carceral expansion / Judah Schept.
pages cm. — (Alternative criminology series)
Includes bibliographical references and index.
ISBN 978-1-4798-1071-0 (cl : alk. paper) — ISBN 978-1-4798-0877-9 (pb : alk. paper)
1. Punishment—United States. 2. Corrections—United States. 3. Imprisonment—United
States. 4. Criminal justice, Administration of—United States. I. Title.
HV9471.S356   2016
365'.973—dc23   2015021429

New York University Press books are printed on acid-free paper, and their binding materials are chosen for strength and durability. We strive to use environmentally responsible suppliers and materials to the greatest extent possible in publishing our books.

Manufactured in the United States of America

10 9 8 7 6 5 4 3 2 1

Also available as an ebook

MIX
Paper | Supporting
responsible forestry
FSC   FSC® C013604

CONTENTS

CONTENTS

ACKNOWLEDGMENTS

This book was written with the support of many people over many years. In my attempt to organize my experience of writing it and to acknowledge the iterations of support I have received, I consider the process in two broad stages, corresponding to its development first as my dissertation research and second as the book you now have in front of you.

In the first stage, I owe a great deal to several groups of people. I worked with a remarkable group of scholars at Indiana University, including Stephanie Kane, Khalil Gibran Muhammad, Phil Parnell, Hal Pepinsky, and Kip Schlegel, all of who provided rich insights, intellectual challenges, and important support. I drew inspiration from Stephanie Kane's writing and adventurous spirit for field research; her edits offered a fantastic point of departure for the reconceptualization of this project as a book. Hal Pepinsky has been a model of scholar-activism related to the specific issues that this book examines. His analyses of power and violence and his work on abolition have been influential to my development and certainly influence these pages. Khalil Muhammad pushed me to consider how the discourses of liberal carceral expansion continued the racial project of mass incarceration and helped in the development of my reflexive lens, particularly in examining how my positionality shaped my understanding of the data. Kip Schlegel has been a constant support over many years. The rigor with which Kip approaches social theory has made me a better scholar. Finally, my deepest gratitude and heartfelt appreciation goes to Phil Parnell. Reading drafts of every chapter and providing meticulous line editing, engaging me in discussions about hegemony and resistance that challenged my analysis and introduced me to important literature, and providing much-needed humor, Phil was more crucial to the success of this project than anyone else. He continues to be the epitome of a mentor, confidant, and friend, and I am profoundly grateful for it all.

While crafting the initial draft of what would later become this book, I benefited greatly from an experience helping Khalil Muhammad, Micol Seigel, and Michelle Brown organize a workshop at Indiana University examining the carceral state and the conditions of its existence. This book's insistence on the interdisciplinary study of carceral expansion owes a great deal to participants in "Carceral Studies across the Disciplines: Scholarship at the Nexus of Art and Activism," including Khalil, Michelle, and Micol as well as Lessie Jo Frazier, Sarah Haley, Ashley Hunt, Jenna Loyd, Dylan Rodriguez, and Rashad Shabazz.

The members of Decarcerate Monroe County (DMC) constitute a third group of people whose influence greatly shaped the analysis found in this book. Their names appear in these pages as pseudonyms and thus they don't receive the acknowledgement they deserve, but DMC kept me intellectually stimulated and politically inspired. Many of its members' insights enliven and enrich these pages as some of the most incisive analyses this book has to offer. DMC members were energetic and thoughtful and welcomed my dual role as both activist and scholar.

This first stage of the project occurred during a particularly emotional year for me: the loss of five loved ones over the course of fourteen months and, right in the middle of it, the birth of my first child, Talula. I needed some help managing the grief and the joy and lack of sleep. Conversations with Mattie White provided necessary relief. I did some of my hardest and most rewarding work with Mattie, and her encouragement of this research and her belief in me were crucial to my confidence and mental health.

I began to consider the project for a book almost as soon as I arrived at Eastern Kentucky University (EKU) as a new assistant professor. As it began to take shape in this second stage of the project's life, other people provided a variety of support. I am fortunate to work in an environment saturated with critical and thoughtful faculty members engaged in important scholarship. Avi Brisman, Victoria Collins, Kishonna Gray, Travis Linnemann, Gary Potter, Ken Tunnell, and Tyler Wall are amazing colleagues, and my work is better because of their influence. Conversations with Tyler in particular have forced me to think more fully—both historically and theoretically—about the political economy of carceral expansion. I am also lucky to work under the leadership of people like Preston Elrod, Victor Kappeler, and Peter Kraska, whose friendship and mentorship I greatly appreciate. In addition, I am thankful to the numerous graduate students who contributed assistance to and commentary on this project at various times, including Maria Bordt, Ryan Carr, Conrad Lanham, Jordan Mazurek, Bill McClanahan, and Melissa Pujol.

In the last several years, I have benefited greatly from friendships with colleagues across time, space, and discipline. Conversations with these scholars and activists in various contexts—on conference panels, through e-mail or the phone, during morning coffee breaks or over evening drinks, and in some cases on playgrounds with our children—have been productive, challenging, and affirming for me. In these ways, I am indebted to Lindsey Campbell Badger, Carla Barrett, Anne Bonds, Michelle Brown, Eamonn Carrabine, Alex Chambers, Alexandra Cox, Michael Coyle, Alessandro De Giorgi, Stefania De Petris, Danielle Dirks, Bronwyn Dobchuk-Land, Rachel Dotson, Jeff Ferrell, Jill Frank, Tim Goddard, Lisa Guenther, Kate Henne, Michael Hoerger, Grace Audrey Hunt, Jenna Loyd, Chris Magno, Erin Marshall, Bryce Martin, Jennifer Musto, Randy Myers, Justin Piché, Judy Rohrer, Sylvia Ryerson, Viviane Saleh-Hanna, Micol Seigel, Rashad Shabazz, David Stein, Brett Story, Lauren Taylor, Emily Troshynski, and Rob Werth.

Several people who contributed in important ways to this book passed away during its completion. Warren Henegar and Sophia Travis kindly spent time with me, offering honest appraisals of what they envisioned for the community and providing important local history. Hal Taylor and Mike Andrews modeled selfless and dedicated community activism. All four worked hard to create a more socially just community, and I am thankful to have had the opportunity to engage with them.

I owe a lot of thanks to New York University Press, in particular Jeff Ferrell, editor of the Alternative Criminology Series; Ilene Kalish, the press's executive editor; and Caelyn Cobb, assistant editor. My experience with them from start to finish has been rewarding. They deserve a lot of credit for carving out a hospitable, encouraging, and productive home for critical work. I am thankful for my experience with all three and wish to thank Ilene in particular for all of her support.

There are also individuals whose early influence in my young adult life deserves acknowledgment. I continue to find inspiration in the words, stories, insights, and analysis that Eddie C. and the other men from the Green Haven prerelease center in 1999–2001 shared with me.

Vassar College educators and scholars like Bill Hoynes, Eileen Leonard, and Larry Mamiya helped me channel some of my activist energy into serious study and critique. Activists and scholar-activists I met during my time as a summer intern at California Prison Focus planted important intellectual and political seeds. Their work, from afar, has continued to cultivate their initial influence on me. I am also grateful for the rich framework and analyses offered by the members of Critical Resistance (CR).

Throughout both major stages of this project, Michelle Brown's readership, support, and friendship has been sustaining and affirming. Michelle formally introduced me to EKU and to New York University Press and provided brilliant feedback on various iterations of this work. I owe her a great deal and remain very thankful for everything.

There are seven people who also have stood by me unconditionally for the duration of this project. I owe a great deal to my parents, Ken and Susan, for their love and encouragement and for modeling both quality writing and wonderful parenting; to my other mother, April, for all of her support over the years; and to my sister, Rebecca, for her fierce sense of humor and dedication to social justice. Her text messages and G-chats punctuated my writing and editing with much-needed comic relief as often as they shared links to political analysis that furthered my own. Finally, there are three people I am thrilled to see every day, whose inquiries into and observations of the world inspire me, and whose seemingly unconditional love for (and patience with!) me is returned so much more—around the sun, around the moon, and back. I am, of course, talking about Brooke, Talula, and Rhea, to whom this book, as everything, is dedicated.

Introduction

More judges and more "experts" for the courts, improved educational and therapeutic programs in penal institutions, more and better trained personnel at higher salaries, preventive surveillance of predelinquent children, greater use of probation, careful classification of inmates, preventive detention through indeterminate sentences, small "cottage" institutions, halfway houses, removal of broad classes of criminals (such as juveniles) from criminal and "nonpunitive" processes, the use of lay personnel in treatment—all this paraphernalia of the "new" criminology appears over and over in nineteenth-century reformist literature.
—American Friends Service Committee, *The Struggle for Justice*

It is in the nature of the calamitous situation existing today that even the most honorable reformer who recommends renewal in threadbare language reinforces the existing order he seeks to break by taking over its worn-out categorical apparatus and the pernicious power-philosophy lying behind it.
—Max Horkheimer and Theodor W. Adorno, *Dialectic of Enlightenment*

Thus, unconsciously, often incoherently, in thinking [about] the question of crime within the framework of common-sense ideas, the great majority of us have no other mental equipment or apparatus, no other social categories of thought, apart from those which have been constructed for us in other moments of time, in other spaces in the social formation. Each of the phases in the development of our social formation has thus transmitted a number of seminal ideas about crime *to* our generation; and these "sleeping forms" are made active again whenever common-sense

thinking about crime uncoils itself. The ideas and social images of crime which have thus been embodied in legal and political practices historically provide the present horizons of thought inside our consciousness; we continue to "think" crime *in them*—they continue to think crime *through us*.
—Stuart Hall et al., *Policing the Crisis*

The history of liberal law-and-order matters because the same proposals for better administration, proffered with the same good intentions, are likely to reproduce the same monstrous outcomes in the twenty-first century.
—Naomi Murakawa, *The First Civil Right*

A Disorienting Moment

In the spring of 2008, just a few weeks before county Democratic primary elections, I sat in the audience in a meeting room at the public library in the vibrant center of downtown Bloomington, Indiana. I was one of perhaps forty-five community residents who had gathered on this evening to hear current and campaigning Democratic county politicians speak about the local criminal justice system and the recently announced plans for its expansion in the form of a so-called justice campus. Although firm details of the plan had yet to emerge, the general contours of the facility had been made available to the public. The justice campus would sit on eighty-five currently vacant acres and would consist of three institutions—a new jail, a juvenile facility, and a community corrections work release center—accompanied by new offices for the county sheriff's department. The jail would more than double the capacity of the existing facility; the juvenile facility and work release center would create two entirely new institutions in the community. The justice campus would constitute the largest carceral expansion in the county's history.

I had been puzzled by the proposal for expansion. I had been living in Bloomington for three years and had come to regard as well deserved its reputation as a progressive—and certainly a college—town. A small city of 130,000 residents that is home to Indiana University, Bloomington had a lively local art and music scene, a downtown commercial district with a limited number of chain stores and thriving small businesses, and a strong network of community and nonprofit organizations. The governments of Bloomington and Monroe County boasted sustainability commissions, a peak oil task force, and a human rights commission. There was also a Bloomington City Council resolution condemning Arizona's anti-immigrant Senate Bill 1070 and symbolically boycotting the state. And there was an extensive, year-round farmers market and a strong local food movement. Dramatic carceral expansion seemed incongruous with this political and cultural identity.

The first official to speak that evening in the library was a long-time county politician named Reuben Davison, who was running for a seat on the Monroe County Council—the fiscal body of the county government. Davison had served in various political capacities in the county previously, including an earlier term as a council member and as a member of the Monroe County Board of Commissioners—the local executive leadership body. He was an outspoken liberal Democrat who frequently integrated his autobiography into his political speeches. Often, he invoked his military service in World War II and its radicalizing effect on his politics. He had returned to the United States from Germany and become a Quaker peace activist. On that night in the library, after introducing himself, he paused and then spoke again into the microphone positioned in front of him, offering a passionate condemnation of mass incarceration in the United States: "The shame of this country in the eighteenth century was slavery. The shame of this country in the nineteenth and twentieth centuries was Jim Crow. The shame of this country in the twenty-first century is the prison-industrial complex."

Davison's use of the term "prison-industrial complex" to describe a historical trajectory of racializing and racist institutions would seem to clearly identify his views regarding incarceration. First introduced into the public lexicon by Mike Davis in a 1995 article for the *Nation*, the term has gained popularity among mainly leftist academics and activists who find it useful for analyzing the growth of mass incarceration; its relationship to changes in American capitalism, including its entanglements with private capital; and its location on a continuum of strategies used by the state for control, detention, and surveillance. Mass incarceration has recently become the province of debate and criticism among a wider swath of the American public, but the term "prison-industrial complex" still signifies a certain committed political view.[1]

Davison followed his politicized condemnation of mass incarceration with a seemingly incompatible second point: an emphatic and passionate plea to build the justice campus. He noted: "We've been talking and planning for too long. It is time to build the justice campus." In fact, Davison was only the first speaker that evening to endorse Monroe County's plan for exponential carceral expansion. Democratic candidates for county commissioner, county council, and judge repeated much the same points: The American criminal justice system, in particular its system of incarceration, was broken and corrupt. The war on drugs was a dismal failure. The local system, in stark contrast, was not only functional but also benevolent, rehabilitative, and *in need of significant expansion*. The justice campus, in their view, would greatly enhance the county's abilities to provide therapeutic justice, education, and other treatment to its most needy citizens.

I felt disoriented. I had attended the event anticipating some degree of support for the justice campus proposal. But as a student of mass incarceration and as an activist against it, I entered the field in Monroe County inevitably mapping my prior experiences examining and fighting carceral expansion onto the local context. Most scholarly, journalistic, public policy, and activist accounts locate the exponential growth of imprisonment in the United States in the context of "tough on crime" public policy, corresponding cultural and ideological shifts to the Right, the neoliberal withdrawal of the welfare state and rise of the security state, the rural lobby for prison siting, and the criminalization of communities of color.[2] When this *oeuvre* does refer to liberal politics and politicians, it is usually to observe their competition with conservatives for who can be the most punitive in rhetoric and policy.[3]

I had mistakenly assumed that the justice campus proposal was at least partly the product of calls for punishment and the law and order politics I had come to associate with the rise of the carceral state. Sitting in the public library that evening, I was surrounded by liberal Democrats and civic leaders, many of whom I recognized as members of the energetic social service community and as outspoken progressives. I was confused by such stark and prevalent inconsistencies. More important than my personal bewilderment was the fact that the people I expected to be allies in challenging incarceration all appeared to be passionately committed to ensuring its local expansion.

A History of Expansion

As it turned out, dramatic jail expansion had substantial local precedent. In 1977, Monroe County employed a not-for-profit, nonpartisan national research company to study and assess the county's incarceration needs and project them into the twenty-first century. The jail at that time had a maximum of forty-four beds and, while not suffering from overcrowding, was universally denounced for its decrepit state. The company, the National Clearinghouse for Criminal Justice Planning and Architecture (NCCJPA), found that a county jail with a capacity of 37–64 inmates would suffice through the year 2000. That is, the 1977 study found that a jail similar in size to the one in use at the time of the study would likely have met the community's needs through the next twenty-three years.[4] Yet throughout the first half of the 1980s, the county pushed for the construction of a new and larger facility. By 1986, after hiring a different consultant who proposed increased carceral capacity, the county had built a new jail with a capacity for 126 inmates—double the need identified in the NCCJPA study—and it was almost immediately overcrowded.[5] By 2008, the county had renovated the jail twice, double-bunking every cell, and the official capacity jumped to 267, although no additional space had been added. In the last several months of 2008 and the first months of 2009, the daily population was consistently over 300 individuals. In the early part of 2008, a jail inmate who had served time for a misdemeanor charge filed a lawsuit against the jail, citing unconstitutional overcrowding. A federal judge granted the lawsuit class action status. In the lawsuit, the plaintiff, Trevor Richardson, cited grievances that included "unsafe and hazardous conditions" resulting from overcrowding; tension; violence; "dirty showers and living conditions;" cold food; and "complete lack of recreation."[6] The lawsuit itself animated local efforts to construct the justice campus. Indeed, it was the explicit intent of the lawsuit to force the county to build a bigger jail. "You always hope in litigation like this that everyone will agree to build a new facility to rectify the situation," the state's legal director for the American Civil Liberties Union told a reporter for the main county periodical, the *Bloomington Herald-Times*. "But the jail still seems to be seriously overcrowded" (quoted in Nolan 2008).

Toward the end of 2007, two decades after the new jail had opened its doors, its daily population had grown to over 300 with no added physical capacity. Under the threat of the lawsuit, the county hired Program Administration and Results, Inc. (PARI), a private firm based just outside Indianapolis that specialized in corrections construction, to research and plan the justice campus. Importantly, the county commissioners instructed PARI to consider only one site: an eighty-five-acre part of a larger plot that until 1999 had been home to an electronics production plant owned then by Thomson Electronics and before that by Radio Corporation of America (RCA). Following the rapid liquidation of the property, the county had bought the eighty-five acres at what county council member Tom Redmond, speaking at a hearing about the justice campus, called "a fire sale price," for the express purpose of building a justice complex. PARI would proceed to propose the construction of a new jail with double the capacity of the current one (478 beds), a new 72-bed juvenile facility, a 100-bed work release center, and various new offices for criminal justice professionals. Built into the proposal and the architectural rendering of the campus was each facility's ability to double in size (Nolan 2009d).

The growth of local incarceration, the pursuit of new carceral institutions, and the expansion of carceral strategies from 1977 through the present are by no means unique to Monroe County. In fact, it is precisely this pattern and its logics that connect Monroe County to the thousands of other stories of carceral growth that occurred during the same period. From the time of the NCCJPA study to the PARI proposal for the justice campus, the United States engaged in a massive expansion of incarceration, with the jail population alone jumping from 183,988 in 1980 to 748,728 in 2010, a growth rate of 324 percent (Clear and Frost 2014, 18). With a similar rate of growth in the prison population (from 319,598 in 1980 to 1,543,206 in 2010, a growth rate of 373 percent), the United States has become the global leader in incarceration in terms of both sheer numbers and per capita rates. As of this writing, the prison and jail population hovers at just under 2.3 million people, with 1,483,900 in state and federal prisons and 744,500 in local jails (Glaze and Herberman 2012), numbers that approximate the *combined* total of the next two largest incarcerating countries, China (with 1.5 million prisoners) and Russia (874,000).[7] In addition, and also directly relevant to carceral expansion in Monroe County, at the end of 2012 a total of 4,781,300 people were under some form of correctional supervision in American communities, including probation (3,942,800) and parole (851,200) (Glaze and Herberman 2012). Indeed, I was in the middle of research for this book when the Pew Center on the States released its report titled "One in 31: The Long Reach of American Corrections." The report called attention to the fact that the rate of Americans under some from of correctional supervision, including probation and parole in addition to jail and prison, had doubled from 1 in 77 in 1982 to 1 in 31 in 2007; in Indiana, that rate had quadrupled from 1 in 106 to 1 in 26 (Pew Center on the States 2009).

The Aim of This Book

The seemingly contradictory stances taken by local officials that evening in the library—one of my earlier fieldwork observations—would become the central phenomenon in need of examination. Indeed, as I illustrate throughout this book, county politicians, criminal justice officials, and civic leaders were quick to offer informed criticism and a denunciation of the prison-industrial complex. Carceral growth in Bloomington complicates the reigning explanations that cite explicitly conservative politics and punitive discourses as the engines of mass incarceration. Democratic politicians, civic leaders, and nonprofit workers who identified themselves publicly and in interviews with me as "progressive," in the "liberal wing of the Democratic party," and even as "anti-authoritarian" and "socialist" led the local movement for carceral expansion. These leaders expressed a vision for local incarceration that attempted to distinguish it from the national narrative of prison growth. Local officials spoke of the need for more carceral space in terms of therapeutic justice, rehabilitation and treatment, and education, concepts that resurrected Progressive era notions of "penal-social laboratories."[8] In the name of the imagined facility—the justice campus—proponents of expansion harnessed the collegiate and bucolic image of the community to a call for the largest carceral growth in county history. Although the justice campus would have increased the county's formal control systems at an estimated cost of $50 million, it nonetheless had the support of the Democrat-dominated board of county commissioners and county council, the executive and fiscal bodies of county government.

In examining the logics, discourses, spatial dimensions, and historical contexts of the justice campus and other carceral expansion initiatives in Monroe County, this book has several objectives in its pursuit of a deeper understanding of incarceration in the United States. First, in centering the discourses of therapeutic justice, rehabilitation, and social justice in its critique, this book considers the role of liberal benevolence in the politics of carceral expansion. In a related vein, the book also examines how the carceral was constituted beyond the institutional formations of incarceration through so-called alternative sanctions that, in fact, extended carceral logics and practices into the spheres of social service and education. These revelations provide empirical support for several important concepts in criminology and the sociology of punishment that have been used in attempts to explain and theorize the extension of the carceral state beyond the prison: Michel Foucault's (1977) carceral archipelago, Stanley Cohen's (1991) net widening, and Katherine Beckett and Naomi Murakawa's (2012) plea to map the "shadow carceral state." In these respects, I hope the book contributes to the important projects of further theorizing the continued growth and transformation of incarceration and the constitutive complicity of liberals and progressives.[9] A second objective of the book is to insist on locating this story in two broader contexts and to examine them: the carceral state of which it is inevitably a part, and the global patterns of neoliberal capitalism that attempt to naturalize carceral expansion as part of the "common sense" of deindustrialized communities reeling from the departures of capital and industry.[10] The book aspires to present a multiscalar perspective, incorporating local, national, and global understandings of carceral regimes in a single case study while unpacking the political economy of incarceration at the "glocal" level. Here, the book pays particular attention to the relationship among economy, politics, and ideology. It was the economic relations of capital under what we refer to as neoliberalism that resulted in the closure of the RCA/Thomson plant, along with several other previously stable local industries, at the end of the twentieth century. Those economic changes operated locally also as political processes in that they affected—by reproducing—class positions vis-à-vis the loss of about 10,000 working-class jobs and the subsequent proposal for exponential carceral growth that everyone agreed would ensnare almost exclusively poor and working-class residents. But these economic and political processes *required* ideological work to aestheticize—that is, normalize—the same patterns that many proponents of local expansion were quick to criticize elsewhere.[11]

A third objective of the book—perhaps the most important—is to examine and offer strategies of resistance and intervention undertaken to oppose the policies and practices of carceral expansion as well as to challenge the logics that provided important legitimacy to them. The material and discursive conflicts and contests between expansion and resistance in Bloomington highlight a particular theoretical tension, between the naturalization of carceral expansion and a trenchant abolitionist critique that circulated and articulated in the same community and among interacting groups. While I encounter, examine, and attempt to unpack that tension, I also admit that it will likely not be fully resolved in these pages.

More simply, *Progressive Punishment* concerns the roots and routes of carceral logics—their origins and their circulations—as they set the conditions for and animate continued growth in Bloomington and beyond. The book critically examines how neoliberal ideology naturalizes carceral expansion into the political common sense of communities reeling from crises of deindustrialization, urban decline, and the devolution of social welfare.[12] In addition, the book chronicles community activists' attempts to destabilize that common sense and shake the community's reliance on incarceration. Bloomington is simultaneously the community under study in this book and a heuristic for a broader consideration of the logics underlying and animating continued carceral growth.

Theorizing Carceral Expansion

Over the course of my two years in the field, my experiences with such events as Reuben Davison's statements in the library accumulated, and my initial discomfort and confusion became a growing appreciation of the incongruities and an intellectual urge to appropriately contextualize and analyze them. At meetings of various county political bodies, in my interviews with civic leaders and politicians, and at four hearings about the justice campus, local officials consistently presented the justice campus and other expansion initiatives as separate from the politics of the carceral state. I felt that this presented a formidable challenge to my own intellectual capacities and theoretical vocabularies. It became apparent that carceral expansion in Bloomington and Monroe County did not fit neatly into the frameworks offered by the rich and interdisciplinary literatures on incarceration. Officials seemed to filter dominant discourses and practices through local cultural and political logics that rendered those discourses and practices palatable in the progressive context of Bloomington and Monroe County. I needed an analytical scaffold that could accommodate both the general power of mass incarceration and its distinctive iterations in the community.

In her ethnography of transnational illicit trade routes, Carolyn Nordstrom (2007) introduces the concept of "il/legal" to describe the permeable borders between legal and illegal channels through which commodities travel. Following her conceptual lead and linguistic maneuver, I came to understand local officials' simultaneous advocacy of carceral expansion and rejection of the prison-industrial complex as "dis/junctures": dispositions toward incarceration and punishment at once distinct and, crucially, bounded by and inscribed with the logics and practices of mass incarceration.

Once I understood them in this way, a particular analytic emerged as a clear way to theorize and historicize the justice campus and subsequent expansion proposals: "carceral habitus," or the corporal and discursive inscription of penal logics into individual and community bodies. In rhetorically rejecting mass incarceration but materially replicating it, local officials and others in the community demonstrated the capacity of carceral logics to structure individual, community, and institutional dispositions (Kramer, Rajah, and Sung 2013). The internalization of neoliberal responsibilization, racialized constructs of criminality, and cultural embraces of punishment can explain much of the way communities come to participate in the carceral state even as they purport to resist and reject it. Indeed, carceral expansion in Bloomington suggests that existing scholarship may underestimate both the hegemonic functioning of mass incarceration and the important roles that individual actors and communities play in adopting, reformulating, and rearticulating hegemonic carcerality to fit the specific common sense of particular political and cultural contexts.

Importantly, original writing on the prison-industrial complex recognized its capacity to structure a "state of mind" (Schlosser 1998). Recent work by the leading criminologists Todd Clear and Natasha Frost has also observed the "structured intellectual economy" (2014, 45) brought about by the four decades of what they refer to as the "punishment imperative." In addition to examining the political economic and cultural phenomena that gave rise to the justice campus in Bloomington, this book also examines the carceral logics that circulate in and through communities, structuring American subjectivities regarding crime and punishment. Indeed, carceral logics both framed and limited local responses to social issues, so that incarceration was simultaneously the problem and the solution.

Despite the power and scope of mass incarceration, little work has explored how communities acquiesce to or contest it. Certainly, there has been scant attention paid to the way that the logics we have come to ascribe to the carceral state may conceal themselves in distinctive discourses in different communities. By focusing on one unlikely node of the carceral state, this book examines the structuring power of carceral logics and maps some of the political, epistemological, and media routes through which they travel. My challenge has been to write the connective tissue that binds seemingly disconnected practices in one small and openly progressive community to the structuring logics of the carceral state. In the course of this ethnographic process, my hope is that carceral habitus emerges as a useful analytic to think through the work that mass incarceration performs in this country in structuring its own reproduction.

It is important to state here that habitus is not a concept predicated on objective reproduction of structures. Pierre Bourdieu, the French sociologist, is credited with developing the concept the furthest. He argues that habitus is best understood as a set of boundaries or limitations of consciousness or ability, within which an infinite number of iterations of given practices or institutions are possible, albeit constrained. He writes: "Habitus is never a mere principle of repetition. . . . As a dynamic system of dispositions that interact with one another, it has, as such, a generative capacity; it is a structured principle of invention, similar to a generative capacity . . . or generative grammar able to produce an infinite number of new sentences according to determinate patterns and within determinate limits. . . . The habitus generates inventions and improvisations but within limits" (Bourdieu 2005, 46). The justice campus proposal was viable because it was articulated through a palatable discourse that was aligned with local politics. Yet to focus only on the local liberal logic of social control ignores the ways in which national hegemonic logics permeated and constructed the boundaries of local habitus. Local leaders and their governmental, private, and nonprofit organizations embodied both the distinct liberal logics of the community and the translocal practices of social control articulated more broadly in the contemporary politics of mass incarceration and clearly in circulation in the county (Garland 2001). Bourdieu writes of this "meeting" between habitus and what he calls "objective structures," arguing that "in all the cases where dispositions encounter conditions different from those in which they were constructed and assembled, there is a *dialectical confrontation* between habitus, as structured structure, and objective structures. *In this confrontation, habitus operates as a structuring structure able to selectively perceive and to transform the objective structure according to its own structure, while at the same time, being restructured, transformed in its makeup by the pressure of the objective structure*" (2005, 47; my emphasis). In Bloomington, a broad array of structural forces—the hegemony of the institutional paradigm of the prison, the circulation of the neoliberal logic of individual responsibility, and the dominance of technocratic epistemologies—inscribed and constrained the range of possibilities.

Local liberal logics of social control were not ahistorical. Rather, the local carceral politics that respondents frequently positioned as exceptional were, in fact, a repository of penal logic from different historical periods. When local discourses of the correctional capabilities of the justice campus are placed in the historical context of penal welfarism or Progressive era "socializing" (Willrich 2003) of criminal justice, for example, they appear closely aligned with those (at one time) national hegemonic paradigms of social control. Anthony Platt notes that, "unlike earlier specialists in social control, [Progressive reformers] viewed the criminal justice apparatus as an institution for *preventing* disorder and *harmonizing* social conflicts, as well as simply *reacting* with brute force" (2009, xxvii). According to Platt, Progressive reformers were critical of the criminal justice system yet focused their efforts on "profes-sionalizing the police and other agencies of social control, diversifying their methods of operation, and extending the coercive functions of the state into new areas of working-class life."[13] When local politicians and civic leaders endorsed growth, they did so through a distinctly differ-ent discourse that usually rejected punitive rhetoric in favor of thera-peutic justice, treatment, and education as the central concepts driving expansion. Moreover, local leaders actively championed the increasing encroachment of criminal justice into "working-class life." Thus, it is imperative to note that the very construct of what I call "local liberal logics" and what county officials proudly claimed as exceptional politics related to incarceration were actually deeply embedded in historical and ideological ideas about crime, punishment, race, and poverty.

The ability for local officials opposed to incarceration to reproduce its physical structures and practices required them to make important intellectual shifts. With the departures of industry and jobs in the de-cades preceding the justice campus proposal, officials had to ignore or overlook the ways that the campus could complete a spatial and politi-cal trajectory from industry to incarceration. That is, officials could not articulate locally what they consistently offered nationally: a critique of capitalism and its structuring of poverty. This "forgetting" of local trans-national history was accompanied by what was perhaps a greater intel-lectual feat: the dislocation of local carceral politics from the national history and contemporary circulations of mass incarceration. Bourdieu notes that it is precisely this forgetting of history—"history turned into nature" (1977, 78)—that brings objective structures into a practical rela-tionship with what he calls the conjuncture, or the place where habitus and its field(s) reside. He writes: "The 'unconscious' is never anything other than the forgetting of history which history itself produces by in-corporating the objective structures it produces in the second natures of habitus. . . . It is because subjects do not, strictly speaking, know what they are doing that what they do has more meaning than they know. The habitus is the universalizing mediation, which causes an individual agent's practices, without either explicit reason or signifying intent, to be nonetheless 'sensible' and 'reasonable'" (1977, 78–79). Carceral habitus suggests that the logics and practices of mass incarceration reside not just "out there" (in media representations of crime and criminal justice, in the racialized "tough on crime" rhetoric of politicians, and in the everyday operations of criminal justice systems) but also "in here" (that is, in our everyday negotiations and productions of the social world). Put slightly differently, carceral habitus in Bloomington illuminates the hegemonic work that carceral logics perform at the level of personal dispositions. Understood in this way, officials' proposals to produce a carceral solution (the justice campus) to admittedly carceral problems (jail overcrowding and sending young people out of the county for detention) had an internal logic and could seem, as Bourdieu notes, "sensible" and "reasonable."

David Garland, a sociologist of punishment, has written: "The forms which punishments take, the symbols through which they claim legitimacy, the discourses in which they represent their meaning, the organizational forms and resources which they employ, all tend to depict a particular style of authority—a definite characterization of the power which punishes" (1990, 266). Officials such as Davison misunderstood their advocacy as somehow operating outside the techniques and logics of punishment. Through Garland's historical lens, we can instead consider the officials' advocacy for therapeutic justice and rehabilitation as a characterization of the local power that punishes. But how did that misunderstanding occur? How did officials who were acutely aware and critical of the carceral state arrive at a set of dispositions that allowed them to suspend their critique of the prison and embrace its dramatic expansion? It is obvious that their critique had less to do with the inherent qualities of the technology of the cage and more to do with an argument against the specific application and scope of its contemporary use. But that seemingly obvious observation is itself revealing, for it then becomes clear that officials believed that the same techniques could have been employed locally but animated by distinctive and principled ideas. In short, it becomes clear that officials believed that the carceral state stopped at the boundaries around the county; that its circulating logics could be rebuffed by a dynamic and progressive community; and that as a result, the community could engage in significant carceral expansion without replicating the same racialized and class-based results that they attributed to the carceral state. Such revelations give credence to Naomi Murakawa's recent explanations for distrusting and discounting the intentions of individuals and policies in her study of what she calls "the civil rights carceral state": "the actual pain of punishment as experienced by individuals and groups . . . varies least by what the partisans value most: the 'message' of punishment. Stated interests in minimizing bias or increasing rehabilitation do not necessarily mitigate penal harm" (2014, 19). Indeed, connecting Murakawa back to Garland, Foucault noted in *Discipline and Punish* that it has become "useless to believe in the good or bad consciences of judges" since it is the "economy of power they exercise, and not that of their scruples or their humanism, that makes them pass 'therapeutic' sentences and recommend 'rehabilitating' periods of imprisonment" (1977, 304).

This book thus examines how the logics and forces keenly and brilliantly revealed by scholars of mass incarceration "trickle down" through communities and are strained through local discourses and practices that can transform their appearance to fit the locality. But make no mistake: while terms like "rehabilitation," "therapeutic justice," "treatment," and "education" appear far more frequently in these pages than "punishment" and "law and order," it is this book's position that in the context of carceral expansion these seemingly distinct positions in fact articulate very similar, and very racialized and class-based, beliefs about responsibility, criminality, and social control.[14] This book cautions against the narrow focus on the punitive turn that characterizes much of Western criminology and sociology (Moore and Hannah-Moffat 2005) and instead attempts to illuminate the ideological and historical linkages between contemporary projects of carceral expansion in the name of treatment and earlier forms of paternalistic, racialized, and class-based coercive justice as well as the modern punitive carceral state.

Indeed, looking beyond Bloomington to the national landscape of incarceration in 2014 reveals the importance of critical carceral studies attuned to the connections between carceral expansion and constriction, as well as to the logics that may appear to support the latter while in fact producing the former. As public policy, media attention, and even political capital accrue around a changing discourse of incarceration, with politicians and think tanks on the Right supporting prison reform,[15] it seems especially appropriate for critical and activist scholarship to interrogate the carceral state's ability to reconfigure itself. Couched in terms of fiscal conservatism and inflected with religious redemption, the political Right's embrace of reform may indicate the next installment of neoliberal withdrawal: carceral devolution (R. Miller 2014). Following the lead of California's Assembly Bills 109 and 117, collectively known widely as "Public Safety Realignment," the county jail may come to play an increasingly important role in solidifying the carceral state. An example from my time in the field illustrates the importance of a critique attuned to the political logics that support a carceral state in the process of reshaping itself. Late in the fall of 2010, the *Herald-Times* published an Associated Press story announcing that Indiana's Republican governor, Mitch Daniels, "strongly endorsed" a study proposing significant prison reform in the state, including diverting many offenders from incarceration (Associated Press 2010). In the context of the sweeping Republican victories in state and federal elections in November 2010, it would seem significant that a Republican governor of a traditionally Republican state was heralding the turn toward prison and sentencing reform. At a holiday party during the same week that the story appeared in the *Herald-Times*, Ian Ozymandias, a member of Decarcerate Monroe County (DMC), a local activist group challenging the justice campus, raised the topic of the study and observed that Daniels's reaction represented a great moment of intervention with the local municipal government. "We need to write something," he argued, "something to say to folks [such as local officials]: 'here is somebody to the far right of you initiating substantial change. And you're not only *not* saying the same things, you're arguing for *more* cages, a *larger* system. If Daniels is saying this, then [Monroe County officials] should be out in front!'"

It is tempting to view Daniels's embrace of reform as a victory for decarceration. But as I note above, such an assessment would be both premature and neglectful of the unpredictable ways that communities adopt and express the logics of incarceration. Indeed, Daniels's endorsement revealed the fact that a Republican governor of a conservative state had initiated a statewide partnership with a research firm to examine and propose reforms to the state prison system while that state's most politically progressive county had just come to the brink of the largest expansion of criminal justice in its history. With that said, Ozymandias was correct in pointing out the opportunity—and the urgency—for the Left to struggle over the framing of reform.

An important part of the scholarly project of examining carceral habitus is the study of resistance to it. In addition to its obvious political implications, that study covers rich, if difficult, theoretical terrain. The question, of course, is how does or can resistance occur when there is such a heavily structured intellectual economy of responses to crises of neoliberalism and imprisonment, and when the solutions to those crises always seem to be more neoliberalism and more imprisonment?[16] If, as this book hopes to show, carceral habitus is deeply embedded in Monroe County, how are abolitionist interventions able to emerge and, according to my account, sever carceral habitus from its anchor to the hegemony of the cage? I engage these questions along the way, particularly in the final section of this book. It is worth noting here that because I consider carceral habitus to be a shifting and historically dynamic concept, it is by definition open to contestation. Constructed by material conditions as well as cultural frameworks and their discursive signifiers, carceral habitus can be vulnerable to campaigns that disrupt the sedimentation of its constitutive logics.[17] The questions to be asked, then, are what does it take, and what would it look like, for the disruption of carceral habitus to be followed by the inscription of an abolitionist habitus?

A Note about Terminology

As indicated by Davison's comments at the forum in the library, the term "prison-industrial complex" was used in Monroe County by both supporters and opponents of the justice campus proposal. The term appears in this book because of its use by my informants, because I find it to be a useful analytic in connecting local to national and transnational practices of imprisonment, and because of the trenchant and activist critique inherent in it. I have chosen, however, to rely most heavily in these pages on the term "carceral." Indeed, I have already used this term to describe the local phenomenon of expansion and as a modifier for the theoretical analytic of habitus. I prefer "carceral" to "incarceration" or "imprisonment" because I find it to be a nuanced and powerful concept that can speak to the strategies and linkages that connect incarceration to other spheres of state punishment and social control.

As Foucault (1977) observed, strategies of social control and repression can and do extend beyond a formal institution and into other spheres of social life. In Monroe County, officials and other proponents of the justice campus worked hard to present its three constitutive institutions as distinct from each other, even suggesting that a work release facility adjacent to a jail constituted a legitimate alternative to incarceration. Moreover, as this book discusses at length in chapters 1 and 2, one popular vision for the justice campus expressed to me by several officials would have moved all of the county's social services onto the site with the three institutions, spatially and conceptually collapsing welfare and criminal justice. Readers familiar with *Discipline and Punish* might recognize in this vision a modern version of Mettray, the penal colony that Foucault studied in that book's final chapter, "The Carceral," and about which he writes: "It is the disciplinary form at its most extreme, the model in which are concentrated all the coercive technologies of behavior. In it were to be found 'cloister, prison, school, regiment'" (1977, 293). The eventual defeat of the justice campus proposal led to new efforts to expand a youth shelter into a sort of juvenile facility, to create a truancy court alongside other existing problem-solving courts, to expand technogical correctional so-called alternatives, and to substitute videoconferencing for in-person visitation at the current jail as part of a larger renovation. "Carceral" is the term that can best present both appreciation and critiques of the common punitive strategies and justifying logics that animate projects like the justice campus, as well as the archipelago of punishments and alternatives that surrounded it.

(Counter) Carceral Ethnography

I became active in the issues that this book examines in 2008, when the Monroe County government first announced the possibility of the justice campus and a partnership with PARI. With other concerned residents, I cofounded an organization dedicated to jail reform. After a year as a community organizer with Decarcerate Monroe County, I transitioned into a role as an ethnographer, while remaining active with the organization. My prior involvement shaped my research focus; participating in meetings with local officials during that first year sharpened my sense of the dis/juncture between local and national discourses and politics of incarceration. Excavating the dis/junctures and locating such contradictions within the implicating and structuring work of neoliberal capitalism and racialized mass incarceration was a task especially suited to an ethnographic approach acutely attuned to local process and to the structural patterns and structuring work of the carceral state.

This book is perhaps less a traditional ethnography than it is a study of the localizing effects of the neoliberal carceral state—that is, a study of the way Bloomington and its contests over carceral expansion were a "crossroads... for the interplay of diverse localizing practices of national, transnational and even global-scale actors, as these wider networks of meaning and power come into contact with more locally configured networks, practices and identities" (M. Smith 2001, 127). This is more than a semantic difference. Traditionally, ethnographies of particular communities include neighborhood descriptions, in-depth character development, and a substantial community history. While this book does describe particular microgeographies of the community, focuses on certain recurring figures, and describes selected local histories, I avoid some of the more traditional ethnographic descriptive and analytical terrain to focus on the circulating logics about capital, culture, and the carceral that, while contested, resulted in the justice campus proposal and subsequent attempts at expansion. Following Pierre Bourdieu and Loïc Wacquant (1992, 113), Stuart Hall and coauthors argue that their concern with mugging in the transcendent *Policing the Crisis* was "to use such a starting point—concrete events, practices, relationships, and cultures—to approach the structural configurations that cannot be reduced to the interactions and practices through which they express themselves" (2013, xi). My hope is that *Progressive Punishment* can be read similarly, both as a study of the politics of carceral expansion that is situated in a particular place and as a larger commentary about the political economic, spatial, and cultural work of carceral logics and how they shape, and are shaped by, American communities.[18] My methodological approach needed to approximate and appreciate the fluidity of capital, ideology, and logic in circulation in the community across time and space so that I could perceive and trace the routes and roots of local carceral expansion.

I conducted two dozen in-depth, semistructured interviews with county and city politicians, civic leaders, criminal justice officials, corrections consultants, and community activists. Most of these informants were instrumental in shaping the local discourses about the justice campus, either because they strongly supported it or because they were involved in DMC and its energetic opposition.

In addition, I conducted over a hundred hours of fieldwork at various gatherings in the community, including official public hearings about the justice campus hosted by the Monroe County Criminal Justice Coordinating Council (MCCJCC), the bimonthly meetings of the MCCJCC, political forums for campaigning politicians, activist meetings, and visiting hours at the county jail. The fieldwork at community meetings provided important entries into the terrain of carceral habitus, as I was able to observe its work beyond the confounding contradictions of informants' orientations to incarceration that came out during the interviews. Officials, civic leaders, and community organizers were present at many of the meetings I attended. There were many times in the field when I observed officials present a vision of the justice campus, community organizers contest it, and officials then slightly alter either their original vision or what had just been offered by organizers to pacify them and alleviate their concerns. In these processes, participant observation sites also were meaningful to the project beyond what was said about carceral expansion. The meetings I attended also provided insights for examining the culture and geography of public spaces, the construction of knowledge and expertise, and the distinct organizational structures and decision-making processes between groups.

Finally, I collected numerous county reports and over a hundred articles from local periodicals to provide a historical context for my inquiry and to examine the role of local media in establishing carceral habitus. Articles covering the history of jail overcrowding, the decades-long discussion of a youth facility, the justice campus proposal, local resistance to it, and local crime provided important insights into how the media represented these issues and contributed to the larger discourse of carceral expansion.[19]

Stuart Hall (1982, 1996, and 1997; Hall et al. 2013) identifies representation as distinct from reflection in its role in creating meaning. Hall writes: "Representation . . . implies the active work of selecting and presenting, of structuring and shaping; not merely the transmitting of an already-existing meaning, but the more active labour of making things mean" (1982, 64). In *Policing the Crisis*, Hall and coauthors expand on the specific role of the media in representing dominant meanings: "[The media] are frequently not the 'primary definers' of news events at all; but their structured relationship to power has the effect of making them play a crucial but secondary role in *reproducing* the definitions of those who have privileged access, as of right, to the media's 'accredited sources." From this point of view, in the moment of news production, the media stand in a position of structured subordination to the primary definers" (2013, 62). The *Herald-Times* played a key role in circulating and legitimating the justice campus vision. Over the years, the newspaper supported local officials' carceral expansion projects, endorsing and representing the construction of local institutions as emblematic of county liberal benevolence. Hall and colleagues write of this relationship between media and criminal justice institutions, observing in their study that newspapers' usage of terms from the police to describe mugging and muggers produced "a transformation into a public idiom [that] gives the item an external public reference and validity in images and connotations already sedimented in the stock of knowledge which the paper and its public share . . . the publicizing of an issue in the media can give it more 'objective' status as a real (valid) issue of public concern than would have been the case had it remained as merely a report made by experts and specialists. . . . This is part of the media's agenda-setting function. Setting agendas also has a reality-confirming effect" (2013, 64–65).

The power of the media to construct meaning and set agendas was evident in the numerous articles and op-ed pieces that the *Herald-Times* published concerning carceral expansion. Articles frequently relied on the framing offered by local officials, and editorials reliably endorsed expansion. The tight circuit of authority between local media, politicians, civic leaders, and outside consultants effectively insulated and circulated a form of what Hall and coauthors have called "cultural power," which they argue "awards command over the process of 'definition' within our society" (2013, 32).

My fieldwork and analysis operated as semiconcurrent processes. Transcriptions of meetings and interviews often led to longer expositions; initial analyses of the field inevitably affected subsequent interviews and observations, and sometimes I intended that they should do so. The central theoretical claim to emerge from my research—the existence of carceral habitus—was the product of an ongoing and iterative process of indexing data, exploring emerging themes, and reflecting on their ability to account for and explain the social world I was examining. In short, my process included the "grounded field research and critical ethnography" advocated by Ferrell and Hamm (1998b, 11) and the "multilayered process of systematic brainstorming and intellectual bridge making" offered by Dimitri Bogazianos (2012, 150).

Conducting ethnographic fieldwork in a community in which I was already living and concerning issues in which I was already politically engaged certainly challenges the traditional anthropological and criminological traditions of objectively studying others. Indeed, many of the people I interviewed, observed, and spent time with in various meetings were people I already knew through my involvement with DMC. Thus, my fieldwork was certainly conducted among the familiar: I was with people I knew, was asking about issues with which I was already acquainted, and was based out of my own home. Yet, perhaps as a testament to the importance of such a close perspective, the research process destabilized the recognizable field site and the familiar became unfamiliar. The explanations of mass incarceration I was accustomed to employing did not fit the political and cultural contours of the discourse and politics of carceral growth in Monroe County. In addition, the community politics I had come to see as reliably leftist were incongruent with the proposal for such drastic expansion. The incongruities of the research raised methodological and personal challenges and imperatives.

My active role with DMC required a reflexive approach to the research that could account for my own positionality. In my fieldwork, I did not presuppose that different spaces were sites for unadulterated perspectives about carceral expansion. On the contrary, I operated from the assumption that the research sites for this project would reveal spaces where meanings of imprisonment were subject to contestation and conflation. With that said, there is ample support for engaged and politically committed ethnography in anthropology[20] and impassioned, if more sparse, endorsement of it in criminology.[21] Bourdieu has observed of scholars that "those who have the good fortune to be able to devote their lives to the study of the social world cannot stand aside, neutral and indifferent, from the struggles in which the future of that world is at stake."[22] Jim Thomas, in explicating reflexivity in his work on critical ethnography, refers both to the impact of the researcher's position on the study and the impact of the study on the social world. The first acknowledges the importance of the "truth quotient" (Thomas 1993, 47)—that is, the validity of a given study, which is fundamental to all research, including critical ethnography, and which involves interrogation of the effects a researcher's priorities and politics may have on a given study. This is especially important in disaggregating, or at least being accountable to, the relationships between our findings and ourselves. The second asks what impact our work has on challenging injustice, furthering a counternarrative, hastening social change, or contributing to social justice. It was the more robust and socially accountable vision of both of these aspects of reflexivity to which I tried to adhere during my fieldwork and writing.[23]

Issues of reflexivity, accountability, and representation were also paramount after my fieldwork and during the writing of this book, especially since I needed to decide whether to name the city in which my research occurred. My decision to name Bloomington was made after years of thinking about the issue. In fact, earlier versions of this manuscript, as well as articles I have published on the material, use a pseudonym for the city. Ultimately, however, I arrived at my decision to use the name through several related conclusions.

First, informants and the institutional review board at Indiana University had given me permission to use the name of the community. Second, the role of RCA and Thomson as well as the material and cultural geography of its site in Bloomington was too rich to be presented with pseudonyms. There is an archival trove of articles about the plant, its closing, the site's redevelopment, and local flirtation with carceral expansion there, and I felt that the book would have suffered from too shallow an engagement with this material if I did not reveal the name of the community. At the same time, there were inevitably so many details that remained that I suspect most readers wouldn't have had trouble identifying the community anyway. Third, I name the community to think through with greater historical and regional specificity what carceral growth in liberal American communities means. Fourth, I have great respect for the tradition in ethnography, and certainly in ethnographies about incarceration, to maintain anonymity out of fear of both harming informants and hampering future access to conducting research.[24] But *Progressive Punishment* is not prison ethnography in any traditional sense. The book is not about prisoners' adaptation, acquiescence, or resistance. Many of my informants were elected officials who invited me to use their real names. I ultimately made the decision to use pseudonyms for all individuals and some organizations to preserve basic anonymity.

Ethnographic scholarship is uniquely positioned to examine a phenomenon such as the promotion of carceral expansion through discourses of therapeutic justice, treatment, and education. It was clear that in Bloomington the "organizing cultural framework" of incarceration was integral to the wide support the justice campus enjoyed among liberals and progressives, a testament to the symbolic work incarceration performs to regulate our abilities to perceive it (Garland 1990, 252). My approach needed a concurrent focus on the material and representational work of local social control efforts. In the latter effort, this book looks to "the ideological and cultural power to signify and thus give events a social meaning, and to win society to their 'definition of the situation'" (Hall et al. 2013, xii). In line with critical scholarship that intervenes in the "common sense" of prisons,[25] this book follows calls by scholars such as Mariana Valverde (2010), who argues for more detailed case studies, and Lorna Rhodes, who claims that "the most pressing need for the study of prisons is to challenge the terms of the discourse that frames and supports them" (2001, 75). In tracing the way the "terms of the discourse" can change across time and space and yet produce remarkably similar policy, this book also follows recent calls to study "contexts that challenge traditional understandings of the penal realm" (Hannah-Moffat and Lynch 2012, 119).

The Outline of the Book

There are a number of key entries into this examination of carceral expansion that reveal the ways carceral habitus is formulated, expressed, insulated, and at times contested and even reconfigured. This book is structured in such a way as to tell the story of the justice campus and other subsequent attempts at carceral expansion in Bloomington and, simultaneously, to interrogate carceral habitus, examine its contours, and consider attempts to disrupt and undo it.

The book is organized into four parts. Part 1, which contains chapters 1 and 2, examines the historical and material geographies of the justice campus proposal. Chapter 1 examines the eighty-five-acre site planned for the justice campus. The ideological work of incarceration (A. Davis 2003, 16) succeeded in part through its reliance on certain tropes resonating in the community that framed carceral expansion as inherently a project of therapeutic justice and rehabilitation rather than of punishment. But this was only possible because of a particular historical geography that had produced a spatial and political landscape on which officials could project their visions. The eighty-five-acre space for the justice campus had been home to the largest television production facility in the world, first bought and run by RCA in the 1940s, owned briefly by General Electric, and then sold to the French company Thomson Electronics in 1984. Following that company's departure from the community in 1999, officials began to envision a carceral future for the derelict site.

In examining the trajectory from industry to incarceration that characterizes Bloomington and Monroe County, chapter 1 locates the community in the transnational neoliberal processes structuring post-Fordist American society, particularly around issues of poverty and security.[26] Locally, the county lost three major employers in the decades preceding the justice campus proposal. The Thomson site offers a particularly poignant illustration of the political economic and spatial connections—and contingencies—between capital departures and carceral arrivals. Indeed, mapped onto this specific history is a story that should sound familiar to those with a sense of the growth of mass incarceration: the exodus of manufacturing jobs, shady partnerships between private capital and public policy, and incarceration as the catchall solution to problems raised by capital's departure. Using testimonies of local planners and architects who spoke of seeing natural carceral contours in the eighty-five-acre site, this chapter examines the ability of carceral habitus to enable the forgetting of history and to structure the way that nature and space are perceived.

Chapter 2 builds on this history to further theorize carceral expansion beyond its most obvious institutional formations. Proposals for expansion did not stop at the three institutions that comprised the justice campus. Numerous visions and policy implementations offered dramatic restructurings of local practice. In one, several officials suggested locating county social services on the same site as the jail, juvenile facility, and work release center. In others, officials looked away from the jail and juvenile institutions and toward specialty courts and other so-called alternatives, proudly locating them and various programs on the same continuum on which they placed the justice campus. This chapter examines the spatial articulations of various logics that collapsed welfare and carceral into a singular vision and that imagined an archipelago of alternatives extending beyond the justice campus.

Part 2, which contains chapters 3 and 4, focuses narrowly on the logics of crime and punishment that constructed both a population in need of carceral treatment and a benevolent complex of facilities to provide it. Chapter 3 examines these logics as they gave shape and structure to the proposal for the new jail. The chapter looks at the ways supporters of the justice campus justified expansion through an imagined jail(able) population of county residents described in terms that conflated economic and moral poverty. While many of these same research informants frequently identified the structural conditions of capitalism as the central problem underlying mass incarceration, they constructed a local individuated, unacculturated, and pathological criminal and proposed solutions grounded in individual, moralistic, and redemptive change. In constructing the county poor as not only occupying fragile economic situations but also as possessing a set of racialized and inferior behavioral and cultural practices, local leaders justified a facility predicated on education, treatment, and acculturation to middle-class status. Importantly, this chapter contrasts ethnographic data with available local statistics on the jail population to interrogate the local construction of crime and criminality.

Chapter 3 also examines more closely the rehabilitative logics that officials positioned as endemic to the county and thus distinct from the logics of the carceral state. Using testimonies from local officials in interviews and county meetings, the chapter examines the structuring logics that guided discussions of jail expansion while also interrogating how such logics located the community as a nodal point in the diffuse articulation of mass incarceration.

Chapter 4 looks at the discourses and practices of juvenile justice policy in the county. A new and large juvenile facility enjoyed substantial and passionate support in the community, including from the few local leaders suspicious of or hesitant about the overall justice campus proposal. Through discourses of child saving, racialized notions of so-called real criminals inhabiting facilities outside of the city, and a belief in the capacity of the community to create benevolent institutions, local officials at once imagined an exceptional community capable of extraordinary incarceration and relied on racial and class tropes from prior eras to justify increased detention of youth. This chapter looks at the expansion of both institutional and noninstitutional capacity for adjudicated youth as reflecting once again the work neoliberal punishment performs in structuring its own reproduction.

Part 3 moves away from the discourse and politics of expansion and focuses instead on the political and epistemological processes that made expansion possible. Chapters 5 and 6 examine the production of local knowledge about crime and incarceration to better account for the role of that knowledge in shaping the county's carceral politics. Chapter 5 looks at the circulation of technocratic discourses in and through local experts and media that restructured local knowledge into support for the campus. Chapter 6 is devoted entirely to a close examination of the substantial history of national and state corrections consultants in the county, paying particular attention to the two consultants whose work was instrumental in shaping the expansion projects I studied. Both chapters engage debates about exclusionary languages and practices of late modernity and map them onto ethnographic examples of policy discussions that abstracted human lives into penological concerns with management and control and that privileged experts at the expense of alternative—and very real—understandings of incarceration.[27] In examining consultants' official reports, practitioners' testimonies, and editorials and news stories in the media, these chapters trace the epistemological processes by which local carceral politics came to embrace and resemble the carceral state, even as many people in the community claimed a certain degree of knowledge about mass incarceration that absolved them of any complicity in its local replication.

Chapter 7 examines some of the governmental and nongovernmental bodies, processes, and relationships in the county to better understand the political contexts in which the production of carceral knowledge and conversations about expansion occurred. The production and articulation of knowledge, and the structuring of spaces to promote and insulate that knowledge, are two aspects of the same phenomenon of what Bourdieu (1991) calls symbolic power, in which agents justify and support the given social order through practices that assign it symbolic capital. In chapter 7, I focus on the structuring of political spaces and discourses so that narratives of expansion were reinforced and insulated while appearing to be open to contestation.

Most of the chapters in *Progressive Punishment* offer glimpses into how dominant discourses and practices of incarceration expansion were also planes of contestation. There are places in the book where I include the ways people intervened in and disrupted the would-be hegemonic discourses of carcerality. Part 4 ends the volume with a more robust examination of local resistance to liberal carceral expansion. Chapter 8 looks primarily, although not exclusively, at one group, DMC, and the resistance it articulated and engendered among other community members. Most accounts of activism against mass incarceration focus on the challenging of explicitly right-wing and punitive politics of carceral growth. DMC's work in Bloomington was considerably different, as the group's members found themselves at odds with would-be allies and needing to construct a critique that disrupted the local liberal narrative of exceptional incarceration. Chapter 8 includes examinations of DMC's internal politics and processes as well as the group's interventions into county carceral politics. In addition, the chapter includes a brief insurrectionary interlude to discuss some sabotage and other higher-risk activities undertaken in the city to halt incarceration.

With the conclusion, I have chosen to end the book by expanding on ideas generated by DMC during the course of my fieldwork. These alternatives are rooted in an abolitionist framework—that is, they are expressly committed to decarceration and to shrinking (and ultimately ending) our reliance on incarceration. There are several sources of inspiration for ending in such a way. First, in the context of the book, nonreformist reforms, or abolitionist alternatives, create a productive theoretical and political tension with the way expansion and reforms were often mutually constitutive in Bloomington. In other words, the alternatives move toward and perhaps begin to inscribe an abolitionist habitus. Second, my choice to end the book with this material was influenced by other scholars who have chosen to end their books with (or frame them entirely through) hopeful gestures toward radically different ways of engagement.[28] Following their lead, I hope that the conclusion and part 4 more broadly will contribute to the scholar-activist movement toward abolition.

At this point, I anticipate that some readers may question the foresight and strategy of a book that focuses its critique on approaches to imprisonment and social control grounded in well-meaning ideals and intentions. After all, some might wonder, isn't a system with a conscience, steeped in progressive ideals and notions of therapeutic justice, qualitatively better than the alternative approaches that characterize most prisons and jails in the United States? As one response to such a question, I turn to the historian David Rothman, whose critical appraisal of Jacksonian and Progressive era reform cautions against the embrace of penal benevolence: "Let it be clear from the start that . . . Progressive reforms did not significantly improve inherited practices. To raise but one theme to which we will frequently return, innovations that appeared to be substitutes for incarceration became supplements to incarceration. Progressive innovations may well have done less to upgrade dismal conditions than they did to create nightmares of their own" (2002, 9).

As an iteration of mass incarceration, the justice campus raises important considerations for understanding twenty-first-century carcerality in the United States. Support for carceral expansion by progressive and liberal community leaders who imagined benevolent local institutions reveals contours of mass incarceration that scholarship has yet to excavate. This book suggests the need for examining the locally situated ways in which the logics and practices of hegemonic carcerality take shape, at times in contrast to its more familiar forms at the level of the state and nation.

PART 1

Neoliberal Geographies of Progressive Punishment

As a powerful site of state sovereignty, cages are places in which a variety of territorializations of economic and state power converge. The nation-state (border) and the city hold host to the powerful dialectics of fixity and flow, incapacitation and mobility.
—Jenna Loyd, Andrew Burridge, and Matthew Mitchelson, "Thinking (and Moving) beyond Walls and Cages"

The "unconscious" is never anything other than the forgetting of history which history itself produces by incorporating the objective structures it produces in the second natures of habitus. . . . It is because subjects do not, strictly speaking, know what they are doing that what they do has more meaning than they know. The habitus is the universalizing mediation which causes an individual agent's practices, without either explicit reason or signifying intent, to be none the less "sensible" and "reasonable."
—Pierre Bourdieu, *Outline of a Theory of Practice*

Sight and Site Lines

In the fall of 2008, the Monroe County Criminal Justice Coordinating Council (MCCJCC) hosted four public hearings about the justice campus to present initial design concepts to the community and receive feedback. The MCCJCC was an advisory body comprised mainly of senior officials from county and city criminal justice agencies that served both to coordinate interagency collaborations and to make formal recommendations to the county government concerning criminal justice policy. During my time in the field, the MCCJCC had played an integral role in identifying corrections consultants for the justice campus and subsequent expansion proposals and ultimately contracting for their services. All four of the justice campus hearings featured representatives from the county's consultant, Program Administration and Results, Inc. (PARI), and from prominent criminal justice administrators. The first three hearings focused on the three major pieces of the campus: the juvenile facility, a work release and community corrections center, and the new jail. In the fourth and final hearing, the content turned to the actual design concept of and architectural plans for the eighty-five-acre site. Joining Richard Kemp, the cofounder and co-owner of PARI, and Tom Grady, the MCCJCC's chair, for the official presentation was a local architect, Steve Vance, who was responsible for the design of the campus. The architectural rendering of the site and the descriptions Vance and others used to explain it provide important insights into the work that planning, design, and landscaping perform in the service of carceral expansion.

As had been the case with the three previous meetings, Kemp spoke first, after brief introductory remarks by Grady. Kemp began by saying: "Back in April, the commissioners asked us to look at the criminal justice system and how that fit together and established that they wanted us to look at the RCA site. They stressed three items: [first, it had to be] comprehensive, far-reaching beyond itself. [Second, i]t had to be flexible, meet today's needs and future needs. Something we could grow in. Something that met the needs of staff. Had to be something the community had input in. [Third, it had to] target juvenile, work release, and jail at that RCA site."

A man in his mid-fifties, Kemp spoke haltingly and stumbled through his testimony, showing little of the authority, confidence, or polish that one might expect from a private corrections consultant. Nevertheless, perhaps because of his rather unthreatening demeanor, the MCCJCC had him begin each of the four hearings. His remarks above, incomplete as they are, demonstrate the important role of the particular landscape sited for the justice campus. The site was chosen in part to accommodate current and projected future needs. Quite explicitly, the county's representatives communicated to PARI that they wanted a complex that could house the three constitutive institutions in dramatically expanded form and that the site needed to be able to accommodate further expansion. In official county discourse and imagination, carceral expansion lay in the realm of common-sense community planning.[1]

The naturalization of expansion is an important indicator of the ways that ideological processes have a material and geographical presence. In the series of excerpts below, Vance followed Kemp's remarks by displaying and describing to hearing attendees the rendering of the proposed justice campus site, noting the ease with which the new carceral geography would both use the land and be integrated into the surrounding landscape. As Vance brought up a PowerPoint slide showing a satellite map of the land to orient the audience to the RCA site, he first located the justice campus in relation to surrounding subdivisions, municipal infrastructure, and businesses: "You can see we're adjacent to the subdivision to the south, RCA park is here [also south, next to the subdivision], the Sudbury farm is west of us here, and [the biotechnology company] Cook Pharmica is here, Schulte [a home storage company] is here, and the new road that was built for the Indiana Enterprise Center and right next to Cook comes right down to the edge of the [justice campus] site right there. So there's a new road right here."

In locating the campus next to its proposed residential, recreational, business, and agricultural neighbors, the county could further the narrative of a truly community-based project. In pointing especially to Cook Pharmica, Schulte (now known as Organized Living), the Indiana Enterprise Center, and the new road, the architect at once attached the campus to the narrative of new economic development that followed on the heels of the RCA/Thomson departure and, crucially, pointed to the infrastructural development that would make a modern facility possible.

Changing slides to a blueprint of the proposed campus, Vance continued:

> This is our early site plan. There are a number of features here I'll explain. First of all are the roads. This site is at the end of the roads right now; over time, roads are planned to crisscross the site so it will be part of the roadway network. This east-west road that would come from Rogers Street and pass through the site would continue through Sudbury and to Wiemer Road [and] would be a secondary arterial in the city's system. Just off of our site Adams Road would come from the north and connect up, and on our site the new Indiana Enterprise road would come from the north and connect up. So this would become part of the roadway grid.

In this vision, the justice campus would further develop a blighted dein-dustrialized zone in the process of revitalization. The campus would stimulate further infrastructural development, connecting north-south and east-west roads and in the process facilitate more connections between newly forming high-tech business, surrounding residential spaces, and rural agricultural land. The justice campus, then, must be understood beyond the discourses of rehabilitative and therapeu-tic justice that expressed a vision of distinctive incarceration; carceral expansion was not just about crime and justice policy. Rather, Monroe County looked to the justice campus as a central municipal project through which to funnel various infrastructural and economic policies, a local example of a much broader pattern that scholars have called "car-ceral Keynesianism."[2]

Finally, Vance turned his attention away from how the campus would animate investment in and commitment to the immediate vicinity and toward the specific geography of the eighty-five-acre site. The concept map of the campus showed the site divided into eight lots of varying sizes, three of which would house the individual facilities, one of which would house a large warehouse that would serve all three facilities, and the remaining four of which would be available for other municipal uses or sold to private developers. In what follows, Vance describes the va-riety of topographies contained within the site but carefully notes how the terrain could work in the service of the proposed carceral function:

> This particular master plan shows lots ranging from three acres to twenty-three acres. The land out there—I don't know if anyone has been out there on the land, but it has a wide variety of types of land. Lot 1 and lot 2 there is a larger, flat ridge top. Down here in lot 6, same thing: large, flat, ridge top. But the other properties are a little bit rougher. This space right here [pointing to the lot between lots 1, 2, and 6] is full of big boulders and rocks. [Showing photos of the actual site] We really have a variety of spaces out there. The trees you see on here are pretty much what are there now. Some pretty heavy woods over here. Sloped land here, open flat meadow. These sites over here [pointing to the western edge] are [a] bit more broken up. There is a big utility easement that goes through here, large overhead power lines. But these lots are very usable. Usable space on lot 7, lot 8. The [lots] over here [pointing to the eastern edge] are not

as easy to use; they have slope going this way and slope going that way, so they're a little bit more difficult to use for a big structure. There's acreage there for smaller buildings that could be stepped down a slope on those sites, whereas these sites [pointing back to lots 1, 2, and 6] are adaptable to some pretty large buildings. These rough areas [pointing to the trees that apparently separate several lots on the western part of the property] actually provide the opportunity for some separation and some barriers that we'll talk more about later. This is an opportunity to [have] separate land use and a significant buffer between various activities.

Vance noted that the site offered a variety of topographies, including large ridge tops, rougher properties full of boulders, and open spaces. Interestingly, the very bucolic nature of the landscape—no doubt part of what allowed this expansion project to be labeled a campus—also would animate the site's carceral functions. Vance argued at the meeting that the open spaces were "adaptable to some pretty large buildings," that the boulder-strewn and other rough areas of the property "actually provide the opportunity for . . . barriers. . . . This is an opportunity to [have] separate land use and a significant buffer between various activities," and that more heavily wooded areas would operate as "sound barriers." Thus, Vance and presumably others saw specific carceral features in the natural grade of the land. In their view, the site could not only accommodate expansion but would also perform the work of carcerality. In addition to considering this as part of the ideology of landscape in general, I submit that the carceral landscape in this case performed similar functions to the historic role of prison architecture.[3] The landscape would naturalize—that is, normalize and beautify through nature—its carceral functions. The name of and philosophy behind a justice campus could only garner support if it appeared to have some integrity. And what better way to demonstrate that the symbolic would match the substantive than to locate the campus on eighty-five acres and deploy a vocabulary and visual register that saw the landscape as naturally carceral? This illuminates important features of carceral habitus and raises critical questions about how the ways in which the world is visually perceived are subject to the structuring logics of the neoliberal state.[4] In Monroe County, local derelict landscapes, structured into that form by capital's migrations, became naturalized carceral opportunities.

The justice campus was possible in Monroe County only because local critics of mass incarceration believed that they would build and operate something distinct from that and characteristic of the community. The ability to believe in the idea of a community unmoored from any spatial or ideological connection to the carceral state (or even to neighboring counties) is clearly a geographical and ideological feat.

But justice campus advocates also had to extract the site from its temporal context. During my three years of engagement in the issues this book examines, I heard virtually no mention of the political and economic history of the county that, once known, would seem to be of essential importance to discussions of incarceration expansion. This particular history implicates the relations of production and representation on which the justice campus was contingent. Perhaps just as important, this history indexes the very spatial connections between capital departures and incarceration growth under neoliberal capitalism. At the core of the dominant vision of expansion, then, was a carceral complex and a set of corresponding logics that proponents would have themselves and others believe operated outside of time and space, separated from the histories and corresponding geographies on which it was dependent.

Chapters 1 and 2 subject the justice campus and carceral expansion to historical and spatial analyses. Understanding carceral expansion as a geographical phenomenon opens the justice campus and various proposals for alternatives up to important material and symbolic scrutiny. Monroe County officials' creation of the justice campus on the site where industry once stood; their plan to centralize social services alongside the constitutive institutions of the campus, imbuing the complex with both welfare and security functions; and their belief in the encroachment of alternative sanctions into family and community life by locating them on the local continuum of care all point to a need to analyze the spatial articulations of carceral habitus.

1

Capital Departures and the Arrival of Punishment

Focusing analytically on the eighty-five-acre site for the justice campus reveals the land to be a spatial index of the community's broader historical and economic lineage. That site, a mile south of downtown Bloomington, locates the justice campus in a larger story of globalization and migrations of industry, capital, and jobs into and eventually out of the community. The site was known colloquially in the county as "the old RCA site," referring to the Radio Corporation of America—the well-known multinational corporation that makes household electronic products—that had bought the property in 1940 from the local Showers Brothers furniture company.[1]

RCA's arrival at that historical moment was met with great excitement locally. Unemployment was high—above 40 percent—and the community also had high rates of foreclosures and dependency on federal assistance.[2] As one work of local history notes, "for many in Bloomington, the Great Depression ended on February 22, 1940 when they learned that the Radio Corporation of America had purchased one of the Showers plants for a new factory."[3] The company had identified the community as a source of cheap and semiskilled labor. Employing three hundred local residents, its plant started producing domestic radio receivers as early as June 1940. Production continued until 1942, when the plant began to convert to war production. According to the "RCA Handbook of Information in Bloomington," from 1960, "the first product in this program was a tank receiver for the US Army. Later, civilian production was further curtailed and work was started in the production of the proximity fuse for the Navy. In 1944 civilian production was completely curtailed and the plant was devoted to the production of war materials. Several other items were placed in production along with the proximity fuse."[4] After the end of the war, RCA shifted production rapidly to household consumer products, for which the company would become world-renowned. In 1949, the company produced its first television set; five years later, it would produce the first color television set in the United States. By the mid-1950s, Bloomington was known as the "color television capital of the world."[5] The company's presence in the community had expanded tremendously. The workforce had grown to 3,000 and would expand to 8,000 just years later. RCA was the largest employer in the county.

But in 1968, the company opened production facilities in Ciudad Juarez, Mexico. In 1977, as the company and the local media celebrated the production of the twenty-nine-millionth television at the Bloomington plant, the International Brotherhood of Electrical Workers (IBEW) was filing for trade-adjustment assistance for 1,100 local workers at the plant because of actual and threatened layoffs due to increased imports. The US Labor Department investigated and found for the IBEW, observing that "the average number of production workers at the Bloomington facility declined 18.1 percent in the second half of 1976 . . . and 22 percent in the first quarter of 1977" and that "production of eight television components was transferred from Bloomington to RCA's foreign facilities during 1976 and production of monochrome televisions was transferred from Bloomington to RCA's foreign facilities during the second quarter of 1977."[6] The last three decades of the twentieth century found the company—sometimes slowly but sometimes quite rapidly[7]—shedding jobs in Monroe County.

Critically, the shift in what Jefferson Cowie calls the "international division of labor" was attributable to the growing globalization and mobility of capital (1999, 127). More specifically, RCA's relocation of production to Ciudad Juarez came on the heels of the expanding labor power of Bloomington's workforce and the attraction of accumulating more capital by hiring nonunion Mexican workers in maquiladoras who were accustomed to making fifty cents an hour, much less than the union wages Bloomington workers were paid.

In 1984, RCA sold its production facilities to General Electric (GE), which already had a presence in the area, for $6.4 billion. GE sold the facility to the French electronics company Thomson within a year, but the original sale still resulted in wage cuts and 272 job losses. In February 1985, the Monroe County Council passed a tax abatement plan for the site, saving Thomson $100,000 a year for five years and establishing the site as an economic revitalization area, a designation set up by state law that provides tax breaks to companies for varying periods of time for making different improvements. Ironically and somewhat bizarrely, both Thomson executives and county officials recognized that the abatement—which the company had requested in order to upgrade its equipment—would likely lead to even more layoffs, because new equipment would mechanize tasks that humans had been performing. Bob Arnett, the plant's manager at the time, insisted that the new equipment was necessary for the company to "become more competitive in the market (which) would mean more jobs for Bloomington in the future."[8] Four years later, in an address during an elaborate ceremony to celebrate the fifty-millionth television produced in Bloomington, Bernard Isautier, the chairman and CEO of Thomson, appeared to reject the notion that the company was succumbing to the pressures of neoliberal globalization and to claim that instead it was committing itself to the community: "For Thomson, Bloomington is not just another plant. It is not a pawn on a chess board that happens to be sitting on a square called Indiana, waiting to be moved as circumstances dictate to some other square across some border or halfway around the world. This is not so much out of some sense of loyalty to the community, although that factor is far from being insignificant, as it is an acknowledgement of how valuable that community's accumulated experience in television manufacturing has become in the global competition." [9] In the ensuing decade, the manufacturing plant continued to reduce its production. Then, in the spring of 1998, Thomson finally closed its doors in Bloomington for good and laid off the last of its 1,100 workers there.[10]

In addition to the departure of Thomson, Monroe County lost thousands of industrial jobs during the 1990s with the downsizing of its two other major employers outside of the university: Otis Elevator and GE. *Herald-Times* articles from the late 1980s note that GE employed 2,100 workers, RCA just under 2,000, and Otis close to 1,200. At the time of the justice campus proposal, RCA had been gone for almost ten years. Otis had shifted all of its production to other places, including China and Mexico; it officially shuttered its Bloomington plant and laid off its remaining 200 employees during the writing of this book. GE offered one economic bright spot. Although the company had announced it was shutting its plant in 2006, it cancelled that decision in 2009, instead laying off 200 more workers and bringing the number of its local employees down to 500. Then in 2010 the company announced it was making a new investment in the local plant to manufacture new refrigerators that used green technologies. The investment from GE would bring job security to the remaining 500 workers and offered some hope that new jobs would be created. Still, having lost over 1,500 jobs in twenty years, the plant was a shadow of its former self.

Despite the spatial and temporal continuity of the justice campus to RCA and Thomson through the eighty-five-acre site, not a single informant spoke of this history as having any bearing on the contemporary debates over the justice campus. Important work in geography suggests that this silence is not surprising. Don Mitchell (2000, 94) has written that landscapes should be considered as both work (the product of labor and social contests over space) and as something that does work (a social agent that develops particular representations of places). Part of the work that landscape performs is the naturalization and even erasure of the relations of production and social struggles that created it (Mitchell 2000, 103–4), an ideological function that includes a "particular means of organizing and experiencing the *visual order* of those things on the land" (Mitchell 2003, 242). Importantly, in its symbolic burial of RCA and Thomson and the history of departed capital and labor under the pastoral and benevolent campus, the proposal performed a necessary moralizing and aestheticizing of the imagined carceral landscape.[11]

Despite the absence of these histories from official justice campus proceedings and from media coverage of them, the migration of capital and jobs that followed companies out of the county—particularly in the case of RCA and Thomson—would seem to be a critical part of the justice campus story. First, officials imagined a pathologically poor jail(able) population, rendering local poverty and crime as ahistorical phenomena (and thus attributable to moral and cultural failure) rather than as situated in the historical and transnational operations of capital that structured the local political economy. In looking to build the justice campus on the very site from which 8,000 jobs disappeared and a factory was razed, local officials proposed an answer to the question of what is left for the children and grandchildren of the class of skilled (if narrowly so), un- or undereducated, and now jobless workers in the wake of migrations of capital and jobs into and out of the county: carceral futures.[12] Indeed, one story in the *Herald-Times* following up on the plant's closure noted that Thomson's departure affected surrounding businesses that depended on the factory; and a second article, a year after the company left, noted that the 1,100 workers it had laid off had either taken lower-paying work or were still unemployed.[13]

Second, the very ability to imagine a justice campus was predicated on the ways in which transnational structural forces had shaped the spatial and political possibilities in the county. Quite literally, the justice campus concept relied on Thomson's departure and the resulting loss of jobs and capital for its material and spatial potential. Local officials, business leaders, and justice administrators sought to resolve crises brought about by neoliberal globalization and neoliberal state devolution through carceral expansion. This pattern of using carceral growth to resolve issues of political economic crisis and resulting surpluses of land, as well as replacing lost industry and jobs, is not unique to Bloomington and the county; in fact, it connects the events in the community to similar stories around the United States.[14]

There is more. By the series of hearings about the justice campus in 2008, some of the original 200-acre Thomson site had already been developed and repurposed. Proponents of the campus frequently referred to the eighty-five acres as an "infill site," locating it rhetorically and spatially in terms of its existing neighbors. Articles during the ten years between Thomson's departure and the justice campus proposal in the *Herald-Times*, including several by its business editor, and in the main alternative news source in Monroe County, the *Bloomington Alternative*, chart the development of the surplus land from abandoned industrial zone to the spatial icon of the new high-tech and life-sciences local economy.[15] These stories detail questionable public-private partnerships involving the mayor's office, the quasipublic Bloomington Economic Development Corporation (made up of local business leaders but funded in part by tax revenues), and a group of local investors (also local business leaders and developers) to market and sell the property. Indeed, the local investors, operating through a separate company called Patterson Management Group and a subsidiary, First Capital Investments, purchased the two-hundred-acre site and two million square feet of warehouse space from Thomson in 1999 for $12 million. First Capital, with the city's help, aggressively marketed the site and sold three-quarters of it to investors affiliated with the Baptist Foundation of Arizona, a nonprofit religious foundation that would eventually collapse under the weight of its own fraudulent Ponzi scheme in the largest bankruptcy of a nonprofit organization in American history.[16] The sale, for an undisclosed amount but no doubt profitable for the Patterson Management Group, occurred in 1999, the same year that the foundation filed for bankruptcy. After the private property was sold to the new private investors in the foundation, the president of the Bloomington Economic Development Corporation—again, a quasipublic entity focused on economic development—would note in the *Herald-Times* that the organization was looking forward to marketing the site to new tenants.[17]

At this point in the chronology of the property, the story continues along seemingly distinct tracks: financial development and carceral expansion. Of course, the tracks are not the least bit distinct. The municipal investment strategies that channeled county growth plans through the major infrastructural development required to accommodate an eighty-five-acre justice campus brings into relief that what was happening at the Thomson site—relationships between developers and county officials; tax abatements and creative districting and financing to attract and subsidize corporations; and, of course, plans for massive carceral expansion—was the restructuring of the state itself, scaled to the county level.

Financial Development

Over the ensuing years, First Capital Investments would continue to develop the acreage it owned as well as move into one of the existing structures on the property. All along, the organization enjoyed important support from the city. First, in 2000, a key legal and financial advisor to the mayor left his post to join First Capital as a partner. One year later, First Capital concluded that the building it was in—one of RCA's original production facilities—was unsalvageable and economically impractical to renovate. First Capital approached the city, including the mayor's office and the city council, for financial assistance in demolition and reconstruction. In a move that raises questions about political patronage and public financing of private capital, the city obliged via several sources of what the *Herald-Times* would call "creative financing" in the form of multiple tax incentives.[18] These included the designation of the area as a Tax Increment Financing (TIF) District by the county government and a Community Revitalization and Enhancement District (CRED) by the state of Indiana.[19] TIF funding pools the property tax revenue of those properties housed within the TIF District and allocates it to the designated entity, in this case First Capital, as developer of the site. CRED funding comes from sales, income, and local option income taxes.[20] In addition to assisting with the demolition of the old building, the TIF funding was intended to be used as incentive for existing businesses to relocate to the site. The location was also in Bloomington's Urban Enterprise Zone, a business-friendly district that provided a variety of tax breaks to local businesses within it. Financial records for the state indicate that the Thomson site had captured $4.5 million in revenue between 1999, when the CRED zone was established, and 2011.[21]

First Capital planned a new business park for the site, to follow on the heels of the original furniture plant and RCA and Thomson. As a *Herald-Times* article from early 2001 noted, the site "already has moved from being a vacant wasteland to a quietly thriving warehousing center," with several local business using the space. However, at this point the site was destined for "high-tech businesses, providing employment opportunities for area residents." The article quotes the CEO of First Capital predicting that the business park, now dubbed the Indiana Enterprise Center, would become a premier urban office park: "We believe this development will attract high-tech companies that need flexible space to grow their businesses. With the city's help, we're going to transform this site into an employment center for high-skilled and highly paid workers." The prediction foreshadowed the larger change from unionized and industrial labor to high-wage, white-collar work.[22] Indeed, after eight years and significant site development, multiple businesses occupied parts of the original two hundred acres. In October 2008, almost on the same day as the first of the four PARI hearings about the justice campus, the mayor, the governor, and executives from First Capital announced plans to build a research and office campus with Leadership in Energy and Environmental Design (LEED) certification on the former Thomson site, close to the projected location of the justice campus. The first tenant would be a life sciences biotechnology company that promised to create seventy-five new jobs over the following three years.[23]

A 2009 editorial in the *Herald-Times* notes another business in particular, a pharmaceutical manufacturing company, whose presence had resulted in about four hundred new jobs. The editorial's celebration of the company's success is instructive because it reveals the dramatic economic restructuring at play in the community. In lauding the new jobs, the editors note the "importance of the life sciences sector to the local economy" and point out that Bloomington "has lost thousands of 20th Century-style manufacturing jobs over the last three decades. Let this celebration also serve to remind us that the transition to a new kind of local economy is continuing."[24] Indeed, as Cowie had noted about this transition ten years earlier, "jobs for college-trained professionals grew to define Monroe County, while locals with little or no higher education shifted from industrial to low-paying service work" (1999, 140).

Carceral Development

As First Capital prepared the property as a site for local businesses, an Arizona court appointed a new group called New Assets Subsidiary to liquidate the Baptist Foundation of Arizona's assets. In March 2002, the commissioners of Monroe County voted to purchase eighty-five of the two hundred acres from New Assets Subsidiary for $1.2 million dollars, a fraction of the parcel's original price. Multiple sources indicate unequivocally that the county purchased the acres for one reason: to build a juvenile facility, a work release center, and a new jail. First, *Herald-Times* articles covering the public hearings and the subsequent county commissioner vote during that spring include numerous quotes from public officials' testimony explicitly discussing the carceral future of the site.[25] Subsequent county and consultant reports between 2002 and 2008, including one from an ad hoc juvenile justice task force comprised of county leaders, confirm that the county had never considered using the site for any other purpose and had never considered constructing the facilities anywhere else.[26] Importantly, it would seem that by locating the justice campus on the site with the existing businesses, the campus would be eligible for the same tax breaks and creative financing that were used to develop the land for private investment. In the *Herald-Times'* story covering the release of the official PARI report in May 2009, Richard Kemp of PARI noted that the campus would be eligible for both federal stimulus money and the same TIF monies on which First Capital relied.[27] Finally, in my ethnographic work from 2008–10—in particular, my attendance at the PARI hearings—I heard testimonies from officials and consultants that the eighty-five acres had been bought with a justice campus in mind and that carceral expansion had been considered only on that site. Indeed, one of the few county politicians to challenge the justice campus proposal made this very point. Speaking up at the end of the first PARI hearing, which had been focused exclusively on the juvenile facility, Tom Redmond—a member of the county council who would become one of the few officials to work in a partnership of sorts with Decarcerate Monroe County—briefly addressed the gathering:

> As far as the discussion tonight about the building, I just heard [Juvenile Court] Judge Randall say the building would be a community decision . . . [but] the decision on where that building will be built is not a community decision; it's a county commissioners' decision. The commissioners have already unilaterally decided that it will be at the RCA property and the RCA property only. No matter if it's an industrial brown zone that has no infrastructure in it, and they will be putting the jail and the youth detention center together. Now this will be discussed at the final hearing. There is a reason that it's at the end. They're gonna be putting the young people in the same piece of real estate as the adult criminals. And that has been stated by Commissioner Richards, that is the only option. They are not willing to look at what the postal service did here, and that is to survey all of the properties to see where is the best place we can put this at, because they want to put it there because that is what they own and they bought it at a fire-sale price. That is my basic concern.

In the three years of my involvement in this issue, this was one of the very few times that someone spoke directly about the important role of the eighty-five-acre site in determining the carceral politics under discussion. Although Redmond's comments were fleeting and quickly muted, his series of points radically disrupted the silence imposed by the imagined carceral landscape.

While the justice campus proposed for the former Thomson site is the most obvious way that local economic restructuring affected local carceral politics, there are other examples. Bloomington's Urban Enterprise Zone marked important transitions in the local economy from manufacturing to high-technology and life sciences, changes that few officials questioned. With this transition at the former Thomson site, about a mile south of downtown, came community revitalization efforts in the downtown itself, including significant high-end residential development in the form of rental and condominium units targeting wealthy university students and young professionals.[28] Along with such development, in recent years, the city police have explicitly prioritized so-called quality-of-life policing, an approach that focuses on aestheticizing the downtown by removing signs of homelessness, poverty, and disorder that constitute the proverbial "broken windows."[29] This approach reflected a town caught between a visible underclass and an elite and was a form of "individualizing disorder" (A. Feldman 1991, 109) that obscured the disordering effects of gentrification behind the criminalization of poverty. In one instructive example of this approach, in the summer of 2013 the city installed 1,400 parking meters all over the downtown, where none had existed before. Of course, metered parking will not affect the residents of downtown rental and condominium apartments who have the luxury of private parking. According to the city's website, the meters generate up to $30,000 in revenue a week.[30] Part of the revenue generated from the meters funds new downtown police patrols, including "uniformed, plainclothes, squad car, bicycle, [and] foot patrol[s]"[31] specifically focused on "public intoxication, vandalism and panhandling."[32] In addition, the city's announcement of the parking meters also noted "graffiti eradication" and "panhandling enforcement" as programs separate from the patrols that the meters would fund.[33] The *Herald-Times* endorsed this plan in an editorial titled "Extra Focus in Downtown Bloomington on Public Safety Is Welcome, Cameras and All."[34] Such an endorsement resonates with recent observations by leading scholars of the geography of punishment about practices of urban banishment in Seattle, where that city's "social control regime lies in sharp contrast to its progressive image."[35] Indeed, the deployment of the police to use arrest as a form of moral regulation reflected county priorities about capital accumulation and a certain chic downtown aesthetic.[36]

In many respects, the patterns of capital investment and divestment in the community illuminate central characteristics of what Neil Smith has called the "see saw movement of capital" (2008, 198; see also 1996).

He argues that the development of a particular area leads to the development of a productive workforce, which in turn leads to lower unemployment, increases in wages, and the development of unions—all of which lower the rate of profit and take away the impetus for development in the first place. At the opposite pole, lack of capital leads to high unemployment, low wages, and reduced organization by workers. Thus, Smith concludes:

> The underdevelopment of specific areas leads, in time, to precisely those conditions that make an area highly profitable and hence susceptible to rapid development. Underdevelopment, like development, proceeds at every spatial scale and capital attempts to move geographically in such a way that it continually exploits the opportunities of development without suffering these economic costs of underdevelopment. That is, capital attempts to seesaw from a developed to an underdeveloped area, then at a later point back to the first area which is by now underdeveloped . . . [capital] resorts to complete mobility as a spatial fix; here again, spatial fixity and spacelessness are but prongs of the same fork. Capital seeks not an equilibrium built into the landscape but one that is viable precisely in its ability to jump landscapes in a systematic way. This is the seesaw movement of capital, which lies behind larger uneven development practices. (2008, 198)

The arrival of RCA in "anything but an industrial town,"[37] the rapid development of a productive and organized labor force, and the loss of 8,000 jobs and departure of RCA's successor, Thomson, illuminate this process. But I would add that the subsequent reinvestment in the community through finance capital and in the form of high-tech and biotech jobs, to say nothing of the justice campus, illuminates how uneven development is "social inequality blazoned into the geographical landscape, and it is simultaneously the exploitation of that geographical unevenness for certain socially determined ends" (N. Smith 2008, 206).

The migration of industrial capital and jobs out of the community and subsequent attempts at carceral expansion is a familiar story in the United States, and it comes with distinct consequences.[38] Locally, the attempt to complete the continuum from industry loss to carceral growth aligns closely with what geographers have noted about conceptions of space under neoliberalism. Steve Herbert and Elizabeth Brown, for example, argue that "conceptions of space help underwrite contemporary practices of exclusion," that " space is not just impacted by neoliberal policies, but that its conceptualization importantly helps legitimate those policies," and, most important for present purposes, that "popularized conceptions of space affect how neoliberalism conceals inequality while simultaneously promoting its spatialized entrenchment" (2006, 756). In addition to structuring the county to lose the Thomson plant, neoliberalism also structured the very ways in which officials could perceive the now-empty space.[39]

Ruth Wilson Gilmore (2007, 11) has proposed that the view of prisons as sitting on the physical edge—at the margins of social spaces and containing marginal people who are marginalized in fights for rights—belies the reality that prisons are interfaces of spaces, peoples, and issues, connecting noncontiguous places into relationships. The justice campus enacted a similar place-making function, connecting (and collapsing) local, national, and transnational histories and forces into a singular institutional complex. In contrast to officials' attempts to distance the justice campus from the politics of mass incarceration, the complex's spatial and temporal interfaces with capital connect it intimately to national trends of incarceration.

The history of the site owned by RCA and then Thomson is more than just part of the community's political and economic context. The departure of capital produced the very spatial conditions necessary for the justice campus vision and proposal. The landscape weaves into and through the community a much larger story of deindustrialization, fluctuations of labor power, the growing consolidation of corporate power and liquidity of capital under neoliberalism, and the transition from Keynesian economic development to carceral Keynesian investment. The growing power of incarceration to shape local priorities inscribed the landscape with the spatial, security, and welfare logics of carceral expansion. Moreover, in an ironic and ahistorical articulation, officials imagined the justice campus as a new and central mechanism for extending educational, rehabilitative, and acculturating programs to the county's poor and incarcerated people, preparing them for precisely the kind of work that had left the community a decade earlier from the very location at which they would now be incarcerated.[40]

2

Consolidations and Expansions

Welfare and the "Alternatives" Archipelago

Carceral Welfare

The landscape of the proposed justice campus would have worked to structure social relations in the county in a number of ways.[1] Perhaps the central expression of carceral habitus in Monroe County was a specific vision of the justice campus that integrated penal and welfare logics into one articulation of carceral expansion. Early in my fieldwork, Monroe County Chief Probation Officer Carrie Donnelly sought a meeting with two community organizers from Decarcerate Monroe County (DMC) in order to clarify her position on the justice campus. She was interested in hearing DMC's perspective, but she also believed that the organization was misinformed and had been overstating the problematic nature of the justice campus proposal. My field notes from our meeting convey Donnelly's vision for the campus:

> During the meeting, Donnelly laid out her personal and more expansive vision of the campus: to erect on the 85 acre site a complex that would include not only adult and youth jails, but also centralized social services. She explained that such a configuration would enable the poor of the county to visit their loved ones in jail while also accessing the food pantries, housing and employment assistance, and social work offices that formed the important components of their safety net. In this vision, the justice campus would constitute a one-stop-shop for poor people, a bucolic strip mall of incarceration and social service.

At least two other officials important to the justice campus proposal—Bill Rusch, a former juvenile court judge whom many officials credited as the campus's intellectual architect, and District Court Judge Anne Lakewood—expressed a similarly expansive vision for the eighty-five-acre site. Rusch proposed a concept in which it would house the justice campus alongside social services and alternatives to incarceration. He explained to me the logic he used while "working it in this community" to push his vision when he sat on the county bench: "The RCA site offers us smart growth. We've got this asset, close to town, and with room to grow. It satisfies our needs now and for decades into the future." The county had indeed bought the site for the express purpose of building some permutation of a justice complex, and Rusch did his part to push the project through in its most expansive iteration. Lakewood, who had expressed some reservations about locating both youth and adult facilities on the campus, nonetheless embraced a hybrid welfare-carceral concept. At the same Democratic Party candidate forum held at the downtown library where I first heard Reuben Davison speak, Lakewood appealed to voters by delineating her vision: "I believe that this center that we have talked about—a justice center—could be one-stop community programming . . . where we have child care for single women and parents who desperately need it . . . and laundry facilities. As we create the center, we will bring in the people who haven't necessarily seen the system."

Landscape performs important work in these visions. First, the eighty-five-acre site would be able to structure expansionist carceral policy for the foreseeable future. Rusch consistently raised the importance of the size of the site, arguing that it could both satisfy the correctional needs of the county now and for decades in the future, as the county could add on incrementally as needed. It was precisely this prospect, and its naturalization into community habitus as so-called smart growth, that community organizers and others opposed to the justice campus feared: having larger facilities with room to grow would structure carceral policy for the foreseeable future, neutralizing any need to decarcerate and enabling continued expansion.

Second, these officials believed a more capacious vision for the campus would do the county poor a favor by offering a streamlined and efficient experience of negotiating the social service bureaucracy. Of course, this vision also suggested a subsuming of the actual needs of people in favor of concerns about bureaucratic management and operations. Donnelly, Rusch, Lakewood and others collapsed welfare and the carceral into one spatial and political articulation, a model that expressed a "single policy regime aimed at the governance of social marginality,"[2] and envisioned a larger bureaucratic model of governing though incarceration.[3] While no doubt attempting to alleviate some of the burdens of travel for people accessing the community's safety net, officials nonetheless envisioned a physical carceral continuum where the jail, juvenile facility, and work release center ensnared food pantries, housing assistance, shelters, and other services in their domain. Indeed, Donnelly noted that the justice campus would help poor people by "allowing them to visit their loved ones and then go get their food stamps," and Lakewood hoped that the services that would be located at the carceral space would pull into their orbit "the people who haven't necessarily seen the system." This offered a narrow and potentially harmful geography of poverty by identifying and attempting to instantiate the carceral facility as the central organizing mechanism of poor people's lives.

Robin Trotter, the juvenile probation supervisor, offered similar comments at the first justice campus hearing. After speaking passionately about the positive relationships her officers had with the young people on their caseloads, she commented on the expansive role of probation in the lives of the families mandated to them and the potential she saw in the facilites of the justice campus for an increased presence:

> We provide educational support to every kid in Monroe County that's involved in our system. That could be GED prep, we provide resources, some of the families we deal with don't have a computer. "Hey, come and use our Internet!" Maybe they don't have a color printer. We help kids learn study skills, organizational skills, we partner with Indiana University to provide functional family therapy, which is a blueprint, evidence-based, internationally renowned program. . . . Some of our families have never been on the university campus, so simply to be exposed to the campus is fabulous. We also provide aggression replacement training, which again is an evidence-based program and very cognitive. We provide a similar program for parents. It talks about problem solving, it talks about anger chain, it talks about how you practice having a difficult conversation, how do you make a compliment, how do you deal with stressful situations, 'cause we know if someone bumps you in the hallway we all don't bump back. So what happens in some of our heads to prevent that and what happens in some of our heads that doesn't? We are extraor-

dinarily treatment-oriented, we are extremely rehabilitation-focused . . . and the number one barrier to us providing additional programming for kids is space. The thing I'm looking forward to with this facility is space: day treatment programs, opportunities for parenting classes, opportunities for kids to learn different skills—life skills, homemaking, all of those different skills that we know are critical for them to be successful.

I will leave aside for the moment the ways Trotter described the population with whom she worked (a task that chapters 3 and 4 take up). Monroe County juvenile probation clearly offered substantial services and programs for young people, but Trotter's testimony is instructive in that it reveals the intimacy—even the interdependency—between program provision and increased carceral space. Indeed, Trotter and many other officials spoke of the centrality of expanded carceral space to providing such programs and the need for such space. That is, community programs for young people were channeled exclusively through the probation office and juvenile court. Expansion of those programs and services appeared possible only through expanding the carceral infrastructure.

Theorizing Carceral Welfare

In the vision of the three constitutive carceral components alongside centralized social services, the justice campus would perform a clasping of the left and right hands of the local government, suturing social welfare to penal policies, geographies, and individuals (Bourdieu 1994; Wacquant 2009b and 2010). In remaking carceral expansion as a welfarist policy initiative, county officials conceptualized their project as operating outside of the logics of mass incarceration, even as the justice campus and the local discourse clearly relied on established—and even previously hegemonic—ideas about punishment and welfare.[4] Theorizing the local articulation of the justice campus as an attempted disarticulation from the carceral state requires an examination of how penal, education, welfare, and other fields structured local individual and community bodies in such a way that they would both endorse carceral growth and maintain that they were, in fact, doing exactly the opposite.

The collapse of welfare and neoliberal state logics into one project produced a carceral model with a number of contradictions. In consistently eschewing punishment for rehabilitation and insisting that the justice campus and its constitutive elements would be based on therapeutic justice, officials resurrected penal welfarist approaches to crime and delinquency, all the while implicitly positioning county carceral politics as distinct and exceptional.[5] Moreover, in the visions of Donnelly, Rusch, Lakewood and others, the justice campus would serve as a hub of welfare, a centralized location of incarceration and social services around which the lives of the county poor could orbit.

Of course, such a vision is complicated and co-opted not only by the problematic rendering of poverty and carcerality as interchangeable and colocatable conditions, but also by the underlying neoliberal logic of creating massive new exclusionary spaces that physically confine populations perceived as risky and subjects them to coerced treatment. Indeed, as Bernard Harcourt has noted, "the logic of neoliberal penality *facilitates* contemporary punishment practices by encouraging the belief that the legitimate space for government intervention is in the penal sphere—*there and there alone*" (2010, 80). Loïc Wacquant has written extensively on this idea, arguing in an article that his book *Punishing the Poor* "insert[s] the police, the courts, and the prison as core constituents of the 'Right hand' of the state" and suggests that scholars "need to bring penal policies from the periphery to the center" in our analyses of neoliberal poverty (2010, 201). Indeed, in *Punishing the Poor*, he argues that the United States has shifted priorities, discourses, and resources from the social to the penal wings of the state and, in doing so, has enacted a "colonization of the welfare sector by the panoptic and punitive logic characteristic of the postrehabilitation penal bureaucracy. The slanting of state activity from the social to the penal arm and the incipient penalization of welfare, in turn, partake of the *remasculinization of the state*" (2009b, 289–90).

While the penalization of welfare to which Wacquant refers is the gradual erosion of public funding and the growing reliance on so-called workfare, the conceptualization of a social service hub located within a carceral complex suggests a similar phenomenon. Donnelly and other officials may have intended to ease the burdens of people in need by colocating carceral punishment and social service, but they no doubt relied on a construction of "kindred problem populations" requiring "people-processing institutions" (Wacquant 2009b, 291). In the inclusion of so many county residents in one vision of carceral space, it is perhaps instructive to consider the campus as a centralized site of exclusion through which the community would reproduce and commingle the social categories of criminals and poor people.[6]

But the justice campus doesn't fit neatly into Wacquant's reconceptualization of the relationship between the left and right hands of the state. He argues that the new government of social insecurity has changed the notion of "poor relief" to mean relief "from the poor" through punitive containment and "by forcibly 'disappearing' the most disruptive of them, from the shrinking welfare rolls on the one hand and into the swelling dungeons of the carceral castle on the other" (2009b, 295; 2010, 204).[7] Wacquant's larger claim about the expansion of penal approaches to problems of poverty is certainly apposite. Yet framing this transition to penality solely as a function of the ideological control of the neoliberal state misses the ways in which, in Monroe County, the same institutional shifts were framed as an expansion of welfare. As I noted above, county politicians imagined the justice campus to operate outside of punitive carceral politics. None of my respondents sought to minimize social services; on the contrary, many were critical of "workfare" politics in Indiana and around the country. Locally, they sought to route county welfare through the carceral apparatus. The campus, they argued, would further instantiate a locally robust social service network and safety net while imbuing the neighboring carceral facilities with an ethos of therapeutic justice. The transition from the "kindly 'nanny state' of the Fordist-Keynesian era to the strict 'daddy state' of neoliberalism" that Wacquant (2009b, 290) observes was, in Monroe County, actually a transmogrification: the community safety net would become the carceral apparatus.[8]

This vision of the justice campus straddled more than a century of carceral ideology. On the one hand, it unmistakably revived Progressive era conceptions of a fundamental trust in the state, even in matters of criminal justice. As David Rothman notes, Progressive reformers "saw no reason to circumscribe narrowly the discretion of the state because there was no opposition between its power to help and its power to police" (2002, 61). Thus, Rothman argues, "the state could be trusted with expanded powers because the problem of crime, as of poverty, *was merely a managerial one: to make certain that the benefits of American society reached all citizens*" (ibid., 60–61; my emphasis).

On the other hand, the subsuming of welfare (the "power to help") in incarceration (the "power to police") is characteristic of the contemporary politics of what Simon Hallsworth and John Lea have called the "post-welfare hegemonic project" of securitization (2011, 144). The vision of hybrid carceral governance that resurrected welfare state logics but confined them to the expanded coercive and punitive institution enacted an important dis/juncture: a politics reminiscent of Progressive era criminal justice but animated by the distinctive logics of neoliberal penality (Harcourt 2010).

Yet it would be myopic to lay the vision of the justice campus solely at the feet of neoliberal punishment. An argument could be made that the justice campus vision of carceral welfare was not surprising, contradictory, or novel. Following work that traces the genealogy of the logic of security,[9] the campus can perhaps best be understood as a rather explicit expression of a connection between social and national security that often goes uninterrogated. In the state's efforts to manage the disordering effects provoked by both the operations of capital and the state's responses to those operations—precisely what Bloomington was experiencing through the rapid departure of capital, the loss of jobs, and the gentrifying downtown—the securitization of surplus workers and others who might pose a threat to the aesthetics of order becomes paramount. Crucially, in this treatment, carceral and welfare perform similar functions for the state, albeit through different means: securitizing threatening bodies through direct violence or pacification.

Alternatives and the Carceral Archipelago

Perhaps there is no better illustration of this hybrid carceral governance—and its archipelagic spatial expression—than county officials' construction of alternatives to incarceration. In the context of criminal justice politics in Monroe County, everyone endorsed alternatives to incarceration. Many people—from the most conservative judge to abolitionist community organizers—invoked alternatives as integral to solving problems of overcrowding and overincarceration.

The consensus about the importance of alternatives belied the contested terrain of what "alternative" actually meant. For many officials, alternatives to incarceration primarily referred to sanctions within their arsenal other than jail, including the components of the justice campus. For example, Judge Allan Barrett, a member of the bench in Monroe County since 1979 and at the time of this writing the circuit court's presiding judge and lone Republican, observed that the larger size of the campus and its housing of community corrections would permit multiple programs, such as day reporting, to be located there. At one of the public hearings about the campus, Barrett explained:

> Day reporting requires daily "blow and go's" at community corrections to see if they have been drinking and periodic drug screens. Again it's a lesser form of monitoring so they can be out of the jail and we can monitor them. We've gotten to the point with this in pretrial diversion where we have about 200 offenders reporting each day between 7:00 and 9:00 a.m. We do have some problems. We don't have funding to operate this on the weekends. When are people most likely to drink and use drugs? The weekends. And we can't monitor them, so we need additional funding for that.

For Barrett, the spatial capacity of the campus held the potential to widen the scope of alternatives available to him and other members of the county bench. The justice campus could house the three constitutive institutions and increase the community's control and surveillance of community members not incarcerated at the site.

As I briefly mentioned above in this chapter, Rusch envisioned the site as housing alternatives to incarceration adjacent to the carceral facilities, a concept that required some intellectual gymnastics to overlook all of the spatial continuities that would seem to violate the very distinctions supposedly in place between incarceration and its alternatives. As Rusch explained to me, his vision of the site included "a hybrid public-private partnership that created a continuum of care, including the offices for CASA [Court-Appointed Special Advocates], the welfare department, other nonprofit agencies, inpatient treatment, group homes, and detention and jail." Angrily, he insisted that the concept of a "continuum of care," a trope in frequent circulation in the community, had to include jail and juvenile detention.

These kinds of visions enumerate and enliven Michel Foucault's famous construct of the carceral archipelago. Foucault notes that the continuum refers not only to the seepage of logics from the prison into other structures of society but also to the physical continuities between the institutions, including "public assistance with the orphanage, the reformatory, the penitentiary, the disciplinary battalion, the prison; the school with the charitable society, the workshop, the almshouse, the penitentiary convent; the worker's estate with the hospital and the prison" (1977, 299).

The conceptualization of one site housing maximum-security carceral facilities, nonpunitive alternative programs, and social welfare agencies as points on a continuum of care permits a deeper engagement with the spatial expressions of local carceral habitus. Moreover, the integration of the diverse, contradictory, and perhaps incompatible logics of carceral punishment and social service treatment brings up again the county's articulation of security and welfare in one spatial complex. In contrast to officials' plans and proclamations, important scholarship has noted that, in addition to the institutions whose explicit mission is incarceration (jails and prisons), the military, child guidance centers, detention halls, and welfare offices are also "branches of the carceral society's apparatus for controlling the deviants; and few of them retain a true rehabilitative program."[10] Despite the benevolence that officials believed was embodied in their visions of alternatives, their proposals would expand and consolidate the county's capacity for social control.

Problem-Solving Courts: Drug Court

The creation of the justice campus was not the only way in which county officials attempted expansion through alternative sanctions. Many local leaders expressed pride in the alternative court model in operation in the county, which included drug and truancy courts. At the time of this writing, more were under consideration, including mental health and reentry courts. Many county officials boasted about the success of the local drug court, which offered what they called "chemically dependent adults" an alternative to jail that focused on a rigorous treatment program. During my fieldwork outside of the county jail during visiting hours, I heard numerous people praise the local drug court for helping them or their loved ones begin to lead sober lives. Indeed, the Monroe County drug court had won national recognition, and studies had demonstrated that it had important results with implications for lower recidivism and cost reduction. In particular, a study of the court by the Northwest Professional Consortium (NPC), based in Portland, Oregon,[11] included the following findings:

- The local Drug Court reduces recidivism by 67% and saves taxpayer money.
- The program demonstrated a graduation rate of 56% compared to the national average of 48%.
- The recidivism rate for Monroe County's participants (including drop-outs) was 17% while the rate for the comparison group was 33%.
- Drug Court participants (regardless of graduation status) were found to be half as likely to have had any arrests in the 2-year follow-up period relative to the comparison group.
- Drug Court graduates had an even lower recidivism rate of 11%.
- NPC found that program participants were arrested 3 times less often than those who qualified but chose not to participate.
- NPC projected $7,040.00 in cost savings for avoided criminal justice and victimization costs per participant in the local drug court program. (Wiest et al. 2007)

These statistics are compelling and suggest that drug court offers important, perhaps invaluable, support to community residents. However, for the present purposes it is also important to examine drug court beyond the story that these numbers tell and to consider its function as an extension of the county carceral apparatus, simultaneously widening its scope and inscribing the so-called alternative with punitive and coercive logics.

The drug court model relied on several core elements. To be eligible for the program, participants had to plead guilty to a felony. This policy excluded people accused of misdemeanor charges who might have desired drug treatment while also requiring people accused of felonies, but interested in drug court services, to abandon their right to a trial. Moreover, there was no agreement to a reduction in sentence; time in prison hung over drug court participants for the two years they spent in the program should they fail to comply with what was demanded of them. Finally, participants were required to find a job and remain employed, as well as pay all of the fees associated with their two years in the program, including whatever therapy was assigned and the costs of the random drug tests to which they were subjected.

The dubious nature of these requirements was reflected in some of the qualitative data contained in the Northwest Professional Consortium report, which was somewhat conspicuously relegated to the appendices and not mentioned in the executive summary. The following are statements from a focus group conducted by NPC of participants in the Monroe County drug court program, including some of those who completed and some who did not:

- "The intrusive part of drug court for me was when they asked, 'What are you doing with the rest of your time?' I felt that it wasn't a fair question, because I was doing everything that they asked me to do. The rest of my time is my time. When you're on other types of probation, they're not all up in your business."
- "Transportation challenges are probably the toughest thing for participants to deal with in the drug court program."
- "Therapy costs (are a challenge)."
- "Drug Screen costs add up and become a stressor."
- "If you don't have a [driver's] license, you have to figure out a way to get to everything."
- "The program requirements made it hard to find a job and keep a job that pays well. There really wasn't anything that was helpful in the area of employment assistance. I found a job on my own."
- "The majority of people [in the program] don't work full-time; they work part-time jobs because there's not enough full-time employment to go around in this town."
- "I had 3 or 4 interviews where someone said, 'Yeah, if you weren't in drug court, we'd love to give you a job. Come back when you're done.'"
- "I got fired from a job because I'm in the drug court program."
- "Some of the sanctions are too much; like the jail sanctions. I understand that you have to be responsible for your actions, but I think they can find other, more productive ways [to provide consequences] rather than sending the person to jail, which is overcrowded and nasty."

- "I think that, if they [program staff members] would have given me a little bit of credit for talking to them, and not tried to change everything, but instead let me figure out what I needed to do [sic]."
- "It almost felt like you signed your life away when you joined Drug Court. We don't have any control; we do what they want us to do." (Wiest et al. 2007, 57–61)

These testimonies complicate the quantitative evaluation of drug court. Participants noted that the costs were burdensome; employment expectations unrealistic; the stigma of participating in the program could jeopardize employment opportunities; and the program felt patronizing, coercive, and intrusive. Drug court's individualizing approach—broadly characteristic of all of Monroe County's programming—not only ignored the material conditions of its clients but actually exacerbated them, increasing costs, adding to financial stress, and even inhibiting entry into the already contracting labor market.

My point in raising these criticisms is not to engage in an evaluation of drug court's effectiveness or to criticize the motivations for its implementation and growth. Indeed, after talking with people involved in the operation of drug court, it is clear that they genuinely believed it could be a positive intervention into the lives of people with substance abuse problems and could keep people out of jail. Rather, I bring up drug court here, in particular the analyses of it offered by its former participants, to draw attention to the ways in which its status as an alternative belied its very central place on the carceral continuum, both in terms of its logics and values and its location under the looming and coercive shadow of jail or prison time.

Problem-Solving Courts: Truancy Court

In addition to referring to their beliefs about drug court, many officials with whom I spoke cited the growth of a local truancy court, officially known as the Education Compliance Court, as a marker of the county's dedication to progressive solutions and alternatives to incarceration. Notably, some officials who were skeptical of the justice campus were advocates of truancy court. One especially prominent official in this category was David Hillman, the county prosecutor, whose background as a community organizer and activist in Bloomington was well documented and who enjoyed significant support among liberal and leftist county residents. Indeed, I suspect that I was able to interview him for this project because of an overlap in our respective social circles.

At the beginning of our interview, Hillman made a point of informing me that he had purposely stayed out of the justice campus discourse because he found the proposal so troubling. Unlike many of his colleagues, he explicitly located the campus in the larger national trend of increasing prison construction and said that he found the consultant firm, Program Administration and Results, Inc., to be a "scam from the beginning."

Importantly, the existence of Hillman and others shows that any attempt to dichotomize people into officials versus activists would be oversimplified: Hillman was part of a small minority of county officials who criticized the justice campus proposal. Yet Hillman's work also animated the expansion of the carceral net. In this excerpt from my field notes written directly after our interview, I reflect on how to reconcile the contradictions of Hillman's alignment with DMC against the justice campus with his work on behalf of the truancy court:

> Understanding David Hillman in the context of his own personal narrative and self-image provides some insight into how these two seemingly disparate parties perhaps have much in common. Twice during our interview, David self-identified as "anti-authoritarian." Once was somewhat jokingly as I remarked on the warm orange of his office walls and he responded by saying that you're not allowed to paint your office in the justice building so he made sure that was his very first project. The second was more serious and occurred when he discussed identifying more strongly with community organizations and organizers than fellow criminal justice personnel and prosecutors from other counties. This anti-authoritarian nature also comes out in his indictment of bureaucratic inertia, which he says gets in the way of community collaborations. He specifically mentioned the creation of new specialty courts—such as the truancy court and the mental health court—as receiving full support from community members but heel dragging from colleagues within criminal justice. Interestingly, the creation of specialty courts is itself an initiative that reveals Hillman's conflicted standing. While DMC mem-

bers endorse the differential treatment of people with mental health issues or addictions, they remain critical of the very nature of these issues being addressed in the coercive realm of state power that is the court. Hillman, working within the system, sees these as vitally important steps to take to mold the local judiciary to the specific needs of the people who come before it. He spends his time crafting and pushing these initiatives because he sees them as preventive and as true steps toward public safety.

Hillman saw the development of a truancy court as an investment in preventing further involvement in the criminal justice system. On the one hand, he talked about the importance of prevention, keeping youth out of the criminal justice system and disrupting the relationship between truancy, dropping out, and delinquency. On the other hand, he coordinated the campaign to create the truancy court and thus further cemented truancy's transition from an educational issue to a juridical one.[12] Indeed, Hillman boasted that in addition to the school system, the truancy court involved the prosecutor's office, the probation department, and the board of judges. In a community summit on preventing students from dropping out organized by his office, Hillman argued that the court was important because it gave "kids a sense that there are immediate consequences to skipping school." He mentioned that one of the administrators from the county school system most active in referring youth to the court was an assistant principal at a middle school, thus suggesting that preadolescent youth were among the court's more frequent subjects. Hillman observed that he and the other truancy court founders recognized that "the reasons underlying an attendance issue are often complicated social issues, including families in crises, poverty, substance abuse problems . . . and mental health issues. These are issues that the criminal justice system on its own is really not well suited to address. But someone has to address them, and that requires a comprehensive, community based approach—so we have to work with other service providers in the community to help us address these issues."

There are a number of instructive points in these remarks at the summit. Hillman understood truancy as indicative of many other social problems, much the same way that other respondents tied incarceration to poverty and addiction. Conspicuously absent from this analysis was any acknowledgment that truancy, like other forms of deviance, is a socially constructed phenomenon that reflects different and uneven distributions of economic and social capital. No one at the summit asked, for example, whether private schools in the county operated outside of the agreement between the public school system and the prosecutor. Would truants from private schools receive the same treatment, with a partnership of the probation department, the juvenile court, the prosecutor's office, and the school addressing their absence or tardiness? Ian Ozymandias, a DMC member and teacher at a local alternative private school, confirmed that no amount of truancy at his school ever resulted in a referral to truancy court or juvenile probation, largely because of the philosophy of the school. The local truancy court likely ensnared only one class of truants, signifying coercive state intervention for families without the resources to buy their truant children impunity.[13]

Perhaps the most glaring implication of this issue was the seemingly unself-conscious acceptance by the community that criminal justice officials should handle truancy. Even as Hillman acknowledged that truancy is embedded in complex social problems, he and the community continued to channel their efforts through a criminal justice solution. Again, admittedly social problems would be addressed through criminal justice, in this case facilitated by the prosecutor, the highest-ranking law enforcement official in the county.

Like the drug court model, the truancy court may prove to significantly decrease truancy or dropout rates, qualifying it for the designation of evidence-based. Again, my point is not to challenge its effectiveness, in those ways and on its terms. Rather, I wish to suggest that truancy court can be understood as a site in the larger carceral archipelago of the county, placing absences from school on the expanding continuum of behaviors subject to juridification and criminalization.

Disrupting the Archipelago

The integration of alternatives to incarceration into the official vision of the justice campus revealed an interesting dilemma for narratives of resistance to incarceration expansion. For activists, the term "alternative" signified programs for treatment, counseling, and conflict resolution that were paradigmatically distinct from punishment and incarceration. This distinction speaks to the clear ideological differences between judges and activists, but it also indicates the importance of the meaning ascribed to individual words and terms that comprise discourses of incarceration.[14] Community organizers in DMC, for example, frequently expressed support for alternatives to incarceration and, to present alternatives to building the justice campus, conducted research into various models of conflict resolution that were in operation nationally. Some of this work appears in the final two chapters of this book. In the view of these organizers, there was no question that increased funds for day reporting and specialty courts would expand the scope of court intervention into the lives of people who were either already overly monitored or who had previously avoided supervision. According to DMC's understanding of the prison-industrial complex as including community supervision programs in addition to incarceration, day reporting certainly would contribute to the "wider, stronger, and newer nets" observed by James Austin and Barry Krisberg (1981, 169).[15] The challenge for activists, then, was to distinguish alternatives that broadened the scope of carceral intervention from those that actually provided some measure of autonomy from supervision. The reach of the county bench into the community complicated even this rhetorical and political task, as programs that appeared to provide independent and even paradigmatically distinct services, such as mediation services based on restorative justice, still partnered with and relied on the local criminal justice system.

There were moments during community meetings where activists tried to punctuate the troubling logic that tethered alternatives to carceral expansion. At the second Monroe County Criminal Justice Coordinating Council meeting about the justice campus, which focused on the work release facility, Matthew Harrison—a long-time antijail activist—framed the proposed alternatives as adding to an already oppressive system of control:

> We have an unacceptable rate of incarceration in this county, and the only thing that could be done—I would differ with [sic] some other comments. Judge Barrett listed a number of things which reduce recidivism, some were 12 percent, some were 16 percent, some were 73 percent. There is one thing we can do in this county that would reduce recidivism by 100 percent, and that's reduce the number of slots, because it's socially unac-

ceptable, inhumane, and indecent for a liberal county such as Monroe County to lock up the proportion of the population that we're locking up. I would urge us not to just look at the number of people in juvenile detention, the number of people in jail, but also the number of people on work release—those 200 people that are coming by every day for various types of tests and genuflections—and the number of people we lock up in federal and state facilities, the number of people on parole, the number of people on probation.

Harrison's testimony offers several important insights into the narratives that community organizers used to disrupt carceral habitus. He identified the core problem as overincarceration, and thus the solution as decarceration. He jettisoned the various approaches to the problem that relied on some form of institutionalization, including those offered by some of his long-time friends, such as Hillman. Moreover, Harrison employed the same framework that county officials used in their support for the campus: the county's exceptional liberal politics. Crucially, however, he argued that the county's overreliance on incarceration and carceral alternatives was shameful in the context of its progressive identity.

Harrison's analysis foreshadows the examination in part 4 of this book of local resistance to carceral expansion. The abolitionist orientation to carceral expansion, including the use of alternatives to incarceration, resonates with what former administrators (who now speak with the benefit of hindsight and the freedom afforded to academics) say about so-called alternatives: "Our misplaced reliance on institutions has served only to sap our imagination. The political and the professional relationships it has engendered ensure that alternative programs are seldom considered. We cannot conceive of certain groups of our fellow citizens being safely dealt with in anything other than institutions or quasi-institutions. As a result, alternatives are seldom what they claim to be. They are quasi-institutional additions to an unassailable institutional tradition" (J. Miller 1998, xvi).

Criminologists have offered a similar appraisal of alternatives. Maeve McMahon quotes Lowman, Menzies, and Palys as observing that although community programs were designed as alternatives to incarceration, "these programmes have become a supplement to them. Instead of *fewer* individuals going to prison, there are now more than ever. And instead of directing individuals *out* of the criminal justice system, the new programmes have directed more people *into* it. . . . The bottom line, therefore, is that more and more individuals are becoming subject to the scrutiny and surveillance of criminal justice personnel" (quoted in McMahon 1990, 123).

The local emergence of the justice campus proposal embodied a "misplaced reliance on institutions" as it expressed community values of treatment and education within a sprawling carceral context. In this vision's most robust and most frequently articulated iteration, the campus would not only increase control over the lives of the exponentially greater number of people who would be incarcerated, but it would also ensnare and host the local and vibrant social service network and a variety of quasi-institutional alternatives.

More broadly, the conceptual and ideological work necessary to express such an expansive vision relied on a historically specific material and cultural geography embedded in patterns of capitalist economic and social relations. First, the Thomson plant had to shut down, leaving behind a wake of un- or underemployed industrial workers and two hundred surplus acres. Second, community officials had to see that surplus land as containing particular carceral contours. Third, and perhaps most contentiously, officials had to imagine, however unconsciously, a relationship between the loss of Thomson and the growth of the justice campus on the same site. The carceral-welfare complex would stand in for the loss of industry, both in stimulating local economic development and in managing the surplus population left behind by Thomson and left out of the new white-collar economy.

PART 2

"Poor Conduct" and the Carceral Cure

Prison "reform" is virtually contemporary with the prison itself: it constitutes, as it were, its programme. From the outset,
the prison was caught up in a series of accompanying mechanisms, whose purpose was to correct it, but which seem to
form part of its very functioning, so closely have they been
bound up with its existence throughout its long history.
—Michel Foucault, *Discipline and Punish*

To blame the actions of individuals within a given historical
structure, *without taking that structure itself into account*, is an
easy and familiar way of exercising the moral conscience without bearing any of its costs. It is the last refuge of liberalism.
—Stuart Hall et al., *Policing the Crisis*

The faith placed in the potential of local carceral facilities to embody
liberal benevolence led at times to far-reaching conclusions. Officials
offered visions of the justice campus that imbued the constitutive institutions with capabilities that would seem not only beyond the scope
of what a facility could accomplish but also contradictory to the negative functions these same respondents attributed to the same types
of facilities when operated anywhere else. In what would seem to be
near-Orwellian reasoning, officials suggested that building the justice
campus—adding exponentially more jail, juvenile detention, and work
release beds—would reduce recidivism and end warehousing.

The true Herculean potential that some people ascribed to the justice
campus was on display when I first sat down to interview Tom Grady.
Grady's role in local carceral expansion was of particular importance
and interest to me. A prominent partner in a Bloomington-based law
firm, he was well known in the community for his volunteer efforts on
criminal justice advisory bodies and his service on the boards of promi-

nent nonprofit organizations. Grady was one of two lay citizens appointed by the board of commissioners to the Monroe County Criminal Justice Coordinating Council (MCCJCC), the advisory body responsible for organizing the justice campus hearings. Grady had also been elected to be the group's chair, which meant that he led the MCCJCC's internal meetings and facilitated the justice campus hearings. In my fieldwork at both sets of proceedings, Grady consistently spoke of his "objective" role in these capacities as "just a citizen," although he never hid his support for the justice campus. Indeed, he authored an opinion piece in the *Herald-Times* that both stated his enthusiastic support for the expansion and encouraged more community participation to shape the contours of the programs the campus would house (Grady 2008). After I had spent close to a year in the field, I sat down with him for an interview in the conference room of his law office.

Grady embodied the central tensions at play in the community regarding incarceration. He was harshly critical, even outspoken, about issues of national incarceration. At one point during our interview, as the subject turned from introductory formalities to the growth in imprisonment, Grady strongly criticized the war on drugs. He lowered his voice, leaned across the table toward me, and put out his right hand, holding his thumb and forefinger an inch apart. "I am this close to embracing full-on drug legalization," he said. He then offered his perspective on national imprisonment: "On the one hand, I think we incarcerate way too many people for way too long a period of time in this country. I think it's ridiculous. All our politicians run on the platform of 'tough on crime.' I have no sympathy for that." After indicting incarceration in the United States, Grady then turned his attention to the justice campus: "The exciting thing about the campus issue was the space for programs, a place for rehabilitation, and a place not just to warehouse more people but also to get away from warehousing. So in a perfect world if God came down and said here's $50 million to build a justice campus, I think it would make us a better community."

Having just strongly condemned mass incarceration and advocated ending the war on drugs, Grady offered what can best be described as a prayer for a new and large local complex of carceral facilities that would move the county away from warehousing prisoners. This contradiction was managed, and cognitive dissonance avoided, by Grady's (and others') belief in the community's capacity for truly distinctive and benevolent incarceration that at once avoided the racialized punishment of the carceral state and would be the primary vehicle through which the community delivered social assistance. In the context of the structural constraints imposed on communities by both the loss of jobs and the retreat from welfare that are characteristic of neoliberal states, Grady saw in the justice campus a community improvement project: a carceral complex that could mobilize local residents to work on behalf of those most marginalized in the community, who would now be housed in one central location. According to this vision, Monroe County had the potential to demonstrate to the rest of the country how to do incarceration properly.

The belief in exceptional capacities, institutions, and officials required a concurrent belief in a population in need of them. In other words, for the justice campus to work as a vision of expansive carceral welfare, officials had to imagine a population whose inferiorities could be met by a set of institutions designed to provide moral education, treatment, and acculturation. Later in our interview, Grady clarified his explanation of the exceptional justice officials and practices by noting the pathological behavior of the jail population: "No one is up in the jail as a first-time drug offender. Having said I think we incarcerate far too many people for far too long, I personally think our local justice system is working their butts off to try and keep the jail population as low as possible. . . . 'Cause those folks in the jail are a bunch of folks who are going to continue their behavior that is criminal, and when they're on probation continuously, there's only so much the judges can do."

What was especially curious about comments such as this was that they contradicted the data that the county itself collected about the jail population. Set against the backdrop of arrest and booking records, official descriptions of both the jail population and the imagined population that the justice campus would house—what I call the "jail(able) population"—reveal a rather insidious suturing of observations about economic poverty to judgments of moral poverty.

Chapters 3 and 4 examine further the contours of local criminal justice practices, paying particular attention to the discourses of both just and righteous institutions and the incorrigible and (morally) impoverished local residents who would be incarcerated there. Chapter 3 looks specifically at the discourse surrounding adult incarceration, and chapter 4 at that surrounding youth detention.

3

"Red Neck" and "Unsocialized," with "Subcultural Norms and Values"

Constructing Cultural Poverty and Caring Cages

The Just Jail

In contrast to the absolute replication of social structures, habitus demonstrates the availability of diverse practices within structural constraints.[1] Local officials could push for the expansion of incarceration, yet do so through discourses and imagined practices that offered important distinctions from mass incarceration. Many officials and civic leaders, in fact, criticized the very concept of punishment and laid out what they considered to be an alternative paradigm for corrections.

Begin Again (BA) and Monroe County Justice (MCJ), two local non-profit organizations whose membership overlapped almost completely, were especially vocal in criticizing punishment, although their critique did not extend to incarceration itself. This was both a practical and political choice: while MCJ studied the local system and advocated for reform, BA was responsible for all of the educational and recreational programming that occurred in the Monroe County jail. BA was run almost entirely by volunteers, who facilitated classes and activities for people in jail that included a women's writing group, preparation for the GED exam, and bingo. The leaders of both groups frequently attended any county meetings that were concerned with criminal justice and offered passionate criticisms—more than one person referred to their denunciations as "fiery"—of the criminal justice system and in particular its targeting of the poor. Yet many of the groups' leaders and volunteers were also reliable and vocal supporters of the justice campus. In the dramatically increased size of the complex, in particular the jail, the groups saw the potential for added space for programming and its further integration into the routines of the jail.

MCJ republished Karl Menninger's *Crime of Punishment* and consistently referred to the book in public meetings and personal communications. Both it and BA advocated for therapeutic justice, a philosophical orientation with specific history in the county and which activists in the groups saw as paradigmatically different from punishment but which did not jettison the technology of incarceration. Therapeutic justice was introduced to Monroe County in the middle of the 2000s, when BA and MCJ brought in a consultant from the Center for Therapeutic Justice, based in Virginia. A whole wing—a cellblock—of the Monroe County jail was made into a therapeutic community, and BA and MCJ advocated that the approach extend to the entire jail. Recent work on therapeutic communities in carceral settings has cautioned against embracing the approach as anything other than "strong-arm rehab" and suggests that the model is "considerably more coercive" than programs like Alcoholics and Narcotics Anonymous.[2]

But therapeutic justice also took on a more universal meaning, used by reformers to advocate a rehabilitative and treatment-centered framework and vision for the jail. Viewed through the lens of therapeutic justice, incarceration offered an opportunity for positive personal change following the appropriate interventionist approach that could make the time in jail productive, introspective, and redemptive.

The leaders and volunteers of BA and MCJ consistently promoted therapeutic justice during the four public hearings about the justice campus hosted by the Monroe County Criminal Justice Coordinating Council. At the first hearing, about the juvenile facility, after Richard Kemp from Program Administration and Results, Inc. (PARI) finished his presentation and the floor was formally opened for public comment, a man named Robert Cantor made his way to the podium to speak. A cofounder of BA and MCJ, Cantor was an elderly clergyman and a community activist involved in issues of poverty, homelessness, and incarceration. Notably, his and others' advocacy for therapeutic justice offered both explicit and implicit support for the justice campus; in their view, the increased space of the facilities would make a robust therapeutic approach possible. Cantor raised this point in his comments:

> Please, let's do something in the community for our youth which is positive from the very beginning, and let's move that on up into the jail sys-

tem so that we're doing positive things for them all along the way so that the experience of going to jail becomes a positive one and not one that results in either their being helpless with a continuing type of helplessness, which makes them really not want to get a job when they get out, not want to change their drug or alcohol habits, not want to take on the responsibility of family life, not really want to be good citizens. We put them out angrier than when they came in, and more inclined to do the negative thing than the positive thing.

Although frequently critical of incarceration, including, at times, the prospect of a new adult jail, Cantor affirmed his support for a juvenile facility.[3] Later in the same hearing, he urged that the county pursue such a facility even if the larger campus plan were to be defeated. Cantor's plea for the facility rested on the popular configuration of a virtuous detention experience that performed the necessary work of making people responsible and saving them. Although many BA and MCJ members were outspoken critics of punishment and self-proclaimed leftists—indeed, Cantor was a radical who frequently invoked Eugene Debs—they rarely spoke of getting people out of jail or investing resources in noninstitutional alternatives. They endorsed detention and incarceration—local, nonpunitive, and redemptive—with passion.

The focus by BA and MCJ activists on the ills of punishment and their passionate endorsement of therapeutic justice affected the rhetoric of criminal justice system officials. Two judges—Patrick Randall of the juvenile court and Allan Barrett, the circuit court's presiding judge—spoke during the same meeting to refute Cantor's claim that the local bench and jail were punitive. In other words, the judges disputed the idea that punishment was even part of the system, preferring to consider their work as treatment-oriented (even when mandating a youth to secure detention or an adult to jail) or as doling out consequences for adults who break the law, a rather paternalistic distinction from punishment that seemed devoid of empirical difference. At the end of the meeting about the juvenile facility, Barrett responded directly to Cantor:

[Robert], with all due respect to you, you said that our approach here was punishment-oriented. That isn't true and it's never been true. I've been on the bench thirty years and for thirty years we've done nothing but design alternatives to jail, trying to find ways for people not to be incarcerated, and increasing the number of treatment and rehabilitative programs that exist here. Tonight the focus is on the juvenile facility. It was introduced . . . as a juvenile detention facility. That has never been what we have called it here in the twenty years we've been talking about it. It's been a juvenile treatment center, for programming and services offered to youth to accomplish much of what you're talking about here.

This exchange raises important insights into the political landscape of the county. As noted above, Barrett was the only Republican judge on the circuit court, and according to my personal communications with a number of people whose cases he has presided over, one of the harshest. Yet his reply to Cantor didn't affirm a place for punishment (as one might assume a Republican judge would do); rather, he spoke to Cantor on the rhetorical turf of therapeutic justice, eschewing punishment as something that he and the court had never embraced. This is illustrative of the powerful nature of local discourse, in which tensions between distinct positions of treatment versus punishment were largely absent at the rhetorical level. Instead, there were unlikely alliances between justice officials, county politicians, and activists to advocate for treatment in the context of increased institutionalization.

Just a month after the first hearing, in November 2008, I attended the third of the four hearings, which focused on the jail component of the justice campus. There, Cantor reiterated his assessment of local incarceration—"We're teaching learned helplessness in the jail. We bring them in, we have no program for them that introduces them to themselves or to the essential requirements of society"—to make the larger point that the campus would enable a broader commitment to programming. BA's programs often operated within a philosophical framework and through a discursive register that privileged personal redemption and rehabilitation, minimizing any analysis of the structural problems that the group's members frequently cited as a critical context for understanding incarceration.[4] Indeed, according to the analysis of BA and MCJ members, the central tension and point of departure between them and the jail administrators was how best to organize time and space within the jail, not necessarily the merits or inherent problems of incarceration itself. This, in turn, allowed many BA and MCJ members to lend their support to the justice campus proposal.

Perhaps rhetoric that is most instructive in demonstrating the symbolic power of local incarceration was that used by PARI. The company framed its work in ways that integrated and repeated local concerns. For example, at the same hearing about the jail, Kemp said:

> A building is a tool. That's all it is. It will be as effective as you make it. And that's what we're here about: how do we look at a tool to make it very effective and provide the kinds of things that you guys are talking about? We won't solve all of 'em, but we'll solve a lot of 'em with the kind of input we're getting here. The thing you have to keep in mind is we didn't get here overnight and we won't get out of it overnight either, but we've got to take some positive steps that takes [sic] Monroe County in a different direction. You are not shy of studies. There is [sic] twenty years of history and studies and evaluations. We've never come into a county where there's this much information about the justice system. So what may have been happening is the lack of consensus to take that first step. We need to get those kinds of steps in there and get started on that. But there's a lot of talk about buildings here today, and building will be about what this group decides to do *in* the building, not about buildings themselves.

Kemp invoked the decades of studies suggesting the need for a jail. Relying on the political capital afforded to studies in Bloomington was a common occurrence in these meetings. Chapter 4 examines in detail several of these occurrences and considers their cumulative effect on the construction of local knowledge. In this particular instance, Kemp mentioned the studies to deflect attention from the institution—where there was a high degree of skepticism—and to the programmatic details, where he correctly assumed there would be more support. As a corrections consultant, Kemp stood to profit from construction; to win the community's support and assuage its suspicion, he strategically deemphasized the bricks and mortar and instead focused on what programming the buildings would enable. In the PowerPoint presentation prepared by PARI and shown at the beginning of each of the four hearings held by the MCCJCC, the very first slide introduced viewers to the "guiding principles identified for the Monroe County Criminal Justice

Complex." The first line of this slide read, "Reduce Recidivism," a laudable goal that officials repeated throughout my research. No one at these meetings asked the seemingly obvious question of how building bigger and newer institutions would reduce recidivism.

It was tempting to endorse the partnerships between these actors and their shared discursive register of liberal buzzwords like "reduce recidivism," "rehabilitation," and "therapeutic justice." But the insistence on carceral expansion as a precondition for the expansion of these approaches would seem to dash hopes that an alternative paradigm might emerge. In fact, as the contours of the carceral expand and are reconfigured around different tropes, it seems especially important to trace the ways that larger circulations of neoliberal capitalist and racial logics express themselves differently—cloaked in discourses of therapeutic justice, for example—in different political and cultural contexts.

Consequences, Accountability, and Control

The rhetorical rejection of punishment in Bloomington belied its presence in criminal justice policy and practice. Officials such as Barrett implied that the title and official intentions for a given facility—"juvenile treatment center," for example—would determine what occurred within its walls. This simplistic argument gained surprising traction locally: many people seemed to accept the premise that a justice campus or a juvenile treatment center would be something distinctive, rather than a "repackaging of punishment."[5] For officials, an explicit and genuine commitment to rehabilitation implied an absence of punishment, as if people incarcerated in jail and juvenile detention voluntarily chose their captivity.

In spite of Barrett's adamant stance that the county bench had never been punishment-oriented, there were important moments during my fieldwork that implied otherwise. Barrett winced during statements at the justice campus hearings from members of Decarcerate Monroe County (DMC) and others criticizing punitive county practices. Invariably, Barrett would take the time to clarify that he strongly preferred to consider the criminal sanction a "consequence," rather than a punishment, for people guilty of a crime. He was especially outspoken about consequences for people who violated the law due to their own addictions. Interestingly, he offered a compassionate view that recognized that treatment was more effective and less expensive than prison and that "less restrictive correctional alternatives are cost-efficient and more effective at reducing recidivism." At the third hearing of the MCCJCC he said:

> Accountability for poor judgment and poor conduct is an essential aspect to effective rehabilitation. What you're trying to change is behavior, the way they look at life and the way they deal with situations. And they seldom have been responsible or accountable. Some of the criminogenic factors have to do with the way people who commit crimes think: they are usually self-centered, focused on immediate gratification, have less empathy for other people, and are less concerned about the social rules that the rest of us are conscientious about. So you have to address that thinking, and if you don't make them accountable for their poor judgment or accountable for their poor conduct, then they think that all the bets are off, that this is a meaningless process with no point to it, and they can continue to act as they have. So you have to have a broad continuum of consequences. Richard [Kemp] referred to them as sanctions; I prefer to think of them as consequences because that's the way offenders need to think of it. It's a consequence of their poor decision making and poor conduct, and that has to ultimately include incarceration because we have a lot of people who'll walk through every level of consequence, and you have to be able to ultimately hold them accountable. It doesn't mean long periods of time in jail, but it has to be certain and it has to be swift. So that's one of the reasons you see people recycled a lot.

Barrett offered rather sweeping generalizations about the "antisocial behavior" of the current jail population and, by extension, those the justice campus would "serve." Like many in the community who advocated for the justice campus, Barrett imagined a jail population both economically and morally impoverished and liable to various biocultural pathologies. In line with these beliefs, he advocated for correction to be administered in a tightly controlled and coercive environment. With some disdain, he spoke of "these people" who "seldom have been responsible or accountable," whom he has to "deal with." For Barrett, the justice campus would integrate punishment and treatment but would also play a didactic and moralizing role for a class of people who needed instruction about living in society.[6]

Barrett's observation that "you see people recycled a lot" also helps explain the expressions of local penal philosophies. The use of a waste management metaphor to comment on the consequences of not holding people accountable for their behavior reveals the importance that Barrett and others placed on forms of new penological power. In this way, local carceral habitus articulated a hybrid vision of social control, integrating and conflating seemingly distinct ideological positions of criminal justice, including the "old penology" approaches of individualized treatment and correction and the "new penology" technologies of management and control observed by Malcolm Feeley and Jonathan Simon (1992). Barrett's observations indicated that orientations toward incarceration that might otherwise seem distinct, such as rehabilitation, consequences, and population management strategies, appeared rather fluidly in a single person's brief remarks.

As the justice campus concept began to buckle under the weight of the price tag attached to PARI's formal proposal, other initiatives that had always been on the table but had been deemphasized during the discussions about the campus became more prominent. Many of these initiatives offered less institution-based, if even more expansionist, visions for the integration of criminal justice into other parts of life, including truancy courts for youth who missed school, increased home supervision, and day reporting. In a revealing indication of the local hegemony of therapeutic justice and rehabilitation discourses, officials framed as benevolent and rehabilitative jail policy initiatives that were restrictive, punitive, and designed for increased control and management of the jail population. In the summer of 2009, just weeks after the release of the PARI report on the justice campus with the company's exorbitant price tag of $75 million, Jail Commander Doug Dobson and Sheriff Frank Sullivan proposed substantial renovations to the current jail that were aimed at alleviating the problems of overcrowding and meeting the need for expansion. Included in the proposed renovations were the installation of eighteen videoconferencing booths and the termination of all in-person visits. Anticipating that the price of the justice campus would be too high for the county, Dobson had conducted his own study, promising to stay within the footprint of the current jail by subjecting the structure to much-needed renovations at a cost to the county of just $1 million. In addition to the ending of in-person visits and the installation of videoconference booths, the renovations included placing bars over the windows of the jail so inmates couldn't knock on the windows to communicate to their families who were waiting in the alley below to visit them.[7] Thus, although the justice campus itself was at least temporarily postponed, the carceral logic of county habitus was rearticulated through extending the reach of the county criminal justice system into spheres of education, family, and youth services, as well as by framing the rather punitive restriction of visitation as in the interests of jail inmates and their families.

The shift to videoconferencing would change the experience of visitation dramatically. Visitors would still come to the jail to see their loved ones but would remain downstairs, while prisoners would remain upstairs in their cellblocks. In an interesting complication of Feeley and Simon's (1992) work, this "new technique" of transitioning to videoconferencing did not necessarily occur solely through corresponding "new discourses" or "new objectives," as the authors contend. Of course, the language of population management and control was present, as evidenced by this excerpt from a *Herald-Times* story: "'It's just really unforgiving [*sic*] the way we do [visitation] now,' jail commander Doug Dobson said. Visitation can take hours. Staff have one elevator on which to take prisoners down to the visitation area, usually six at a time. And moving inmates is always a security risk, [Sheriff Frank] Sullivan said. With the video screen system, inmates won't have to be moved, which improves security and reduces staff involvement in visitation, he said" (Brooks 2010).

Concerns with population movement and staff efficiency resonate with the discourse and objectives outlined by Feeley and Simon (1992). But it's also important to note that the *Herald-Times* article had the headline "Staffing, Facilities Still Issues for Sheriff," followed by "Planned improvements could ease visiting time at jail"—language suggesting that the Sheriff's Department and the *Herald-Times* framed the bureaucratic move in ways that attempted to elicit sympathy from those concerned with issues of visitation.[8] Elsewhere, the newspaper noted that Dobson believed the changes would be "huge," observing that "he believes they'll make visiting an inmate more convenient for members of the public, who often spend hours waiting outside or crammed into the jail's tiny reception area during cold weather."[9] Indeed, I heard Sullivan, Dobson's boss, note in remarks to a Democratic Party forum before the county's primary elections that the changes to video visitation "will double the amount of time for visitation" and create a "better experience for those visiting."

The benevolent rhetorical façade given to the policies of ceasing all non-technologically mediated visitations is important to interrogate. Indeed, some visitors to the county jail and DMC members took the position during public meetings of refusing to recognize videoconferencing as a form of visitation. Despite the symbolic intervention into the discourse, the renovations occurred and inevitably affected understandings of visitation and interpersonal communication, as they rendered prisoners less visible to the outside world and more visible to their captors.

The punitive nature of these changes may be best appreciated when viewed in the context of the genealogy of jail architecture in the county. The jail at the time of this writing, the one that the justice campus would have replaced and the one that Dobson and Sullivan renovated, was built in 1986 in order to address serious flaws in its predecessor. That jail, built in 1936 and universally condemned for its decrepit state, was located on the ground floor of a building one block south of the downtown square. As several older informants noted to me, you could walk by and talk with inmates. In the current jail, prisoners live four and five stories above ground, removing from the nonincarcerated public any ability to sense their presence.

The exception to this total removal from the community had been prisoners' abilities to knock on the windows in the cellblock. This occurred most frequently during visitation hours, when loved ones would gather in an alley on the jail's western side while waiting, sometimes for hours, to enter for their assigned visitation time. With other members of DMC, I attended the jail's visiting hours frequently. We saw the time as an opportunity to remain accountable to the people most affected by jail policies in the county. Most often our trips during visitation hours were informal, and we would chat with people at the jail. Sometimes we brought food or coffee, since the jail didn't provide either. Occasionally, the visits were more targeted. We would come with art materials on Mother's Day and Father's Day so children could make cards for their incarcerated parents. Or, during a particular campaign, we might show up with short surveys to obtain people's views about certain policies. Consistently during these visits, we watched as family members and their incarcerated loved ones used a combination of hand signals, knocks, and lip reading to communicate simple but important messages of support and encouragement across the otherwise impermeable border of the jail. Visitors in the alley would step back from the building until the fourth- and fifth-floor windows of the jail became visible. There, they could identify their loved ones by the vague outline of their bodies and the familiar signals. The contact enacted important ties between family members and resisted the implied policy of the jail of maintaining total segregation of the incarcerated from the nonincarcerated. Perhaps because this activity implied that there was a fracture in the armor of power, jail officials integrated barring the windows into their 2010 renovation budget. In less than a month, a justice campus predicated on rehabilitation, therapeutic justice, and education was replaced by jail renovations that further punished and dehumanized the captive population and their visitors.

It would be a mistake to assume that the discourse of the justice campus was easily separable into distinct camps of correction and control, each with its own spokespeople. Although some officials were more inclined to embrace certain vocabularies within the larger discourse, I was struck by the fluidity with which officials and others moved along the continuum of language as they spoke about the campus and its population. Moreover, as I have tried to convey in this section and as other scholars of power and punishment have illuminated, discourses of correction and treatment are frequently discourses of punishment and control.[10]

The Cultural Work of Punishment

One explanation for the insistence on the nonpunitive character of local criminal justice policy was that, in fact, Bloomington's progressive politics and culture permeated and infused the criminal justice apparatus. Indeed, this explanation would follow the logic employed by many people in the community. But, as the previous two sections showed, local benevolent rhetoric still insisted on suturing programming to existing and even expanded carceral institutions. Moreover, as the previous section revealed, there were exceptions to benevolent rhetoric, where the same officials who insisted on the compassionate nature of the system were responsible for instituting policy that was unmistakably, and often quite viciously, punitive.

Placing chapter 1's focus on political economy and geography into conversation with culture reveals the important ways that local contexts play central roles in shaping formations of penality. That is, the massive carceral expansion proposed in the form of the justice campus would not be possible in Monroe County if it was framed within discourses of law and order or crime control. Carceral expansion *had* to be filtered through a vocabulary that could fit its physical contours into a rhetorical mold commensurable with local politics. This understanding is aligned with important work that treats prison expansion as a phenomenon that has to be understood beyond crime and justice policy, but that also cannot fully be explained by overly economistic determinism. For example, Garland notes that "society's cultural patterns come to be imprinted upon its penal institutions, so that punishment becomes a practical embodiment of some of the symbolic themes, constellations of meaning and particular ways of feeling which constitute the wider culture. . . . [S]ources of penal change and the determinants of penal form are to be located not just in penological reasoning or economic interest or strategies of power, but also in the configuration of value, meaning and emotion which we call 'culture.'"[11]

Applied to Bloomington and Monroe County, Garland's argument suggests that local political culture can shape specific formations of penality. Certainly, the rhetorical attention paid to discourses of rehabilitation and therapeutic justice and the policy initiatives around various quasicarceral alternatives to incarceration points to the influence of Bloomington's progressive nature on its orientation toward punishment. But this book suggests that local political cultures—and culture more broadly—are not so easily divorced from the circulating structural forces that Garland positions as distinct.[12] Progressive politics in Bloomington may have shaped the discourses of carceral expansion to fit within an acceptable range of policy. However, the very concept of the justice campus revealed that culture—the configuration of value, meaning, and emotion—operated within a confined register of available vocabularies and policy options heavily structured by neoliberal and racialized logics of crime and crime control.

This observation about the limitations of local discourse and policy vis-à-vis rehabilitation confirms recent work on contemporary penal policy. Some authors have considered the "liberal veil" (Moore and Hannah-Moffat 2005) beneath which central punitive logics animate carceral practices. The local suturing of penal welfarist approaches (Garland 1990 and 2001) to the new penological (Feeley and Simon 1992) imperatives of risk management and other technocratic managerial concerns (Hannah-Moffat 2005) would seem to connect Bloomington carceral policy to larger trends of punishment. This "late-modern rehabilitation" (Robinson 2008) eschews welfarist narratives that supported treatment as an end in and of itself and instead is inscribed into a broader framework of actuarial concerns (Garland 2001). While most Bloomington officials were disposed to favor incarceration firmly rooted in penal welfare sensibilities, the actuarial and punitive mechanisms and discourses on which they relied to measure, justify, and apply those sensibilities in support of carceral expansion cannot be ignored. That is, local officials mobilized rehabilitation logics and filtered them through actuarial mechanisms (including corrections consultants and risk management discourses and policies) to support an inherently punitive project of carceral expansion (Gray and Salole 2006; O'Malley 1999). Such instrumental uses for actuarial mechanisms confirms foundational work on the intimacy between the actuarial and the political (Beck 1992) as well as recent research into the ability of the actuarial to sanitize racially discriminatory sentencing (Starr 2014).

Moreover, work that seeks to locate notions of risk and discipline in historical materialist analyses (Kramer, Rajah, and Sung 2013; Rigakos and Hadden 2001) makes it clear that the actuarial justifications for the justice campus ignored striking evidence that the entire project was predicated on a particular historical trajectory and material geography of deindustrialized and mobile capital. It was a distinctive local discourse that animated a particular landscape that at once aestheticized a massive carceral expansion project through green and liberal rhetoric, justified it through actuarial mechanisms that spun openly corrections-focused and intellectually suspect consultant reports into allegedly objective criminal justice policy evaluation gold, and, crucially, buried the history of the land in the process.

"Poor Conduct" I: Jail(able) Subjects

As a repository of penal ideologies that nonetheless could fabricate seemingly distinct iterations of incarceration, carceral habitus produced a sense of an exceptional locality. It was common for people in the county to comment on Bloomington's identity as "an oasis," a "beacon," or an "island" of progressive politics, a fascinating group of spatial metaphors that projected an exceptional subjectivity onto a geographic dislocation from the communities and larger political structures of which the county was inevitably a part. This construction of self and other took on especially troubling qualities when it was manifested in discussions of race, racism, and class. Frequently, officials imagined Monroe County, and especially Bloomington, as embodying a kind of postracial ethos, an enlightened politics that insulated the community from the racist practices operating elsewhere. In erasing the possibility of racist practices in the community, officials in fact participated in the transmission and calcification of hegemonic racial logics. I introduce this phenomenon here, largely in reference to the construction of the adult jail(able) population. I return to it in the next chapter, when I examine constructions of racialized and class-based youth subjects.

My first experience of this dynamic occurred when I took my dog to a popular dog park. While he splashed around with a friend, I stood with the owners of the other dog, a friendly couple who chatted with me about life in Bloomington and in particular life as an academic. When I formally introduced myself, including my name, they quickly made sure that as a relatively new resident of the area and as someone with a distinctively Jewish name, I knew to avoid the town of Martinsville, a warning they said they communicated to any new acquaintance who is a person of color or a member of a religious minority group.

Martinsville is Bloomington's bogeyman. It is a small city of 12,000 residents halfway between Bloomington and Indianapolis, the closest major city. But that geographical marker is also a crucial sociopolitical symbol of distinction. While the town certainly offers Bloomington drivers any number of gas stations, chain restaurants, or coffee shops that they might need, one cannot ignore the warning of almost mythic proportions reverberating in one's head: "Don't stop, certainly not if you are a person of color, queer, or Jewish."

People in Bloomington were fond of noting Martinsville's racist reputation and observing that the oasis of progressivism and tolerance ended as one reached the dividing line between Morgan and Monroe Counties, rendering us as safe and them as the dangerous other. Of course, Bloomington residents were correct to point out that their community was distinct in various ways and held important, progressive values. They also made astute points to residents of color about being aware of the way legacies of racism—Martinsville has a sordid history of Klan activity and one high-profile murder of a Black woman—can hold communities in their grip, shaping the identities of community residents to perpetuate the town narrative.[13] But Bloomington liberals seemed unaware of the fact that the narrative they told about Martinsville shaped and limited their analysis of Bloomington. For if the problem was there, then most certainly it was not here.

In practice, the belief in an exceptional locality immune from replicating various institutional injustices that were acknowledged to exist—even to be pervasive—elsewhere actually enabled the very injustices that local leaders rhetorically derided. For example, I specifically asked Reuben Davison, a member of the Monroe County Council, about the racial composition of the inmate population of the county jail. Our interview in the spring of 2009 took place a year after the night in the library where I had first heard him speak about the prison-industrial complex as part of a continuum of racist institutions going back to slavery. Since that time, I had attended numerous county gatherings, including four public hearings about the justice campus, county council monthly meetings, and interviews with candidates for public office, which had afforded me several opportunities to hear Davison speak out against mass incarceration in much the same way. In our interview, when I asked him about his thoughts on incarceration, I prefaced my question by noting that I had heard him offer this perspective before. He beamed, chuckled, and said, "You know, that's my line. I'm glad to know you remembered it." He continued:

I think there are similarities [between slavery, Jim Crow, and mass incarceration]. Most of us really know better. It's bad enough that our incarceration rate is so much higher than European countries, but it's also drastically higher than Canada's. You can argue that Sweden and France and all those countries—you have a homogeneous population and can make the argument that they're easier to deal with, but Canada's almost as diverse as we are. They have their own problems with indigenous populations. It's a problem over the world but it's much worse here.

I then specifically asked him if problems of racism in the prison-industrial complex affect Monroe County. He replied:

No. Of course, people would disagree with me. We have about 15 percent African Americans in our jail, which is high compared to our population, which is 3 percent Black. I thought it would be higher than that and in some places it is, like in West Lafayette [another small city and college town in the state]. If anything, I think our judges and our system—they're almost [Davison hesitated] I wouldn't say antiracist, but they would be very careful not [to] do anything that would be considered racist.

This immediately struck me as an unusually revealing comment. Davison categorized local judges not as antiracist but as "careful not [to] do anything that would be considered racist." Certainly, one interpretation of the comment is that judges are vigilant about not being complicit in the institutional injustices of the criminal justice system. But Davison's characterization also could indicate that judges are anxious about the perception of the county bench as being particularly concerned with equality. Of course, Davison also recognized the grossly disproportionate confinement of Black people locally—a rate that was five times their proportion of the local general population—but he said explicitly that there was no problem of local racism. Within the popular narrative of an exceptional community that rejected racialized mass incarceration in favor of therapeutic justice, racism could not possibly explain the disproportionate local incarceration of Black people. This had the consequence of affirming racialized constructs of criminality: in Davison's narrative, if the county jail existed outside of the national racist context of mass incarceration, then following his logic, the disproportionate rate of confinement of Black people in the county jail would reflect their disproportionate involvement in crime. Davison's concurrent rejection and acceptance of structural racism revealed and performed the ideology of race itself: his efforts to explain away the obvious local articulations of a national phenomenon that he correctly analyzed reveals the depths to which we "need a social vocabulary that will allow us to make sense, not of what our ancestors did then, but of what we ourselves choose to do now."[14]

Moreover, Davison's comments implied that because there were no explicitly racist individual judges, there was no racism in the community. This belief that racism is a problem of individual ignorance—rather than a strategy, logic, practice, and product of structural and institutional relations—both encoded local institutions with a high moral character and inscribed local jail inmates with a racialized responsibility for their own incarceration. Davison's comments to me were, in short, an expression of what has been recently called "carceral racial liberalism": an "obscure[ing] of racial power through vocabularies of bland administrative reform and soft racial paternalism."[15] In Bloomington, carceral racial liberalism anchored the addressing and redressing of racism to local carceral expansion.

Discussions about social control are predicated on the social construction of a population in need of controlling. Local support for the justice campus was predicated on an imagined jail(able) population of county residents, often described by my informants in terms that conflated economic and moral poverty, a form of "liberal othering" that Jock Young (2007, 5–6) has explicated.[16] In their analyses of local poverty, local officials, civic leaders, and even some activists endorsed the construct of an individuated, unacculturated, and pathological actor in need of reformation. While many of these people frequently identified the structural conditions of capitalism as the central problem underlying mass incarceration, they proposed solutions grounded in individual, moralistic, and redemptive change. In constructing the county poor as not only being in fragile economic situations but also as possessing a set of racialized and inferior behavioral and cultural practices, local leaders legitimated the need for a facility predicated on education, treatment, and acculturation to middle-class status.[17] This individuation of the structural problem of poverty is understandable in Monroe County. First, the creation of a responsible actor is a hallmark of neoliberal penality.[18] Attached to the promise of a therapeutic carceral regime, local constructions of poor subjects played rather easily into the "late-modern rehabilitation" that Gwen Robinson (2008) has observed as an emerging carceral strategy. Second, the neoliberal classifications of carceral subjects found affirmation from and affinity with the many officials and civic leaders who were current or former members of the social service community. The frequent repetition of themes of individual change and redemption reflected the influence of national strategies for mental health treatment and advocacy. Several local politicians, civic leaders, and the leaders of BA and MCJ, including Cantor, had advanced degrees in mental health and psychotherapy. Important scholarship has pointed out that the mental health model advocates individual change through various interventions as the solution to crime.[19] Third, there is some evidence that the individuation of poverty in the county, and the treatment modalities that invited, was predicated on a particular racialization of the local jail(able) population that "softly otherized" Monroe County inmates while more forcefully otherizing those outside of the county.[20]

Seen in several contexts, then, the substitution of the personal for the structural was understandable, but its implication was dangerous. Faced with the overwhelming nature of embedded poverty, officials looked for ways to initiate some semblance of change. But their benevolent intention does not mitigate the severity of their rhetorical and political choices to personalize the structural: they condemned to incarceration the very people they were quick to identify as victims of past abuses, current addictions, cyclical poverty, structural inequality, and historical racism.

Of course, officials based their determinations about the jail(able) population in part on their own experiences with the local jail population. As I describe below, officials cited certain behaviors, family arrangements, intergenerational recidivism rates, and other indicators of moral inferiority in their rationalizations for the justice campus. That is, officials justified their sweeping indictments of the population based on a sense of legibility; they knew this population and thus could claim that their critiques rested on an intimate familiarity and not the punitive rhetoric they otherwise disdained. Of course, the structuring of personal knowledge, including the vocabularies available for our use in ascribing meaning to such knowledge, is the subject of important theorization about power, including from scholars of habitus.[21]

One representative example of local constructs of the jail(able) population came when I asked Davison to describe his sense of who was in the current jail and who the justice campus would serve:

They're mostly young men from sixteen to thirty-six [years old], and about 80–90 percent are from the socioeconomic lower part of society. Most of them didn't do well in school, didn't do well in sports. For whatever reason, they are basically a subculture. They don't have a stake in their culture. They have different values and different lifestyles. How to deal with that is another question. I've heard it said more than once by people, you can generally tell by third grade which kids are going to wind up in the [criminal justice] system. . . . One of the causes of the problem is that we simply don't deal with the issue that all these people come from the lower class. For example here in Bloomington, what makes our situation here so egregious is that we should have a much lower participation in our system than we do. Half our population never goes to jail except for illegal consumption. If you had a jail for the university related population—there are a lot of kids in the age group [from the community] that sit up in our jail—you would only need five or six cells. So we really need to deal with that and for some reason we've chosen not to deal with it.

Notably, Davison's construction of the jailable population corresponds to John Irwin's observations in his classic study of the San Francisco City Jail (1985). Irwin concludes that two characteristics define most jail prisoners: detachment and disrepute. He writes that jail prisoners are detached because "they are not well integrated into conventional society, they are not members of conventional social organizations, they have few ties to conventional social networks, and are carriers of unconventional social values and beliefs" (1985, 2). Irwin's observations are similar to Davison's construction of the population as "basically a subculture" with "different values and different lifestyles." Both men certainly offer class-based notions of behavior and sociality. But in Irwin's definition of disrepute there is perhaps an important insight into how these individuals and their behavior become jailable. He writes that jail prisoners are disreputable because their behavior is perceived as irksome, offensive, and threatening (ibid.). He expands on this notion, observing: "It is not simply the fact of theft that provokes arrest; it is who commits the theft and what type of theft it is. Our society . . . has been quicker to criminalize covetous property accumulation by the rabble than by other classes. The police are always on the lookout for purse-snatching, theft from cars, and shoplifting, but they almost never patrol used-car lots or automobile repair shops to catch [lawbreaking] and they never raid corporate boardrooms to catch executives fixing prices. The difference between these crimes is not seriousness or prevalence; it is offensiveness, which is determined by social status and context" (ibid., 17)

Davison's comments reveal important ways that advocates of the justice campus made local poverty and class into issues of cultural pathology, even as they articulated positions on national incarceration steeped in criticisms of the structural conditions of capitalism. Davison argues that incarceration is practically inevitable for the local poor since "you can tell by third grade which kids are going to wind up in the system." Such a sweeping statement interestingly justified local expansion by integrating a narrow reading of life-course theories of crime with the practices of some prison administrators to project the number of institutional beds needed based on third-grade test scores.[22]

Moreover, Davison clearly observed that the jail was not for the university population, going so far as to say that a jail for that population (over 30,000 people) would only require five or six cells. He insinuated that little crime occurs on campus, a questionable assertion on its own and one that ignores sociocultural constructions of deviance that criminalize in town the same behaviors that are condoned on campus.

These two issues—the individuation of poverty and the belief that crime is a "locals" phenomenon—reflect tensions captured over decades in the community by both popular cultural production and scholarship. *Breaking Away*, the iconic film featuring Bloomington's famous Little 500 bicycle race, chronicled a racing team comprised of local "cutters," the adolescent and young adult children of local quarry workers, as they battled teams from Indiana University fraternities (Yates 1979). The film used the race to explore more deeply class tensions and larger political and economic issues found in the county. Jefferson Cowie writes in *Capital Moves* (1999), his book chronicling the trajectory of RCA-Thomson from New Jersey to Bloomington to Tennessee to Ciudad Juarez, that *Breaking Away* misrepresents the changing political economy of the county by focusing on the disappearance of quarry work, which, he argues, had disappeared from the area decades earlier. Instead, to be more accurate, the film should have explored the second wave of deindustrialization to hit the town: the loss of 9,000 jobs from the local RCA plant.

Cowie observes of the film that "the constant stream of new college students attending Indiana University in *Breaking Away* are an ongoing reminder of what the local boys will never be, and their situation is complicated by the fact that they won't even have the work opportunities lost by their fathers . . . [the film] clearly portrays the underside of Monroe County's much-celebrated economic success" (1999, 140). Between 1980 and 1990, despite the growth of white-collar, professional, technical, and sales jobs in the county, blue-collar jobs dwindled. Cowie continues: "When the growth of the city's population is taken into account, the percentage of clerical workers, farmers, laborers, equipment handlers, and helpers all showed a net loss during the 1980s. Jobs for college-trained professionals grew to define Monroe County, while locals with little or no higher education shifted from industrial to low-paying service work" (ibid.).

In blaming a subculture of poverty for the representation of a disproportionate number of locals in the county jail, Reuben Davison and others of my informants ignored a variety of complex factors: the criminalization of addictions, the social construction of crime and criminals leading to arrests of locals and little or no sanction of university students, the belief in the local benevolence of the system, and most glaringly, the changing political economy of the community and the steady loss of working-class jobs.

Invoking similar constructs of the jail(able) population in the community was Dan Little, a public defender and biweekly columnist for the *Herald-Times*. In his column, Little referred to clients and potential clients in terms that were at times shocking for their callousness and troubling because they were written by a public defender. Little's statements clearly indicated his belief in his clients' need for lessons in morality. In one example, he used his column to excoriate graffiti artists who had defaced a monument to fallen police officers with the words "Fuck Cops." Little assumed that he knew something about the people who wrote the graffiti, calling graffiti artists in general "idiots with a spray can" and "spray paint morons." About these artists in particular, he wondered, "What kind of mindset leads a person to come to this particular spot to drain the poison from their pea[-size] brain in front of this monument?" (Little 2010). He then listed all of the selfless acts that police officers had performed in Bloomington over the years, never once mentioning that the sentiment "fuck cops" could conceivably be the result of any number of victimizing interactions with officers, the likes of which had been captured by the newspaper for which he wrote. In another example, Little devoted an entire column to the metaphor of involvement in the criminal justice system as education, referring to himself as a "tutor," the courtroom as "my classroom," his client as "the student," and other actors such as police officers as "adjunct professors" (Little 2009). The metaphor specifically and his columns generally are one more paternalistic strand in a larger community narrative that constructed a particularly deficient actor in need of the very moral and cultural education and treatment that the justice campus was imagined to provide.

Davison and Little were not alone in their construction of the jail(able) population. Local media and other officials also invoked a pathological and individuated actor in need of carceral treatment when speaking of current and future jail populations. In the official discourse of the county justice system and the coverage of crime and justice issues by the *Herald-Times*, a jail(able) population emerged that was overwhelmingly poor and possessed various inferior traits. According to both local media and several of my informants, the population was "antisocial" in their behavior and personality,[23] in dysfunctional "redneck romance[s],"[24] "unsocialized" in their interactions with the community,[25] governed by "subcultural norms and values,"[26] and mired in "intergenerational recidivism."[27] That is, despite paying rhetorical attention to criticizing the structural constraints imposed by capitalism, officials and the newspaper often naturalized poverty in the county, mapping various inferior behaviors onto the economic condition of being poor.[28]

Curiously, constructions of the jail(able) population as antisocial, incorrigible, and morally impoverished contrasted sharply with the available evidence from the county. In the Monroe County Sheriff's Office 2011 annual report, the data included a list of the top ten jail admissions by offense. Of the 6,178 people admitted to the jail in 2011, the most frequent charge was for public intoxication, with 1,155 admissions, or 18.5 percent of the total for the year. The next nine admissions by offense were drunk driving (486 admissions, or 7.8 percent), D felony theft (291, or 4.7 percent),[29] probation violation warrants (219, or 3.5 percent), resisting law enforcement (168, or 2.7 percent), illegal consumption of alcohol (144, or 2.3 percent), writ of attachment (136, or 2.2 percent),[30]

A misdemeanor battery (125, or 2 percent),[31] marijuana possession (124, or 2 percent) and criminal trespass (106, or 1.7 percent). While it is not the intention or place of this book to minimize the potential harms of these actions, it is important to point out that at most three of these can be construed as remotely violent (or potentially so), a distinction that I hesitate to even draw because of the variability of that definition.[32] Moreover, by simply not incarcerating someone for being drunk in public, the county could have reduced the jail population by almost 20 percent, to say nothing of the potential diversion options for probation violations, writs of attachment, illegal consumption, and marijuana possession. Indeed, while local officials were correct in observing that the jail population consisted almost exclusively of the county's poor, it would seem that many students attending Indiana University, an institution consistently ranked as among the top party schools in the country, could probably be admitted to the jail for the same offenses.

In addition to the contradictions between officials' explanations of poverty nationally and locally, their constructs of criminality expressed a subtler and more insidious dis/juncture: the racialization of local and nonlocal jail populations, even as officials concurrently spoke out against the racism of the prison-industrial complex.[33] Most explicitly, officials racialized whiteness through invoking the "white trash" identity of the jail(able) population. Recent scholarship on the term "white trash" notes that it "objectifies and stigmatizes whites living in poverty and lacking proper decorum—carving a raced and classed hierarchy from relative homogeneity."[34] The term collapses racism and classism into a single referent, enabling two processes: "it is a way of naming actually existing white people who occupy the economic and social margins of American life, and it is a set of myths and stereotypes that justify their continued marginalization."[35] In Bloomington, constructions of a racialized and class-based "not quite white" criminal subject justified a facility designed for moral education and acculturation to hegemonic whiteness.

The soft otherizing of local crime is conspicuous in the context of census data, which reveals largely white populations in both the city of Bloomington (87 percent) and Monroe County (88 percent). Moreover, when local talk turned to crime and incarceration outside of the community, official constructs of crime changed. My informants often spoke of "real crime" and "real criminals" as being located in other(ized) places, such as Chicago, Indianapolis, and Gary, a phenomenon I explore in more detail in the next chapter.[36]

Before concluding this chapter, and as a segue into chapter 4's focus on youth, I will add a final complicating and important observation about the discursive construction of the local population: community organizers opposed to the justice campus were not immune from relying on racialized and classed constructs. Despite the distinct differences between proponents and opponents of the justice campus and the important ways that activists offered counterhegemonic articulations that disrupted the dominant narrative of expansion, there were moments where people on either side of this issue offered perspectives or analyses that undercut any attempt at essentializing their differences.

One DMC activist who spoke at the first MCCJCC hearing about the justice campus, concerning the juvenile facility, discussed how some young people he worked with made important observations about who would likely end up incarcerated: "One made a very astute observation . . . that this [facility] will probably be full of poor African American kids, poor kids at that to speak more broadly. Because they won't have parents that are there for them and it's not that they're in some other county and they're not involved, they're not involved here." Incarceration certainly can strain relationships, and it is conceivable that detained youth have parents who are disengaged or absent from their lives. Nonetheless, this comment offered a rather narrow and linear connection between absentee parents and detained youth forged through race and class signifiers. The implication of the activist's comment was that parents are not involved because they are "African American" or "more broadly," poor. Notably, this activist didn't qualify his comment by acknowledging any of the structural conditions of poverty that prevent people from being involved, or that alter or limit the ways in which involvement occurs. His comment thus joined the discourse that relied on narratives steeped in cultural and pathological constructs of racialized poverty.

Conclusion

Community leaders relied on several overlapping narratives to justify the new jail and the larger justice campus of which it would be part. First, officials stitched the problems of jail overcrowding and minimal in-jail programming to the solution of new carceral construction. A new jail, they argued, would relieve the overcrowded conditions that were unacceptable and that kept the county under the threat of a lawsuit. Moreover, officials and other leaders saw in a new jail ample space for classes and other programs, as well as offices for the nonprofit organizations that would teach and provide them. Of course, the solution of new construction and the dramatically increased carceral capacity it would bring relied on there being a population to confine. In the discourse of who was and would be incarcerated and treated, county officials affirmed repeatedly the existence of a culturally and morally inferior population, with behaviors and ways of thinking that rendered them in need of carceral treatment. With the exception of some community organizers whose interventions into the discourse I profile in chapter 8, no one interrogated the characteristics of poor conduct except to question whether their origins were biologically predetermined or developed through exposure to peers or family. By locating human actions in an imagined isolated realm of "subculture," local dominant understandings of the jail(able) population severely reduced the possibility of policy conversations and solutions aimed at ameliorating the material conditions of the community. In addition to the absence of such analyses, there was little consideration of the invention of the very population in question.

4

"A Lockdown Facility . . . with the Feel of a Small, Private College"

Even those county officials who were ambivalent about or critical of the ultimate rendering of the justice campus defended the initial concept, which had centered on the idea of a juvenile facility campus. Perhaps the most edifying expression of the original vision for a youth justice campus came from Bridget Markham, a county council member who was running for reelection in 2008. Markham's platform for her candidacy included a passionate commitment to building the justice campus. When I interviewed her at a local café in 2009, she rejected the massive nature of the final proposal but restated her support for a complex that featured "a lockdown facility . . . [with] a progressive and innovative educational component, alternative programming, and with the feel of a small, private college, where there could be school programs, programs related to other disciplines at the university, the kinds of initiatives that exist there—local food programs, things like that."

Markham's vision suggests that diverse structures influenced local carceral habitus. Her references to both education and local food in the context of expressing support for youth detention are instructive. First, in the very terminology of "justice campus" and the programs imagined for it there were clear indications that education, social service, mental health, religion, and sustainable agriculture molded local notions of carceral expansion, along with the influence from criminal justice. But outside influences on the penal and judicial field are not novel and in fact illuminate the unexceptional nature of local justice. As Michel Foucault observed of the changing practices of penality from torture to discipline and the necessary changing logics that accompanied it, "today criminal justice functions and justifies itself only by this perpetual reference to something other than itself, by this unceasing reinscription in non-juridical systems" (1977, 22).

Second, Markham's reference to local food programs while advocating for a juvenile facility reveals the rhetorical and conceptual influence of Monroe County's strong and vibrant local food movement. Bloomington boasted a nationally recognized farmers market, and there were city, county, and nonprofit organizations dedicated to expanding local sustainable agriculture, cuisine, and economy. Many civic and political leaders expressed their support for the justice campus, in particular the juvenile facility component, through a slogan of "keeping local kids local." This was most directly a response to the juvenile court's practice of sending youth out of the county for secure detention. But the slogan certainly relied on the political and cultural capital generated by the "locavore" movement. In a fascinating twist of logics and imbrication of movements, officials mapped the passion and energy related to eating and buying local produce onto a call for increased local "consumption of punishment."[1]

Of course, the influences on carceral habitus from different fields were strategically manipulated. Officials and corrections consultants were well aware of the community's passionate support for sustainability initiatives. They were able to harness some of that support by attaching important signifiers to the campus proposal. For example, every official presentation about the justice campus included Richard Kemp of Program Administration and Results, Inc. (PARI), noting the importance of "green thinking" to the ultimate design. In a testament to PARI's shallow conceptualization of sustainable design, never once did Kemp say anything more elaborate than the word "green" or the phrase "green thinking." Nevertheless, supporters and other community members celebrated the ecologically friendly rhetorical gesture and filled in the many blanks that Kemp left. At the Monroe County Criminal Justice Coordinating Council's hearing about the youth facility, one local director of a youth-serving agency began his comments with an important critique: how his organization could use some of the money that would go toward the campus. He stopped, however, after just a minute and then concluded his remarks this way: "Finally, if you're gonna make it green, please consider solar panels on the roofs, ways to collect rainwater to provide water internally. It would be nice to have moped transportation for staff to and from the courthouse. This property if it is gonna be developed and is gonna go green could in a way pay for itself over time. Please save the taxpayers that expense."

The county narrative about the justice campus took on especially passionate tones and language when focusing on the juvenile facility component. Frequently, county judges and probation officers framed the need for the facility as a moral and political matter: they argued not only that the county had the capacity to create exceptional institutions but also that doing so would be an integral expression of its progressive politics.

The passionate tone of the hearing that focused on the juvenile facility featured officials integrating heart-rending anecdotes into the more often used rhetoric of evidence-based practices. As a result, this came across as an attempt to shame local citizens critical of the proposal into accepting the vision of a local facility. Tugging on his listeners' heartstrings at the hearing, Juvenile Court Judge Patrick Randall told the story of a boy he had just left in court:

> He's never been away from home before. And he had to look at me and ask "Judge, where am I going?" And I explained to him you're leaving to go to detention, and I had to explain to his family that that's fifty miles away. And he asked, "Well, how will I see my mother?" and I had to explain to him [Randall paused and stared at the audience], "Well, you won't." Unless she's able to get down there, and for a lot of my low-income people that I deal with, they're not gonna be able to make it. I have no control over the facility; I have no control over the family's ability to participate in services; I have no control over the programming that the children get. . . . It is not the same as us, this community, taking responsibility.

Randall's concerns about distance and the preclusion of visitation were justified. But there was an unmistakable trace here and throughout his testimony that illustrated his desire for control over the location and treatment of youth. For Randall, the problem was not detention but geography and jurisdiction.

In the following long excerpt from the same hearing, Randall laid out his understanding of the need for the justice campus, pointing to the common presence of juvenile facilities in other counties in Indiana and implying that the lack of a local facility reflected poorly on Monroe County's expressed progressive politics:

I thought I would check to see out of the fifteen largest counties in the state how many [don't] have their own facility for secure detention and shelter care. There is one. Which one would that be? Well, that's us. That's us [Randall smiled ruefully]. I think we pride ourselves on being one of the most progressive counties, [as evident in] our view on corrections [and] our view on dealing with children. I take mine from [previous juvenile court] Judge Geraldine Lane; I know Judge [Bill] Rusch before me also did. We are always oriented toward treatment and rehabilitation. We have the lowest percentage per capita of children sent to the Department of Corrections in the state. We keep our children here if we can. The problem is, we have no facility other than [the] youth shelter at this time in order to keep children in our community and offer them services and programming. So what's the solution? We've talked about it at length. We do need to build a local juvenile facility with beds for secure detention, for shelter care, and for residential care. We need to have the ability to offer mental health evaluations, drug and alcohol treatment, life-skills training, all the things we'd like to be able to offer our children, and we have to do it. It is our duty. It is our responsibility. We can utilize local resources, we can partner with local schools and the hospital. I think we can do a unique job of it. . . . We have struggled with this decision for the last twenty years. We have, in my opinion, the most qualified group of citizens of any county. We have had participation over the years by so many people in trying to put this together. . . . It is time. It's time to, for lack of better words, grow up. It's not right that we don't have a facility for our kids in this county when every other county of our size or smaller does. So I would urge you to consider this. We need to discuss what's the right size of the facility, and that's the kind of input I certainly want to have from all of you, what kinds of programs and services we should offer. I go back to the report from March 1, 2001, by a blue-ribbon panel the commissioners put together, and it has wonderful ideas for programming. I think we could start there and go from there. But I'm sick of planning. I'm tired of planning. It's time to move on this. That's my statement.

Unpacking this quote reveals much about local politics. There was an absence of any rhetoric of punishment or law and order. Instead, Randall and others focused exclusively on family preservation, treatment, life skills, and education—laudable goals, and certainly squarely within a liberal tradition. However, for Randall, the shame of the county was the absence of a facility. He implied that a community that prided itself on being progressive should clearly be able to detain its own youth in its own facilities. Indeed, it was the "duty" and "responsibility" of Monroe County to ensure the construction of such an institution.

Randall made an important rhetorical move at end of his statement by suggesting that the ensuing conversation should focus on what programs should be put in place, not whether the facility should exist (I explore such rhetorical moves, which had the effect of steering the public meeting in particular directions, in part 3). With the paternal tone that Randall took during the meeting, including stating his belief that this community needed to "grow up" and build already, it is clear that he believed he knew what was best for young people, their parents, and the larger community. Rather than separating him from juvenile judges around the country, this belief actually placed him squarely in their midst. The crucial point here is that the political capital for the juvenile facility came through a belief in the redemptive and rehabilitative capacities of local institutions.

Official endorsements of the juvenile facility at times went beyond coherence. At the same hearing, Rose Halverson, then president of the city council, made a public statement. Halverson frequently offered her credentials as a "social justice and antipoverty activist." At the hearing she began by stating her support for the proposed juvenile facility, and she provided her credentials by mentioning her own history as a child protective services worker and as a current volunteer in the jail with Begin Again and Monroe County Justice. She then said:

> I'm now working with individuals in the jail who I had on my caseload as juveniles. . . . We have to consolidate our efforts, from the school system to the wonderful volunteers we have in this community to our public officials to our justice system. It is time. I couldn't agree more with Judge Randall. I will be joining his choir. It is time for us to address the needs of youth and families to be preventative [sic] in our efforts. The amount of money we invest in [the juvenile facility] will save us not only money— we're talking human capital, human lives. That makes me ill as a volunteer working with the jail: people with capabilities, intellect, abilities that have wasted many years of their lives being locked up, without freedom,

without dignity, without the opportunities to be with their families. So I couldn't be more supportive of working on this project. Thank you, Judge Randall.

Halverson offered a clear critique of the toll that incarceration takes on individuals and families. Her support for the juvenile facility matched her defense of the benevolence of the county's criminal justice institutions and personnel in other hearings I attended. But reading her statement reveals a startling reality: she passionately advocated for the juvenile facility as a way to prevent incarceration, arguing for the detention of young people to prevent their incarceration as adults. Officials missed the tautology of this widely accepted vision—incarceration to prevent incarceration—because they saw the detention facility as an essential mechanism for saving the lives of destitute and marginalized youth.

The belief in the transformative capacity of local institutions and officers translated into officials endorsing expansion and encroachment into the lives of individuals in ways that they criticized in other geographical contexts. Frequently, officials articulated this expansion through lamenting the lack of adequate personnel in their respective departments and as part of the overall county justice apparatus. In their narratives, more probation officers, sheriffs, and city police would translate into better and more humanely served residents.

In my interview with Carrie Donnelly—the chief probation officer, who was an outspoken critic of incarceration and a passionate supporter of a new youth facility—she advocated both an expansion of the city police force and an expansion of institutional alternatives to youth detention. She mentioned that in the mid-1990s the state had offered the county $500,000 to build a juvenile facility. According to Donnelly, the county's inability to decide what such a facility should look like, what it should do, and where it should be located had resulted in the loss of those funds and their redistribution to neighboring Bartholomew County. (Ironically, in the summer of 2009, Monroe County hired Victoria Krause, a youth detention consultant. Krause had long directed the facility that Bartholomew County had built with those funds and, at the time of my interview with Donnelly, was assisting Monroe County in its newest attempt to create juvenile justice space.) One consequence of not having a place to send youth, Donnelly told me, was the high number of "street adjustments"—discretionary decisions to leave situations alone because of a lack of detention or treatment options—that police officers were forced to make. This was the second time Donnelly had mentioned to me that the police frequently did not detain enough young people and that the presence of a facility would allow the police to detain more of them.

In one example that Donnelly gave to indicate the problematic nature of street adjustments, officers were called to a location where young people had been caught shooting paintball guns at cars. According to Donnelly, officers ultimately abdicated responsibility for handling the situation to members of the immediate community, who worked with the youth to pay for some of the damage they had caused. For Donnelly, this was an example of law-breaking behavior that went unaddressed by the juvenile justice system and thus constituted a lost opportunity for intervention into the lives of young people and their families. In direct contrast to Donnelly's framing and assessment of the situation, one can interpret the incident as an instructive if isolated example of community conflict resolution that avoided formal justice system processes and resolved problems in a decentralized and perhaps restorative fashion. This particular example offers an insight into important differences between liberal reformers like Donnelly, who advocated expanding systems to treat more individuals, and Decarcerate Monroe County (DMC), whose members looked for ways to shrink the existing systems of formal social control. For Donnelly, this example was one of many instances in which a local facility and a greater continuum of institutional and alternative sanctions would provide police officers with a place to take youth and a continuum of sanctions to employ as treatment and punishment. For DMC and other critics, Donnelly's ideas were a clear example of net widening, the process by which youth who otherwise would avoid ensnarement in the system altogether become caught up in an expanded continuum of alternative sanctions.[2]

Exceptional Locality and the State

Officials' beliefs in their exceptional capacities were nothing new. As David Garland (1990, 249–76) has argued, various symbolic, rhetorical, and material practices of penality help construct the subjectivities of those on both its delivery and receiving ends. In framing local penality as an extension of Monroe County's welfarist policies and overall ethos, officials could inject punishment into the same narrative as social services and project a larger image of the benevolent county (ibid., 267). In this way, officials could also present jail and youth detention officers as social workers and incarceration as an extension of social services. This served the important symbolic function of disarticulating the local, welfarist criminal justice apparatus from the punitive state, although it should be clear that the state—in its historical role in the county, its structuring of the circulating logics, and the reliance by the county on the technology of the cage—was anything but absent.

The slogan of "keep local kids local" and its constitutive message of decentralized county governance over juvenile justice indicated a broader relationship between the community and the state. As compelling work has shown, the state figures heavily in the transmission of logics that structure community attempts at justice.[3] In Bloomington this was especially notable because attempts to govern local youth justice were positioned explicitly in contrast to the state. But the explicit rhetorical rejection of the state in the local embrace of the justice campus ignored the various ways that the state worked in and through the local community in material and symbolic fashion. As various scholars have argued, neoliberal decentralization of the state does not mean that the state withers. Instead, the state can diffuse its power, operate through both brute force and discursive hegemony, and scale back its official presence even as its scope expands and its influence grows.[4]

Moreover, in their rhetorical rejection of the state, local officials ignored a rather startling piece of history: it was the Indiana Department of Corrections (DOC) that originally approached the county about a regional juvenile detention center. In 1990, around the time commonly cited as marking the beginning of studies and conversations about a new juvenile facility, the *Herald-Times* published two stories that I offer as revisionist historical context to the county narrative of a unique youth facility. In the first article, "Correction Officials Seek Support for Juvenile Center," the reporter begins by noting that "state correction officials met in Bloomington Tuesday night and urged other southern Indiana counties to dig into their pockets and support a regional detention center for juveniles. . . . The state wants to see a regional effort in the area of juvenile justice, according to one of the meeting's monitors, [an] Indiana Department of Correction deputy commissioner" (Welsh-Huggins 1990).

The reporter notes that the meeting came on the heels of the $500,000 grant from the state to the county to construct a regional facility. Given difficulty in acquiring additional funds from the county and surrounding counties, the meeting was held to create a plan for gathering the supplemental monies. Just three weeks later, the *Herald-Times* ran an article with the headline "Detention Center Budget Gets Funds." The article noted that the county council had started the appropriation process by which it would budget monies to supplement the state's $500,000: "Morgan County has pledged $100,000 to the project, with the remainder of the funds coming from Monroe and per-day charges paid by counties sending juveniles here" (Higgs 1990).

These same issues persisted even after the justice campus proposal had moved from its central place in community discussions during 2008 and the first part of 2009. In the fall of 2009, a few months after the release of the official PARI report about the justice campus, local officials turned to the Youth Services Bureau (YSB) for space to house some adjudicated youth as well as offices for some juvenile probation officers. Until then, the YSB had served primarily as an emergency youth shelter, a youth counseling service, and as a national Safe Place for youth in crisis. The YSB executive director reported directly to the Monroe County Board of Commissioners; with the changes in the YSB's mission and composition, officials were also eager to transfer control of the YSB from the county commissioners to the board of judges, in particular Juvenile Court Judge Randall. The change in management would bring three probation officers to the site. In the view of officials, this would expand and enhance the services available to youth.

As much as officials relied on the rhetoric of locality and treatment to advocate the importance of both the justice campus and the YSB, unmistakable elements of a larger political and economic strategy were built into their campaigns. Specifically, the mantra of "keep local kids local" belied another motive for the transfer of the YSB to the board of judges, one less easily communicable through a slogan and less likely to generate immediate support: paying probation officer salaries through different monies would save probation jobs and county money.

Because the circuit court housed the Probation Department, Juvenile Court Judge Randall was now able to move juvenile probation officers into office space at the YSB. Thus, the probation officers became eligible for funds from a pool of monies separate from the regular county budget. The county council had passed an ordinance in 2007 creating a special funding stream for juvenile services through a County Option Income Tax (COIT). During the summer of 2009, with the justice campus proposal abandoned and the YSB change proposed, the council voted to raise the COIT, which would fund the salaries of three probation officers, contingent on their placement at the YSB (Nolan 2009e). Integral to understanding the importance of the COIT funding is the fact that the probation department would have lost the three positions without the use of the separate funding stream. Lest there be any confusion, the three probation officers at the YSB were not even assigned to young people who were in residence there. The move was largely financial, with the added dubious result of reshaping the identity of the shelter to correspond with its new carceral component. In contrast to the claims made by some people at the meetings about this issue that "here in Monroe County, we don't make decisions about youth based on money,"[5] it would appear that concerns about saving money and retaining probation officers were of paramount importance in the eventual transition of control of the YSB to the board of judges.

This brief history complicates officials' proclamations about the exceptional nature of Monroe County juvenile justice. The influence of the state Department of Corrections on the initial conversations about a juvenile facility, the importance of state monies, the early consideration of user fees from other counties as income generation, and the transfer of the YSB to the circuit court all suggest that political and economic forces structured local decisions about juvenile justice. This contradicts the testimonies from officials who claimed their local system was separate from the carceral state and made enlightened decisions about youth.

Constructing Local Benevolence

The belief in the redemptive, rehabilitative, and exceptional potential of local youth institutions reveals the ways that habitus framed local perceptions of self—that is, of officials' personal, professional, and organizational identities. Criminal justice officials' presentations of selves as therapists, counselors, and educators (as opposed to their actual titles of judges and probation officers) bring Foucault's observations about the new "army of technicians" (1977, 11) that administer discipline into productive theoretical engagement with Bourdieu and habitus. Writing of the abandonment of torture in the West and the turn away from the body and toward the disciplining of the soul and mind, Foucault argues that "wardens, doctors, chaplains, psychiatrists, psychologists, educationalists" (ibid.) took over from the executioner the administration of the punishment regimen. There was ample historical precedent for framing juvenile punishment as something benign and even benevolent. It was Monroe County officials' ahistorical embrace of this role that highlights the importance of embodied—and forgotten—structures.

The construction of local juvenile justice identity weaves into the discussion of local facilities the historical trajectory of the juvenile court itself. Local officials were correct, historically speaking, in claiming that the court was designed to act in ways that resembled objective structures of treatment and education. Anthony Platt observes:

> The role model for juvenile court judges was doctor-counselor rather than lawyer. "Judicial therapists" were expected to establish a one-to-one relationship with "delinquents" in the same way that a country doctor might give his time and attention to a favorite patient. . . . Juvenile court judges shared the missionary passion of the child savers and approached their work in medical-therapeutic terms. In their efforts to impress juvenile offenders that the court was seeking only their best interests, they were both friendly and firm, offering hope of a better life without abandoning their position of authority and power. (2009, 142–45)

This historical role certainly animated the juvenile justice politics of the community. The reach of this identity was perhaps best revealed during the process surrounding the changes to the YSB. At a series of meetings that DMC organized and hosted in the fall of 2009 to compel elected officials to explain and defend the proposed changes at the YSB, conversations revealed important distinctions between officials' perceptions of themselves and the perception that the community had of them. These distinctions, which were explicitly discussed among meeting attendees, also revealed important differences about the meaning of safety, a concept central to criminal justice. In addition to counseling and other services, the YSB had long been a "Project Safe Place" for three counties—a designated residential location to which youth could admit themselves if they felt unsafe in their home or community. Until the 2010 transfer of the YSB from the board of county commissioners to the board of judges, about half of the young people who resided at the shelter were on probation, although that was incidental to their stay. Many of the people who stayed at the shelter or used its services did so voluntarily and did not have a delinquency case or probation officer.

At times, DMC was successful in contesting definitions of safety and suggesting that community perceptions of official identities differed from officials' self-perceptions, which are important indications of the ability to destabilize and even shift the habitus. Nevertheless, officials were often able to integrate these concerns and criticisms into their narrative, rendering interventions ineffective and appropriating them in ways that bolstered dominant understandings. The officials' concepts of county detention and incarceration allowed them to convince themselves that their roles, the experiences of youth under their supervision, and the nature of their jobs and institutions were qualitatively different from identical jobs and institutions elsewhere and that people experienced them in ways that conformed to both the officials' self-concepts and the official stated nature of their institutions. At a meeting about the YSB hosted by DMC in the fall of 2009, Randall spoke about the formal role of the juvenile court and the way his courtroom manifested that same ethos: "The focus of the juvenile court is to help the children. You know, you don't get a jury trial in juvenile court. Why? Because the goal is not punitive after disposition, the goal is to help you. The goal is to help that child and that family. That's what I'm about, that's what I'm gonna be pushing for." In the judge's view, the juvenile facility would embody the same philosophical approach as his courtroom: help and treatment. County leaders frequently framed their understanding of facilities and the potential of future facilities within the official definition of the system and dismissed both criticism and experiences that called that connection into question. If the juvenile court and juvenile probation operated under a formal and explicit mission of treatment, according to their logic, the officials in those departments, the operation of those departments, and the ways in which youth experienced them must naturally conform to that mission. Importantly, the history of juvenile justice suggests that officials' insistence on an alignment between mission, intention, and reality belied significant fissures.[6]

At the same meeting about the YSB, in response to some criticism and apprehension from shelter staff members who were worried that the YSB transfer and the presence of probation officers would affect the perception and use of the space, Randall responded with visible annoyance that probation shared the shelter's "culture of rehabilitation" for youth. Frustrated, he added, "Come on, guys, probation is like social workers," and "[Bloomington] is a community of purpose. . . . YSB and probation are both delivering services." Donnelly would later ask a DMC member critical of the move, "Where would you get [the idea] that the juvenile justice system is punitive? We are different than the adult system. We deal with treatment." She thus mapped the official mission of the department onto the lived experiences of both the officer and the youth.[7] Officials often claimed that they were "against youth incarceration" and insisted that their positions were the same as DMC's, even as they pushed for policies that would explicitly expand carceral capacities and widen the reach of the juvenile court.

Although the rhetoric of the judge and probation officials dominated meetings, people in attendance offered critical appraisals of the plan for the YSB. Several people over the course of the three meetings argued that the presence of probation officers at the facility, and the knowledge that the facility was under the purview of the judges rather than the county commissioners, would inevitably alter the community's use of and openness toward the services. One professor from Indiana University said, "If I were a homeless youth and knew that there were probation officers at the shelter, I would go nowhere near it." Indeed, two young men formerly housed at the YSB, both of whom had also spent time in juvenile detention, spoke up after comments from Randall. One told the judge and the rest of the attendees that "kids feel nervous around probation; kids feel nervous around judges." The second said that he had been "locked away in an abusive situation from eleven to eighteen years old. Punishment is what I faced."[8] He spoke of the palpable difference in the missions of probation and the YSB, noting that he felt criminalized by probation and supported by the YSB, which he credited with keeping him out of juvenile detention.

In the last of the three YSB meetings, the agency's clinical director, Tony Daniels, spoke of the compromises therapeutic services might have to make if probation officers were to move into the YSB. He noted that his office was next door to the office that probation officers would occupy. Looking directly at the judge and probation administrators present, he rhetorically considered whether the presence of a probation officer would compromise the confidentiality and comfort that his clients currently felt in his office. "With a probation officer literally sitting next door," he asked, "will that client talk about their marijuana usage the previous day or other potentially illegal activities that are part of their need for counseling?" Daniels's point received nods of support and subsequent comments from DMC members who shared his concerns. Randall, Donnelly, and Robin Trotter were sitting directly in front of me and exchanged hushed criticisms of Daniels's points, shaking their heads and noting to one another that kids do not perceive probation officers as threats. In their view, expressed repeatedly during the course of the three meetings, probation officers were no different from social workers.

It appeared that the critics in the room—including members of DMC, YSB employees, young people formerly housed at the shelter, and their parents—understood the probation department and the judge to be components of a punitive system that disrupted and threatened the safety of otherwise noncoercive spaces. The insistence from Randall, Donnelly, and Trotter that probation officers were social workers who existed outside of the system that, by definition, they were a part of attempted to reassure Bloomington residents concerned with mass incarceration and the local expansion of juvenile justice. This discursive construction of the local juvenile court and the probation department frequently succeeded, as it relied on both the historical mission of juvenile justice and the county habitus that articulated local carcerality through objective structures of treatment, education, and rehabilitation. Officials could easily sway what one DMC member characterized to me as "the many well-meaning local folks who just want to help the poor kids."

"Poor" Conduct II: Constructing the Local and Foreign Youth Subject

In addition to articulating distinct practitioner subjectivities, officials also relied on dominant constructs of youth criminality. It is a central feature of the cultural work of punishment to construct subjectivities in such a way as to deem some people normal and others deviant and requiring social control.[9] Local officials were aware of this construction of normal and deviant and spoke with clarity and passion about racialized and class-based markers of difference. Many condemned the institutional racism of mass incarceration and located the roots of criminalization in capitalist inequality. Yet when discussing Monroe County, they often invoked a responsibilized, individuated, and unacculturated actor whose actions were freely chosen and unattached to the structural constraints of capitalism that the same officials recognized as pervasive everywhere else. It was thus the job of the county and its institutions to reconstruct those individuals through a treatment regimen that required their captivity and enforced compliance. While officials could offer existing and potential programmatic options as evidence of their rehabilitative focus, they did not recognize the ways that neoliberal logics sutured punitive and treatment approaches to discourses of criminality.[10]

In one memorable example, I sat down with Victoria Krause, who had been a police officer and a social worker and who had retired from directing Bartholomew County's juvenile facility to open a consultancy practice. As noted above, at the time of our interview, Krause was assisting Monroe County in its attempt to transfer jurisdiction of the YSB. Like many of my informants, Krause strongly condemned incarceration, going as far as admitting to a "hatred" of the criminal justice system. As she told me, "I dropped out of a PhD program in criminal justice because I couldn't see myself studying a system I hated." Nevertheless, Krause could reconcile her politics of incarceration with her occupation as a juvenile justice consultant through a belief in the possibility of incarcerating young people for their own benefit. Indeed, speaking of the institution she had directed, Krause claimed, "I'm passionate about that facility." In her descriptions, a picture of a differentiated and deficient youth in need of detention began to emerge alongside curiously contradictory images of her facility. On the one hand, she took pride in describing the common critique of her facility: that they are "too nice." On the other hand, she explained her "zero tolerance" policy for profanity. When administrators from other counties come to tour her facility, she said, they always question the lack of profanity. Krause then noted that residents who use profanity are sent directly back to their rooms until they "calm down." She said that she views the anger expressed through profanity as evidence of poor socialization and inappropriate behavior. In this regard, she also spoke of the importance of certain therapies in the facility and in frequent use in her county's community-based juvenile justice services to break intergenerational cognitive and behavioral patterns and ways of thinking that land young people in detention. She spoke passionately of the day treatment program operated by the juvenile court, which required young people to report seven days a week, including after school, all day on Saturday, and Sunday afternoons (so, as Krause told me, "families can worship together in the morning"). Noting that "they all have anger issues," Krause explained the high usage of cognitive-behavioral therapy, aggression replacement therapy, and moral reconation therapy in her county. She made no mention of poverty, racism, joblessness, or other structural factors.

Krause dismissed and disparaged punishment, yet she openly endorsed consequences that disciplined youth into certain prescribed performances of deference and comportment. This turned into punishable offenses certain behaviors—even certain words or ways of speaking—that outside of her facility were not necessarily even considered deviant, let alone criminal. Discipline also came in the form of the "examination,"[11] through which young people were classified, studied, and treated according to the biological, psychological, and social needs that the institution and its employees identified.

Krause's endorsement of treatment modalities "to break intergenerational patterns of delinquent thinking" was a popular perspective shared by Monroe County officials. The heralding of cognitive-behavioral therapy and other "evidence-based" approaches (Bishop 2012) as essential to the detention experience affirmed critiques of the neoliberal logics that marry punishment and therapy and that are part of the "novel responsibilizing industry" that has become the "new rehabilitation of late modernity."[12] Moreover, the discipline meted out to young people invoked the "disciplining" of poor youthful offenders from prior eras into their appropriate class positions.[13]

Yet using the need for treatment to mark difference, construct other-ness, and justify an expanded juvenile justice system within the county was simultaneously also used to signify a second set of distinctions. While Krause and others spoke of local youth as exceptional in the un-threatening nature of their delinquency and thus in need of the ther-apeutic carceral services that the county saw itself as able to provide, they also contrasted local people with a racialized "real criminal" await-ing them at the state facilities. Historians of race and punishment have observed this fastening of criminality to Blackness[14] and have charted how such a construct animates selective rehabilitative interventions into the lives of white youth. On the latter point, Geoff Ward has noted the importance of white supremacy in motivating the Progressive era child savers: "Rehabilitative efforts were often reserved for native-born and immigrant Anglo Americans in white-dominated juvenile court com-munities, where common European ancestry and white skin rendered them less threatening, distinctly 'salvageable,' and ultimately more assimilable—culturally, economically, and politically—than black and other nonwhite youth" (2009, 228; see also Ward 2012). Moreover, other scholars have observed the contemporary work this construct performs in the symbolic production of race,[15] in the determinations of correc-tions administrators and institutions to employ or abandon rehabilita-tion strategies and discourses,[16] and as an engine of governmentality and other forms of neoliberal practices.[17]

Given the largely white population of Monroe County, it would seem that the very concept of the justice campus—as a benevolent carceral institution whose mission was the reformation, redemption, and rein-tegration of its inhabitants into the community—was predicated on a largely white jail(able) population and guided by an "invisible hand of racial nepotism that sets the limits of cruel and unusual punishment for white Americans."[18] The question remains as to whether the county's overall approach would be different were its population more racially heterogeneous.

The energetic pursuit of a youth facility illuminates the larger and familiar racial politics of criminal justice at play in the community. Dur-ing an interview, Donnelly remarked to me that another county that was also home to a large university but was an hour closer to Chicago had a much higher rate of youth incarceration, a fact that she speculated was due to its proximity to "criminals from Gary, Indiana, and Chicago." Just a few minutes later, while reflecting on the recent history of juvenile justice in Monroe County, Donnelly claimed that there had been a jump in the number of young people sent to the Department of Corrections in the mid-1990s because of local gang activity. She observed, however, that these were "organized 'wannabes,'" suggesting that real criminals come from outside the community, presumably from the same urban centers she had mentioned earlier.

Other examples of the construction of the county and its youth as distinct from places with "real crime" and "real criminals" abounded, including in the contributions to local discourse made by the *Herald-Times*. Through editorial endorsements of carceral expansion and through its coverage of events related to crime and justice, the newspaper played a key ideological role in the transmission of certain definitions and perspectives of social problems and solutions. In this way, as noted in scholarship of media and crime, the newspaper "provide[d] a crucial mediating link between the apparatus of social control and the public."[19] In a story about a police raid on a house after an investigation revealed several young men with alleged ties to the Chicago Vice Lords were living there and selling crack cocaine, the newspaper quoted a police captain as saying:

> This investigation has revealed yet another group of individuals who have come from out of town for the sole purpose of dealing crack cocaine in our community. Even with these arrests, and the recent arrests of others engaging in the same type of activity, there will be new dealers who will try to fill the void left behind. We are committed to identifying and arresting those whose illegal activity wreaks havoc on the community by contributing to other crimes and the shattered lives they leave behind by exploiting those who become addicted to the drug. *Hopefully, sometime soon the message will reach those other communities that Bloomington is not the place to go to deal drugs.* (Creps 2007; my emphasis)

The message implicit in the captain's testimony was clear: drug dealers come from other(ized) cities and threaten the community's way of life. In ignoring the drug dealing that occurred in and through the local community and certainly at the university, the captain positioned

Bloomington and its residents as innocent and untainted victims of "real criminals." He joined other local officials in the creation of a local delinquent population who were in need of saving—from others as much as from themselves—and who were clearly imagined to possess souls at risk of corruption.[20]

Sometimes coverage and analysis in the *Herald-Times* conveyed surprise when acts occurred in the community that offended the newspaper's sense of an exceptional local youth subject. One editorial took a punitive position against a ten-year-old whose errant toss of a rock hit a school bus: "It's not a real surprise that a middle-schooler rather than an older kid appears to have been the one who threw a rock through a school bus window, slightly injuring a Pike volleyball player following a match against Bloomington South's team. Not a surprise, that is, after the initial shock that such a thing could happen in Bloomington" (Editorial 2009c).

The newspaper's "shock" that such a relatively mundane incident could occur in Bloomington is curious for its naïveté and instructive for its implicit endorsement of exceptionalism. The paper acted as if the community's preadolescent population was of a purified stock that not only abstained from horseplay or delinquency but also never made errant tosses.

Safety, Justice, and Visibility: Disciplined Definitions

Without pulling away from the ethnographic material, I want to take a conceptual step back and consider what local conversations about identities of youth and officials suggest for larger and related ideas. Specifically, I want to point to the ways that common-sense notions of safety and justice were contested during the course of the attempts at carceral expansion.

The contestation of the meaning of safety is central to understanding the discourse and politics of carceral expansion in the community. Moreover, the instability of safety and other important concepts implies that carceral habitus, deposited in the community like sediment, was subject to shifting in response to currents of resistance. Here I ask how the habitus responded to resistance and how it settled again after it had shifted.

Meetings about changes at the YSB revealed that none of the officials had asked young people who were current or former recipients of YSB services if they would feel safe accessing services if the shelter were under the control of the board of judges and if some of the faces they were to see at the site were those of probation officers. Indeed, Krause failed to ask any young people for their thoughts on the matter; unsurprisingly, her final report to the county about the YSB changes concluded enthusiastically that the YSB should be integrated into the juvenile justice apparatus. In the transfer of control of the YSB, it is possible to observe the ability of county habitus to hold off attempts at reformulation: the narrative of safety remained strongly enough rooted in the belief that it is provided for and protected by police and probation officers. Despite DMC's success in disrupting this narrative when it was articulated through the justice campus proposal—when the group convinced enough community leaders to think about safety more broadly, and even to consider the ways in which state officers make people feel less safe—the YSB change had enough political momentum and support to succeed.

In the discourse over the fate of the YSB, different translocal logics of safety affected local definitions. In the case of liberal judges and county politicians, safety came with caring officers, who were a legal manifestation of a larger political identity centered on public service and governmental benevolence. For community organizers, safety took on a more radical political definition. DMC members used terminology and analysis from national organizations such as Critical Resistance to articulate a vision of safety as meeting the basic needs of all community members.[21] DMC also understood safety within a larger anti-authoritarian critique of state power: to the group's members, safety meant being free from the coercion and punishment characteristic of police and probation officers, however caring they might be.

The series of meetings about the fate of the YSB offered a rich display of rhetoric about justice, with Randall and county politicians making claims about the transition at the YSB in a discourse of locality, family, and services. Both Randall and county commissioner John Tierney in particular made efforts to shape perceptions of the YSB change and their larger goal of a juvenile campus by not using the language of detention, prison, and incarceration. In contrast, DMC and other critical members of the public intentionally referred to the proposed facilities as "jail," "incarceration," and "detention" to conceptually and linguistically link those punitive institutions with the models the county promoted. While DMC members understood that there may be important distinctions between detention and treatment centers, the history and coercive nature of the system that operated both entities left members skeptical of either model. In the discourse of justice, the language of DMC (incarceration, detention, and jail) met the language of the county officials (family, locality, services, and treatment), with neither side adopting the frames of the other. This offered a fascinating contrast with national debates about incarceration: in Monroe County, officials, including those at criminal justice agencies, employed the language of rehabilitation, while community organizers challenged it, albeit on the grounds that treatment was essentially a façade for punishment.

Daniels, the YSB's clinical director, offered valuable insights into the contested meaning of terms. Daniels had worked with young people in the community for over a decade, in partnership with Randall and other juvenile justice officials. In response to a question from me about where the differences in perspectives between Daniels and the juvenile justice officials originated, Daniels observed that Randall wanted to "harmonize disagreements." He spoke of Randall being upset over some of the language at the first meeting about the YSB that did not distinguish between "locking kids up" on the one hand, which no one admitted to doing or liking, and placing kids in treatment on the other hand, which is how officials prefer to describe institutionalizing young people. Daniels explained that "if you talk to the kids, that's how they refer to it— 'yeah, I was locked up'—and if you ask them about it, they were actually [incarcerated]. Twenty-two hours or something like that, and then you have a couple [of hours] to walk around. So, you know, it depends on who you talk to. And you know, there weren't any kids [at the meeting]."

With no young people at the meeting and none interviewed for Krause's report, the vision and language of Randall and others circumscribed the conversation, coding the experience of detention in terms of rehabilitation and treatment. The absence of young people from the conversation rendered their experiences of punishment anecdotal and the perspective of Randall and others an evidential, dominant, and uninterrupted narrative.

The absence of young people and their perspectives from these meetings was alarming, especially when understood in the context of local rhetoric of advocacy for a juvenile facility. Advocates predicated the need for local detention on the problem of youth invisibility; officials insisted on the moral superiority of keeping local youth close to home. Former Juvenile Court Judge Geraldine Lane's advocacy for the justice campus best exemplifies the issues of youth visibility.

With few exceptions, my informants who favored the justice campus cited Lane's influence. Indeed, she had a status of mythic proportions in the community and was thought to have unparalleled empathy for young people and energy for working on their behalf. Moreover, she was widely credited with doing the most work to push the justice campus vision during her tenure on the bench. My informants often framed Lane's work on behalf of local youth as a form of resistance to the punitive state. Donnelly recalled annual trips to testify before the Department of Corrections when Lane stood up and announced that she refused to send youth there. This brave gesture of a locality standing up to the state against injustice was also remarkably ironic: Lane's defiance was expressed most acutely through a vision of creating the very institutions she was protesting.

When I interviewed Lane, she explained the origins of her passionate advocacy for youth. As a Black woman from Virginia who grew up under Jim Crow segregation, Lane said that race relations and discrimination were always of paramount importance for her. She said she could never reconcile how a country could rhetorically promote and dedicate itself to equality and freedom while its founding documents legitimized slavery. Because of her experiences, she learned at a very early age to always consider who was left out of the conversation. It was this idea of exclusion that framed her passion for youth:

> I began working with juvenile cases when I went on the bench. I'll be perfectly frank: I had no interest in that area of the law. I had been on the bench for just a short while and listened to some of the conversations that people had, the way they talked about issues and left out children, the ones that I dealt with anyway—the poor people. I became very interested in that. I began to listen to the way people talked about issues and the way they excluded, without even realizing it, the people I dealt with almost every day. That was the beginning of my interest.

In Lane's vision, the Bloomington community, though concerned about social problems and social justice, excluded young people—"children" as she called them—from its vision and self-image as a community that takes care of its own. When young people were left out of the local discourse, Lane argued, they were also excluded from local care:

> When we talk in our society about society's problems we have to listen very carefully to see who is left out, or to ask if everyone is included. And generally, [children] are not [included]. I can never understand why we do not have a facility in this community for our children who have to be removed from home because they need treatment they can't get at home or they have delinquency issues. But we need to keep them here. They are the only group of people who are transported out of our community! Imagine, in our jail we can have a person who committed murder or some serious crime. They can look out the window and see their community; they can visit with their families. Our children go miles away. Now they're being transported by the facility to which they are going, but prior to that they had to be chained and handcuffed and the police would transport them.

For Lane, the juvenile court acted as a positive intervention in the lives of youth heading down a perilous path—in fact, she used the word "saving" in connection to what the court does—and maintaining a local facility imbued with community values and priorities was a logical extension of that approach. Much of what she said implied that people opposed to the facility did not have children's best interests at heart.

Lane's vision and rationale is integral to understanding the larger discourse, as many of my informants saw their support for the justice campus and the YSB change as part of a history of child saving that began with Lane's work on the bench. But the consensus about keeping local youth local was also troublesome. Predicated on correcting the problem of young people's exclusion from local care, officials excluded the very same people and their families from the local political process that determined their future.[22] Moreover, officials believed that the primary way in which to extend local care to youth was through the construction and expansion of the very institutions of exclusion they rejected outside of the community.[23]

PART 3

Carceral Epistemology

Knowing the Jail and Governing the Town

[S]pecific discourses—such as "criminology," "eugenics," or "social work"—are put to work in penal institutions and help organize the practices of classification, assessment, reform, or incapacitation which different regimes adopt. Much of this is internal to the institutions, and is articulated in technical documents and expert decisions, so it might well be considered to be of limited rhetorical significance—to be primarily a method of doing things rather than of saying things. But, once again, these technical discourses and the practices which they make possible are not merely a silent, functioning machinery. They are also . . . a kind of oratory even though they often pass for sheer "information," "knowledge," or "science."
—David Garland, *Punishment and Modern Society*

Theorizing Carceral Knowledge

Examining the local construction of knowledge—what counted as knowledge, what it sounded like, and who was able to claim it and who was not—is necessary for continued excavation of carceral habitus in Bloomington and offers further assistance in understanding the relatively widespread acceptance of the justice campus proposal. Local politics meant that carceral expansion could be justified only through a discourse that framed it as distinct from the prison-industrial complex. But that discourse could not have succeeded without epistemological justification that confirmed the need for a facility and the legitimacy of the therapeutic approach.

Social theorists concerned with power look to the relationship between discourse and knowledge in constructing authority and domination. Various theories coalesce around a central concept: rather than being solely a linguistic register that describes reality, a discourse actually constructs objects of reality. In attaching meaning to the construction, a discourse can create the reality it purports to describe.

John Sloop has examined this dynamic in reference to discourses of incarceration. Writing of Paul Willis's claim that culture "'is the very material of our daily lives, the bricks and mortar of our most commonplace understandings,'" Sloop explains that "Paul Willis provided a double-edged definition of culture: while culture is positive in the sense that life could not be experienced without the bricks and mortar that give it shape and substance, it is also negative or constraining, in that bricks and mortar have a discursive materiality that privileges existing discourses, existing ideology. As discourses and definitions become generally accepted within culture, they are assumed and hence act as sedimented practices" (1996, 4).

Sloop helpfully illuminates how carceral habitus is formulated and instantiated. The discursive bricks and mortar that constructed and maintained local cultural understandings of carceral treatment in Bloomington also served to structure and suture any discussion of reform to the physical bricks and mortar of institutions. Community members in favor of the justice campus adamantly stated that the conversation had to be about more than the architecture and size of facilities and should focus on the programming, but they may have failed to realize that their ideas of treatment—as predicated on an institutionalized population and often being coercive and threatening punishment—still used the cultural and discursive bricks and mortar of hegemonic paradigms of social control. Indeed, as chapter 2 explained, the discursive bricks and mortar that constructed local ideological approaches to crime and social control also constructed and constrained even the noninstitutional or alternative approaches. The implication of this, of course, is that such discursive practices made it difficult to discuss abolitionist change. In this way, Decarcerate Monroe County was engaged in a cultural contestation—or, as Don Mitchell might call it, a "culture war" (2000, 5)—attempting to destabilize the universe of discourse that predicated any discussion of reform on carcerality.[1] Other scholars have injected important insights regarding epistemology into this idea of discourse performing ideological work to shape the very terms we use to construct cultural understandings of phenomena. For example, Pierre Bourdieu writes: "The theory of knowledge is a dimension of political theory because the specifically symbolic power to impose the principles of the construction of reality—in particular, social reality—is a major dimension of political power" (1977, 165). He continues: "Any language that can command attention is 'an authorized language,' invested with the authority of a group, the things it designates are not simply expressed but also authorized and legitimated" (ibid., 170).

Writing about the relationship between Edward Said's *Orientalism* (1979) and Michel Foucault's body of work, Robert Young observes that the two authors understand discourse as "an epistemological device that constructs its objects of knowledge through the establishment of a practice of a certain linguistic register. Rather than simply describing the world as it is, as if language mediates reality directly, a discourse constructs the objects of reality and the ways in which they are perceived and understood: as Said put it, 'such texts can *create* not only knowledge but also the very reality that they appear to describe'" (2001, 388).

Bourdieu and Young argue that discourse creates the certainty that it purportedly reflects. When discourse becomes "authorized," it assumes sole primacy in the construction of reality. Avery Gordon has written that her engagement with haunting as a sociological phenomenon revealed the structured limitations of even critical vocabularies for considerations of what she calls "the dialectic of subjection and subjectivity" (2008, 8). Of course, as she points out, "it is not simply the vocabularies themselves that are at fault, but the constellation of effects, historical and institutional, that make a vocabulary a social practice of producing knowledge" (ibid.).

Such a perspective sheds light on the circulating discourses supporting carceral expansion in Monroe County and begins to unveil how something like the justice campus could conceivably occur. Yet without another piece of this literature, the picture would remain incomplete in the place where it may matter most: the source of discourse's authority.

The role of the state is important both theoretically and ethnographically to this conversation. The state—and with respect to the present conversation, it may be most appropriate to refer to the carceral state—animates the dynamic of knowledge and discourse. The state, after all, is the ultimate "authority group" and source of "authorized discourse" that

Bourdieu (1977, 170) notes. In his treatment of Hobbes, Mark Neocleous writes that "knowledge is an attribute of political order: power is knowledge and questions of epistemology are questions of political power. The Leviathan's power lies, in part, in its role as the producer and regulator of knowledge" (2003, 48). As Neocleous and others have pointed out, the nexus between state and knowledge was forged, or at least honed, through its exercise in the service of colonialism.[2] Since then at least, the state has been imagined as not only the central dispenser of knowledge but also as the body without which knowledge itself is impossible. As Neocleous observes, studying the state requires examining how "sovereignty asserts itself in the sphere of knowledge" in two ways: "first, through the way *the state has been imagined as an institution of and for knowledge* and, second, through the way this *power-knowledge nexus has legitimized state practices over and through civil society*" (ibid., 49).

In Monroe County, the carceral state was the source of the terms, epistemological devices, symbolic capital afforded to those devices, and constructs of authority in circulation. In relying on technocratic terms like "evidence-based" and their underlying positivist epistemology and in attributing expertise and authority to corrections consultants, local officials and local media helped to transmit and strengthen state knowledge and, at the same time, to code that knowledge and the practices it legitimated in a discourse that could win local consent (Hall 1996; Thompson 1984).

Foucault (1977 and 1980) locates the general idea of discourse as an epistemological device within the specific discipline of criminology[3] and the disciplining criminological agencies. Criminology helps construct the very concepts it purports to study, he argues, and then it reifies those concepts by subjecting them to a discourse of scientific study. This process has an interdependent relationship with practitioners of criminal justice, who rely on criminological knowledge to legitimize their work while also providing criminology with its subjects of study.[4] In a famous passage in *Power/Knowledge* in which Foucault responds to criticism of his description of criminology as a "garrulous discourse" of "endless repetitions," he writes:[5]

> I think one needs to investigate why such a "learned" discourse [as criminology] became so indispensable to the functioning of the nineteenth

century penal system. What made it necessary was the alibi, employed since the eighteenth century, that if one imposes a penalty on somebody this is not in order to punish what he has done, *but to transform what he is* .... Once you suppress the idea of vengeance, which previously was the act of a sovereign threatened in his very sovereignty by the crime, punishment can only have a meaning within a technology of reform. And judges themselves have gradually made the shift, without wanting to and without even taking cognizance of the fact, from a verdict which still retained punitive connotations to one which they cannot justify in their vocabulary except on condition of its being transformatory of the person condemned. Yet they know perfectly well that the instruments available to them, the death penalty, formerly the penal colonies, today imprisonment, don't transform anyone. Hence there is the necessity to call on those who produce a discourse on crime and criminals which will justify the measures in question. [Criminological discourse] is indispensable in enabling [judges] to judge. (1980, 47–48; my emphasis)

This passage is particularly relevant to examining the epistemologies that structured and legitimated Monroe County's carceral habitus. First, as previous chapters showed, officials insisted that principles and practices of therapeutic justice and rehabilitation were foundational to the county bench and criminal justice system. Officials justified creating a jail(able) citizen through their belief in transforming "what he is." In this way, officials aligned themselves with Foucault's observation that punishment retains meaning and is justifiable only within a technology and discourse of reform.[6] Second, and especially important to part 3's contentions about the epistemological work of habitus, this passage observes that justifications for such sanctions—literally, justifying judges' judging—relies on a criminological discourse and its creation of problems and solutions.

Chapters 5, 6, and 7 examine the epistemological and political processes through which ideas about local criminality and local carcerality gained political capital in Monroe County. The three chapters examine interrelated themes that emerged during my fieldwork and that served as constitutive parts of the construction of local knowledge about incarceration. Chapter 5 explores the dominance of technocratic, managerial, and professionalized discourses and the priority placed on the institutional expertise of local providers. Chapter 6 examines the prominence of state and national corrections consultants in the contemporary and historical processes of carceral expansion in the county. Chapter 7 looks to the political spaces and linguistic maneuvers that privileged official epistemology and attempted to insulate it from criticism. These chapters map some of the routes that dominant logics of mass incarceration traveled to ultimately structure local carceral habitus.

Although I separate the construction and insulation of knowledge into these three thematic areas, they are in fact mutually constitutive. For example, the reification of local practitioners' knowledge confirmed the expertise of national consultants, many of whom identified themselves as former practitioners. In addition, consultants frequently relied on a shared technocratic register of terms, such as "evidence-based practices and programs." At public meetings, even when the purported goal was public input, this shared vocabulary, along with perpetual budgetary concerns, worked as a form of cultural capital that allowed those with proficiency in such discourses—consultants, local officials, criminal justice practitioners, and long-time civic leaders—to more readily engage in conversations about expansion. Moreover, the official discourse in the county marginalized other forms of knowledge such as narratives of personal experience, a strategic part of the symbolic violence of language that performs ideological work.[7]

5

Seeing like a Jail, 1

Evidence and Expertise

Certain forms of knowledge and control require a narrow-
ing of vision. The great advantage of such tunnel vision is
that it brings into sharp focus certain limited aspects of an
otherwise far more complex and unwieldy reality. This very
simplification, in turn, makes the phenomenon at the center
of the field of vision more legible and hence more suscepti-
ble to careful measurement and calculation. Combined with
similar observations, an overall, aggregate, synoptic view of
a selective reality is achieved, making possible a high degree
of schematic knowledge, control, and manipulation.
—James C. Scott, *Seeing Like a State*

The Semiotics of Expertise

The first of the four Monroe County Criminal Justice Coordinating
Council (MCCJCC) public hearings about the justice campus began
as the remaining three would. The MCCJCC chairman, local attorney
Tom Grady, opened the meeting by describing the role of the advisory
body and the nature of the four hearings. Richard Kemp, of Program
Administration and Results, Inc. (PARI), next briefly sketched the company's plans for the justice campus and described its progress. Kemp
then turned the meeting over to the resident expert for the evening,
Juvenile Court Judge Patrick Randall. In what were some of the first
official remarks about the justice campus public process, Randall said:
"Good afternoon. I feel like I'm having déjà vu all over again. I first
spoke on this issue almost twenty years ago in this room. I think I've
spoken on this issue twenty-five times over the years." Holding up and
then flipping through a five-inch stack of papers, he said, "As you can
see in front of me, we have at least five studies examining the issue of

whether or not we need a juvenile facility to deal with both shelter care and secure detention."[1]

As the reader might remember from the previous chapter, Randall spent much of the two-hour meeting justifying his and many others' belief that a local juvenile facility was both critically important and that its absence belied the community's commitment to progressive politics and social services. Of crucial importance was the fact that there was evidence in favor of the campus: all five of the studies Randall mentioned supported a facility in the community.

In Monroe County, the local discourse of carceral expansion not only described exceptional and benevolent institutions but also enacted the techniques of knowledge that made those institutions imaginable and possible. Conducted by state and national corrections consultants, the studies Randall referred to that night dated back decades. All five came to some version of the same conclusion: Monroe County needed a youth detention and treatment center. The studies worked as important semiotic resources for local officials in favor of the campus.[2] Sitting in county chambers, presiding over the meeting, speaking about his decades of work as an attorney and judge, and holding a thick stack of official reports, Randall commanded respect and had influence as an expert. Such authority, backed by empirical evidence and political support, generated considerable legitimacy for the justice campus proposal.

The Technocratic Discourse of Limited Possibility: Evidence-Based Practices

The following is an e-mail message sent in December 2009 by Peter Bergman, a local jail reform activist and a founding member of Begin Again and Monroe County Justice, to members of Decarcerate Monroe County (DMC) discussing strategy for jail reform, particularly around the issue of the proposed changes to visitation:

> The mantra of people in the system is now "evidence-based." While there is scant evidence that the system as a whole has any evidence supporting its design, particularly lengthy sentences, decision-makers (judges, department heads, elected officials) now refer to scientifically gathered evidence as the criterion for decision-making about these matters. I be-

lieve "evidence-based" presents a powerful tool to challenge the system in multiple ways.

As an example, prisoners that receive support from family are much less likely to recidivate than those that receive no family support. Assuming that lowering of recidivism is an overriding goal then criminal justice policies should encourage family ties. I believe there is a juvenile probation program that is supposed to do that. But the system systematically attacks family ties through high costs of telephone calls, barriers to visitation, lengthy jail stays waiting on the courts, lengthy sentences, and other actions. I think a case could actually be made that inmates be rewarded [for calling] their families to maintain strong ties rather than punished with very high jailhouse phone charges.

I am personally repelled by TV visitation but before rejecting it out of hand I would review the evidence where it has been implemented and with what effects. My understanding is that this is a relatively common approach in newer jails so that this issue must have been reviewed multiple times. What were the criteria used in those other communities? Among decision criteria should be whether TV visitation builds strong family ties that contribute to reduced recidivism in the long term rather than just the operational efficiency of the jail. Perhaps a combination of TV and regular visitation with choice given to the family could address the multiple issues involved.

In Monroe County, the local circulation of technocratic terms such as "evidence-based" integrated neoliberal and actuarial notions of justice into the community's traditional rehabilitation-oriented ethos. County officials and consultants spoke freely to each other and the public in this language that often justified expansionist policies. Moreover, as I witnessed multiple times while attending county meetings, the reliance on discourses of policy evaluation and planning served to marginalize those people—that is, most people—who didn't have the same information or were unfamiliar or uncomfortable with such specialized and bureaucratic terminology. The concept of evidence-based policy thus had significant discursive capital in the county, so that using the terminology coded certain people as more qualified than others to comment on the justice campus, the changes at the Youth Services Bureau (YSB), and other policy proposals. Crucially, the language of an evidence-based approach also limited the articulation of what was possible, steering conversations toward the narrow set of programs that qualified under this designation and that could be implemented in the justice campus or the YSB.[3]

This put community activists in a difficult position, as the terrain of actuarial knowledge constructs was by no means even; clearly, evidence-based designations relied on the individuated and neoliberal programs promoted by local officials. And activists were uncertain how to challenge something that used the language of "evidence." Thus, activists at times chose to rely on the same discourse to present information. This was a contested decision, involving many discussions about what kinds of discourses wielded power among those proposing carceral growth and those resisting it. Many DMC members commented to me at various stages of my fieldwork that they felt disempowered by county meetings where the discursive terrain deflated their attempts at intervention and where they would, dejectedly, defer to county officials to answer questions and frame discussions.

In contrast, in the e-mail message above, Bergman clearly saw some strategic value in using evidence-based discourse to challenge components of the local system, in this case the replacement of in-person visitation with videoconferencing. Bergman argued that the effects of videoconferencing on the preservation of family ties were dubious, and thus the practice would ultimately fail to be classified as evidence-based. For Bergman, a discourse of evidence-based practices was a hegemonic, political, and discursive terrain on which activists could rhetorically challenge unjust practices. There were two corollary components to adopting this strategy. First, it would make the discourse of reform commensurable with the discourse of the system. Second, it would add immediate legitimacy to the work of the activists.

But evidence-based designations can by definition apply only to those programs or practices subject to the work of program evaluation, a process that privileges certain kinds of programs and certain kinds of knowledge. In the case of program evaluation, a restorative justice organization in town, Bloomington Restorative Practices (BRP), scraped by on a meager annual budget while a well-funded, abstinence-based program such as drug court flourished, in part because of its status as a nationally prominent evidence-based program.

In the case of knowledge production, Bergman acknowledged his own affective response to video visitation ("I am personally repelled") but then subjugated that response to the realm of actuarial policy analysis. While he and other activists had the educational privilege of being able to speak from both experiential and evidential epistemological positions, many people in the county—including those most affected by criminal justice practices—spoke from the position that what they had experienced was wrong, a position that several officials marginalized as "anecdotal."[4]

In a powerful attempt to capture some collective experiential analysis of jail visitation, DMC activists Dave Santiago and Victor Whitney attended the all-cellblock visiting hours at the jail to interview visitors about their perspectives on video visitation. The local radio station WFHB provided the activists with digital audio recorders and later played an edited version of their interviews. What follows is a transcript of that portion. I include it here, uninterrupted by my analysis and with only minor edits, to offer a production of knowledge that constitutes a powerful alternative to the evidence-based paradigm:

> DMC ACTIVIST 1 (DMC1): So how do you feel about these proposed changes to the visitation process, to virtual visitation from real visitation?
>
> JAIL VISITOR 1 (JV1): It's bullshit really. I mean, how you supposed to stay connected through a TV screen? Honestly, I mean through a glass is bad enough but at least you're somewhat close while if you're just on a TV, it's ridiculous.
>
> DMC1: What effect do you think that would have for you and your relationship to your loved one?
>
> JV1: It will probably make it a lot harder 'cause I mean seeing him is bad enough behind the glass and is stressful to people, but then just seeing him through a TV and that's it, that would be worse on anybody.
>
> JV2: In some aspects it will be an asset, because like I said it will reduce the number of turnkey operations needed at the jail for accommodating visitation. This concept has been employed in many institutions throughout the county and the country.
>
> DMC1: How do you feel about the prospect of visiting your family through a TV screen?

JV3: I think it's not right. We as people have the right to see our families and to see them through a TV screen is like watching TV. I would personally like to see my family face to face to let them know I'm here. It's pathetic. I really do think this is the worst thing that they'll do to everybody. It doesn't need to be changed; it's fine the way it is. It's crowded, it's a lot to handle, but it's better for everybody. 'Cause us as people who come to visit—we didn't ask for this, you know, we didn't want them to be here but they're here so the least we can do is be here for them.

JV4: Well, my personal feelings are that taking away the humane inter-action of it will set us back a hundred years. I understand that they're incarcerated, but there's no reason to take away what hope they have to see the people they care about. That makes absolutely no sense to me at all. What, to save money? I don't know. You know, I personally think we pay taxes for it, there should be something we have, and that's the right to see the people we love not through a video screen but through face-to-face interaction. I don't know, I would think that being someone in the position to be incarcerated, I would think it would take hope away from me, make a desperate situation worse. Bad enough to be taken away from the people you love but then not to be able to see them, and it's not the same seeing someone on video versus seeing them in person, not at all. I would think there could be a more efficient way of doing this without installing video. One, it seems awfully expensive, you know, if you're gonna do an upgrade such as that you would think you could come up with something moderately cheaper that would both be satisfactory to them and still allow us to see the people we care to see.

JV5: I think it's terrible, 'cause families need to see their family member. It's wrong. People that can't afford to get out? Yes, they need visitors.

DMC1: And what effect do you think it would have if they moved to video visitation on family and different relationships?

JV5: Well the ones that's in here—

JV6 (INTERRUPTING): The reason you come to visit—

JV5: Yeah.

JV6:—is you can see the person.

JV5: See if they're all right, you know? That they're not hurt, getting fed, you know? That's what I think.

DMC1: And you said something about just because they can't afford to get out they should still get a visit.

JV5: That's right. That's right.

DMC1: Would you explain that?

JV5: Well some—like the person I have in there, you can't get out because you can't get up that much money and they have families they got to take care of, so they can't afford to do this. I know it's wrong for them to get in here, but they still need to have visitors.

JV6: Yeah, they got nothing better to do but waste our time and our money and I just think it's unfair, it's ridiculous. They're supposed to be the ones helping the county but the way I see it they ain't helping, they ain't doin' anything.

DMC1: And what effect do you think it would have if they went to video visitation?

JV6 (LAUGHS): A lot. You know, people want to come here and see their loved one in there, they don't want to have to sit there and see them through a screen. It's just . . . and I understand they're probably gonna sit there and say "well you know what, your loved one probably shouldn't have gotten themselves in here." Well, you know what? Sometimes it's just not that easy. You know? It might be for something minor, like a . . . like anything. But I can understand them being rude against a drug dealer [lowers voice] or something, but anything else, no! It doesn't make any sense to me whatsoever. If you're in here you're in here, it's not anybody else's fault, it's not the jail's fault, but everybody has rights and they're just taken rights away.

It sucks. They need to figure something out that works for everybody and not them. 'Cause that's what it is, whatever works for them to where they don't have to do as much paperwork. The way I see it, paperwork is paperwork no matter what. If they got time to sit around and talk inside, then they [don't] got time to get everyone else in to see [their loved one] . . . one [cell] block at a time? That's ridiculous. And then they tell you to come down here and sign the paperwork, well they don't tell you over the phone that you're gonna have to wait another three hours till you can see someone.

DMC1: So you're waiting two to three hours just to sign a piece of paper?

JV5 AND JV6: Yes!

JV6: And then you gotta wait another, what, two to three hours depending on what time that block is able to see their loved ones.

DMC1: So would video visitation affect that at all? Even if it did, would you want to move to video visitation?

JV6: No.

JV5: No, 'cause people want to see their loved ones.

JV6: Yeah, they wanna see 'em face to face, they don't want to look at them over a screen. It's all computerized. Whatever is easiest for the jail and the county is what they wanna do. They don't care about nothing else. They don't. But you know if it was their loved one, it would be a totally different story.

JV7: Well, I feel that it's not right, I feel that every person should be entitled to a visitation, I feel that the inmates are encouraged when their families come in. And I think it's just crazy, you know, that they expect us to visit our family members and friends through a videotape. You know, you need that one-on-one contact. They need to be encouraged. Everyone needs to be encouraged. If they want them to be rehabilitated and helped, then I feel like they should allow their family member to come in. They need friendly faces and that will help them to be more encouraged. I think it's discouraging to people. I don't care if you're in here one day to ten or twenty years, I think if you have family members coming in and they are able to see their family members and to feel that they're loved and that someone's thinking about them, it powers them and encourages them to do better and get their lives together and get out.

DMC1: Politicians are saying that it will cut down on the wait time and that people wouldn't have to come back early in the morning. Would that change your mind?

JV7: No, I don't think so. I think it's crazy, I don't appreciate them even thinking of something like that. With everything going on in the world, they can think of better things than this.

JV8: They have better ways they can spend our taxpayer dollars. They can hire more guards to let the inmates visit and then they can do other things they need to do around the jail.

DMC2: If you had a choice between personal visitation and video visitation, which would you choose?

JV8: I'd take the visits that they have now where you can see 'em through a glass window. Or even get a room with tables like they have [at] the Department of Corrections where you can actually give your visitor a hug or something.

JV9: Well I don't think it's a good idea, I think it's gonna cause a whole lot of problems inside and outside of the jail and its kinda cruel. It's gonna really stop us from really visiting. You get to see 'em behind a glass but that's better than a little camera.

DMC2: So how do you feel about video or virtual visitation?

JV10: I think it's ridiculous. I think it'll be harder for the children who are coming to see their parents up here and the inmates really. Yeah, I don't like the idea of the video one at all, and I know 'cause I bring my children up here and I think it would be really hard on them, too.

The near universal rejection of video visitation by the people who were at the jail to visit their loved ones constituted important and legitimate knowledge. In addition to playing the interviews on the community radio station, DMC activists read portions of the transcript at community meetings to bring the voices from the street into the official spaces where policy was made and where those voices were often absent.

But testimonials about visitation did not align with the dominance of so-called objective knowledge. In the contest over the changes to visitation, DMC's campaign fell short, and the jail renovations—including the change to video visitation—occurred during the spring of 2010.

A little over a year earlier, Grady, the chairman of the MCCJCC and the public face of the justice campus hearings, had noted frequently during the hearings the importance of remaining objective, even as he made his support for the justice campus widely known, including publishing an opinion piece in the *Herald-Times* advocating for it. A BRP staff member spoke at one of the justice campus hearings about the importance of his organization not entering into the politics of expansion in the county and remaining an objective provider of services, but then he praised county officials and institutions as a "model of criminal justice." Scholarly literature makes it clear that objectivity can become an insidious disguise for dominant subjectivity, a particularly important realization for activists working to disrupt habitus, since supposedly objective knowledge can both reaffirm hegemony and further marginalize counterhegemonic claims and methods of conveying them.[5]

Interestingly, even when the political and geographical context changed from official meetings to activist-hosted meetings, the terrain of actuarial discourses did not necessarily shift. That is, it was not surprising to find county officials using a technocratic discourse when discussing the justice campus and its constitutive programs in a meeting held in official county political chambers. But in a meeting held at the public library, hosted by DMC, and featuring shelter staff members and concerned current and former clients discussing concerns about the proposed changes to the YSB, officials relied on a language that immediately separated and attempted to privilege their technical knowledge. At the time, I was struck by the inflexibility of their reliance on the discourse, but I understand it now as a strategic effort to remain on favorable discursive terrain in conversations that could conceivably have seen them cede some power.

At the first of the three meetings about the changes at the YSB organized by DMC during the fall of 2009, conversations revealed tensions between attendees about the possibilities of change and reflected their epistemological differences. According to DMC's flyer advertising the public meeting, it was called to "discuss the needs and desires of community youth and the future of youth services. The meeting will ask broad questions about what we want for all of our youth and will be followed by organizing activities to help create concrete steps toward proposals."

Before the meeting began, DMC members hung posters around the room featuring questions such as "What do kids in crisis need?" and "What makes youth safe and healthy?" and encouraged meeting attendees to go around the room and write answers on the posters. The point of the exercise was to help participants think creatively about core issues that surrounded discussions of youth detention and shelter care. Additionally, DMC members engaged in this practice to democratize and decentralize the space of the meeting. This was done explicitly to reject the so-called expertise that was privileged in official meetings and to promote the belief that the experiential knowledge of meeting attendees—especially those youth and their families who had experienced detention and shelter care directly—could contribute meaningfully to discussions, a variation of the standpoint epistemology offered by feminist scholars to center women's experiences as points of departure for examinations of oppression.[6]

The meeting drew a diverse group of participants. In addition to activists, local youth workers, and some families with direct experience with the juvenile justice system and the YSB, there were three county council members, one county commissioner, two representatives of the probation department, and the Juvenile Court judge in attendance. The officials repeatedly invoked technocratic and bureaucratic constraints on reform, arguing that the tax structure, state laws, and county council actions all dictated that certain changes, including noninstitutional placements for adjudicated youth, were impossible while others—the judicial takeover of the YSB and the subsequent integration of probation officers into it—were easier, given existing funding sources and political agreements.

Given their responsibility for making policy, allocating money, and navigating various levels of bureaucracy, officials' technocratic language made some intuitive sense. But their responses during the meetings revealed their reliance on a technocratic register through with which they considered social issues even beyond the context of policy making. At a community meeting in the public library, where most people in the room were not politicians, local officials still spoke of what was possible or impossible in terms of budgets, tax maneuvers, and bureaucratic constraints.

Departing from officials' language, YSB staff members, DMC members, parents of detained or sheltered youth, and social service workers expressed support for keeping youth services free from punishment and coercion. These meeting attendees spoke about the punishment and pain of juvenile detention and the warmth and support of the shelter. In conversations with DMC members after the meeting, many of them told me they felt that the presence and participation of several parents of youth who were current and former users of YSB services constituted the more powerful and victorious aspects of the meeting. These parents praised the YSB's services highly. One said that the YSB "has been a blessing both for shelter care and for connection to other support services," and another commented that YSB staff members "are extended family to us." The presence of parents and their personal stories offered a direct challenge to the knowledge of statistics, tax revenues, and bureaucratic constraints offered by officials.

Provider Expertise

The discourse of evidence-based practices privileged criminological knowledge that came from being a practitioner. My informants who worked in the criminal justice system often explicitly referred to expertise that could come only from their positions, such as sitting on the county bench, practicing law in the courtroom, or overseeing probationers. But it would be a mistake to narrowly identify this privileged knowledge only with criminal justice officials and workers. Often, informants cited a broader array of "providers" or "stakeholders" whose voices and perspectives informed county initiatives such as the justice campus and the changes at the YSB, an acknowledgment of a community process that previous reports also cited. These providers included people—often executives—from local education, mental health, nonprofit, and business organizations, people whom Foucault has called "the new technicians of behavior" (1977, 294).[7]

The place of other stakeholders at the proverbial table with criminal justice professionals at times was manifested in literal ways. Olivia Krasny—a long-time community activist, nonprofit executive, and small business owner—and Grady were the two long-time citizen appointees to the MCCJCC, traditionally sharing the table in the official meeting room of county government with criminal justice officials and politicians. Since about 2008, however, the MCCJCC had included representatives—often executives—from the local hospital, mental health organizations, and county school system, rounding out its membership with providers from other segments of the community with whom criminal justice agencies partnered.

Of course, these relationships can be interpreted in different ways. Many people I spoke with, including county officials and leaders from reform-oriented nonprofit agencies, viewed these partnerships as a model for other communities. They saw the participation of civic leaders and representatives from different communities of practitioners as indicating a collaborative and even consensus-based approach in the community. Were these partnerships progressive collaborations or the institutionalization and co-optation of reform and an attempt to pacify the more outspoken critics?

One of DMC's frequent criticisms of the MCCJCC and the way it handled the justice campus hearings was that it excluded the voices of both the community's most marginalized residents and those critical of a new facility. In a telling exchange at the first hearing, a DMC member asked several questions about who had been involved in the discussions of the justice campus with PARI. Grady, moderating the discussion, responded to her by saying, "I want to ask Olivia [Krasny] or [Judge] Pat [Randall] to answer who in the community has been involved. It was a lot of leaders and community members, it wasn't just the political people, is that fair, Olivia?" Grady's response pushed Krasny to answer in a certain way and, perhaps unsurprisingly, she responded that the contractor had indeed consulted a diverse group of providers. Randall then listed the names of people consulted by PARI to strengthen the point that the company had spoken with a diverse cross-section of the community. However, the people on his list were Department of Child Services administrators, probation officers and administrators, business leaders, a superintendent of the school system, judges, and politicians. Unwittingly, Randall reinforced the DMC member's original point: the "stakeholders" whom PARI consulted during the information-gathering process were not a cross-section of the community but rather a slice off the top of the political, business, education, and criminal justice classes, precisely the population whose members had agitated for the creation of a justice campus.

County meetings shaped knowledge of local justice issues in other ways as well. Frequently, judges spoke about the knowledge that could come only from sitting on the bench and without which one had a limited understanding of carceral policy. In the second of the four justice campus hearings, for example, Judge Allan Barrett, spoke for the first hour of the two-hour meeting, despite its stated goal of being for public comment. Moreover, the framing and content of Barrett's comments promoted the idea that knowledge was unidirectional, disseminated from providers and practitioners to lay community members, rather than a collectively produced understanding among multiple parties. In response to what he perceived as misunderstandings among the public at the first hearing, Barrett framed his comments in the second as "myth versus fact," aiming to "educate the public in order to produce a more productive discussion." In other words, in an open meeting designed to collect public comments and hosted by an allegedly objective advisory body, Barrett explicitly took control to put community discourse in alignment with his views on acceptable solutions.

Barrett's intervention in the public hearing expressed his concerns with the misrepresentation and misunderstanding of local criminal justice "truth." Indeed, he framed his comments as dispelling myths and presenting facts, subjugating popular knowledge to a version of truth visible from his position as judge. Barrett's view of the privileged position of judicial and carceral knowledge that comes with experience in judicial and carceral agencies resonated with the perspectives offered by other informants who worked in local criminal justice agencies. They also believed that their positions on the bench, in the courtroom, in the jail, and in community corrections provided them with a level of insight especially important to understanding the needs of the community.

In my interview with former judge Bill Rusch, which was most memorable for the volume at which he spoke and the open hostility he displayed toward many people involved in the justice campus issue, he chastised his critics and critics of the campus by arguing that his time on the bench gave him a superior position in a hierarchy of knowledge. He singled out those he viewed as being hostile to juvenile detention, saying that they—professors, politicians, and community residents— were not sitting in his seat as judge: "I'd like to see them hear some of the cases I heard and not put these kids in detention." Rusch evoked the knowledge obtained through sitting as a judge to privilege his perspective and insight. He viewed people removed from that position as naïve or ideological.

After the two-hour interview, in which Rusch spent much of his time banging his fist on the table and using hostile epithets to refer to county politicians (see chapter 7 for excerpts from the interview), we began to wrap up our time together. His parting comment to me did much to summarize the tone of our interview and his own epistemological location. He said that the eighty-five-acre site of the justice campus would meet the county's current needs and would produce a very different conversation decades from now, when further expansion would be required. With the Thomson site, he argued, "we would already have the space and could avoid another forty-year process of indecision, painful conversations, and producing ultimately nothing but PhDs," obviously referring to my study. I found this comment instructive. He seemed to insinuate that community process slowed down the growth that he saw as necessary and inevitable. According to his logic, planning for the future meant thinking creatively only in ways that could expand incarceration. There was no mention of the possibility that planning for the future could involve a decrease in the need for incarceration. Rusch viewed jail and detention needs as proportionate to population growth and as moving inexorably toward expansion. In addition, he believed strongly that only those with the perspective that comes from being a practitioner could accurately assess those needs. Thus, for Rusch and many others, an eighty-five-acre justice campus with double the current capacity of jail beds and the creation of a new juvenile detention facility simply "makes sense."

6

Seeing like a Jail, 2

Corrections Consulting

Consulting Carceral Cities

When I interviewed Carrie Donnelly, the chief probation officer, she and other local criminal justice officials and county politicians had just returned from a visit to Tippecanoe County, the home of Lafayette, Indiana, and Purdue University. The Monroe County delegation had traveled north to visit Tippecanoe County's new detention facilities and returned considering them a model for Monroe County to emulate. According to 2010 census data, Tippecanoe and Monroe Counties are comparable demographically. Monroe County's population is just over 130,000; Tippecanoe's is 167,000. Tippecanoe County has a slightly higher median income ($45,000 versus $41,000) and a slightly lower poverty rate (18.2 percent versus 20.7 percent). Both counties are overwhelmingly white (90 percent), and have comparable populations of Black (3.5 percent) and Asian (5 percent) residents. Tippecanoe County has a more substantial population of Latino origin (7.5 percent versus 2.5 percent).[1]

Proudly, Donnelly pointed out that despite their relatively comparable populations, Tippecanoe County was decidedly more punitive. For example, Tippecanoe County sent many more youth to the state's Department of Corrections than Monroe County. Donnelly reported that, on average, Tippecanoe County had 25–30 youth in detention, whereas Monroe had just 2–3. Tippecanoe County transferred an average of fifty young people from juvenile court to adult court every year, presumably because of the severity of the charges against them; in one particularly bad year, Monroe County transferred seven. Donnelly noted that the accepted explanation of the disparity in rates between the two counties was Tippecanoe's proximity to Interstate 65, which connects Indianapolis to Chicago; thus, criminals from Chicago and Gary, Indiana, had more influence in Tippecanoe—a not very subtle racialization of crime.

Yet for all of the rhetorical efforts to differentiate Monroe County philosophically and politically, its officials sought the advice of officials in the very counties from which they distinguished themselves on issues of carceral policy and practice. While praising Monroe County's progressive approach to justice and restrained use of incarceration and denigrating Tippecanoe County's politics and overuse of jail, Monroe officials were touring Tippecanoe's facilities for architectural and organizational insights into a future juvenile facility. Each administrator with whom I spoke praised what he or she saw in Tippecanoe County. At one of the internal meetings of the Monroe County Criminal Justice Coordinating Council (MCCJCC) that I attended, for example, Juvenile Court Judge Patrick Randall and Monroe County Council member Brian Mulvaney spoke of the trip while updating the advisory body on the transitions occurring at the Youth Services Bureau (YSB). Mulvaney observed that Tippecanoe County is "very detention oriented," bringing every arrested youth into a new intake center in full shackles. He then praised the county's state-of-the-art facility. Randall also celebrated the facility and noted that he perceived a "paradigm shift" in approaches to youth incarceration, with communities that created punitive facilities now coming around toward a more treatment and community-based model—or, as Randall called it, "our approach." The contradictions, in other words, continued. Officials returned from their trip convinced of the overuse of incarceration in Tippecanoe County and the moral superiority of Monroe County's approach. Yet they also returned energized by the prospect of building a new and larger youth facility modeled on what they had observed in Tippecanoe.

Tippecanoe County's model included detention and shelter facilities existing side by side and on the same property. This was of particular interest to Monroe officials since both the justice campus and YSB initiatives would have located the same services together. This was also the model in operation in Bartholomew County, just two counties east of Bloomington. Randall, Donnelly, and others were so impressed with Bartholomew County's facility, in fact, that—as noted above—Monroe County hired the facility's director and founder, Victoria Krause, as the latest consultant to develop Monroe's juvenile justice system. Monroe County's consistent approach to other counties and various state and national corrections consultants would seem to complicate officials' insistence of the community's exceptionalism. In criticizing other counties' carceral practices while simultaneously looking to those counties for guidance on facilities, Monroe County demonstrated an important quality of carceral habitus. The inevitable comparison that local officials were forced to make to existing structures—Tippecanoe's juvenile facilities, other counties' jails, state prisons, and other existing institutions—shaped their articulation of what was possible locally, both positively ("we have to lock up some people") and negatively ("we are about treatment, not punishment"). That is, objective carceral structures offered officials both the physical template for what they envisioned and a symbolic template against which they critically positioned the local imagined campus.

There were also times when Monroe County endorsed criminal justice approaches that would seem entirely out of character for a community that believed in its own exceptionally humane and liberal politics. In the following excerpt from a *Herald-Times* editorial, the paper actively promoted the "broken windows" approach to law enforcement first articulated by James Wilson and George Kelling (1982) but perhaps more infamously implemented by Mayor Rudy Giuliani and Police Chief William Bratton in New York City in the 1990s. The approach has been extolled by law and order politicians but much maligned by social scientists and activists because of its targeting of poor, homeless, minority, and un- or underemployed populations (Harcourt 2001; Herbert and Brown 2006; McArdle and Erzen 2001; Stewart 1998). The *Herald-Times* advocated its implementation locally to address graffiti:

> Paint slapped on the sides of buildings, like it has been in downtown Bloomington with regularity this spring, is not art. It's vandalism.
>
> Some in our community put an innocent face on graffiti. Some examples of it are very colorful and intricate. But except in rare instances in which the painting is invited, it defaces someone else's property.
>
> A vast majority of the graffiti is simply letters or marks sprayed on visible walls or signs. Bloomington police assure the community it's not a sign of gang activity, but it certainly has the look and feel of abject lawlessness. And it's noticeable on main Bloomington thoroughfares, a blight on individual and commercial properties as well as a blow to the general security of the community.

The "broken windows theory" applies here. The idea got its name from a 1982 essay that suggested minor anti-social behavior such as breaking windows and spraying graffiti gave way to an impression of social disorder that led to more and more serious anti-social behavior. The solution: painting over graffiti and fixing broken windows so the unwanted behaviors didn't take root.

While the idea has been debated over the last two decades, many studies, including one done last year in the Netherlands, indicate the theory of quick cleanup works.

Businesses must fight paint with paint, quickly covering over graffiti that appears on their property. *And law enforcement officials must come down hard on anyone found vandalizing other people's property in the name of art or self-expression.* (Editorial 2009b; my emphasis)

In defining graffiti as a "blow to the general security of the community," suggesting law enforcement must "come down hard" on graffiti writers, and baldly advocating "broken windows" policing, the paper's editorial board aligned the periodical and its vision for the community with the racialized and class-based approaches taken by the very police departments from which Monroe County tried to distinguish its own. Curiously, instead of supporting community approaches to crime and quality-of-life issues that resist the broken windows approach and that have been tested and shown to work,[2] the *Herald-Times* instead placed itself squarely in alignment with the politics and discourse of a frontline and unmistakably right-wing approach to the war on crime. Of course, in naming graffiti as a threat to security, the paper also revealed that its primary concern was with preserving the aesthetics of private capital, even at the expense of losing legitimacy to claims of exceptional politics.

Following the publication of the editorial, I wrote a letter to the *Herald-Times* in which I criticized the paper's advocacy of such a maligned and punitive response to graffiti. The letter was published on a Saturday; the following Friday, I attended my weekly basketball game with a group of men, most of whom worked in various capacities for the city of Bloomington. When I entered the gym, several of the men confronted me about the letter, clearly upset by my criticism. "How would you like graffiti on your house?" asked one. "What would you have the police do? You have better ideas?" asked another. "Judah," said the director of a city agency, shaking his head, "You really stirred the pot here." Despite my attempt to explain that I had not been defending graffiti but rather trying to point out the danger of advocating the simple yet loaded response of "broken windows," I was met with skepticism and some hostility. For these Bloomington residents and leaders, and I suspect for many others, the paper's characterization of graffiti—as a blight on an otherwise vibrant and sanitary downtown, a threat to capital, and a signifier of danger and crime, and thus as a transgression that required the formal social control of the criminal justice system—resonated.

The *Herald-Times* played an important role in structuring carceral habitus and reproducing local knowledge. It would be one thing for a local police spokesperson to have argued for the broken windows approach. It is something else for the media to transmit such police propaganda without critique. It is yet another thing—perhaps most disturbing of all—for the media to internalize police propaganda and then, without referring to the police, to externalize it and advocate it to readers in the form of an editorial, now packaged as the measured and even objective opinion of a respected periodical. Seemingly independent from the actual sources on which it relied for reporting, the editorial nonetheless signified the paper's adherence to official police perspectives, but it also added a gloss of legitimacy and perhaps won a small victory in the contest for hegemony.[3] Taken in the context of the *Herald-Times's* largely uncritical support for the justice campus and its frequent endorsement of dominant official discourses, the editorial can be understood as helping structure a carceral habitus at once characterized by discourses of benevolent justice and inflected with some of the more punitive and controversial approaches to criminal justice in the United States.

"Outsourcing Community Decision Making": Carceral Consultants

One of the ways in which the county undermined its own claims to exceptional justice practices was through its historical reliance on state- and national-level consultants. The county spent hundreds of thousands of dollars over the years paying so-called experts in corrections and detention to suggest ways to solve the problems of detaining youth out of the county, chronic jail overcrowding, and the need for expanded alternatives. The presence of corrections consultants in the county put dominant national logics into circulation as it also attached a certain currency to official county perspectives on construction and expansion by invoking the consultants' objective expertise. Insights from Stuart Hall's work on media are germane here. In explicating what he calls the "dominant-hegemonic position" of decoding, Hall notes the importance of the "professional code," the form of representation personified by outside expertise or "objective" media. While "relatively independent" of the dominant-hegemonic code in its application of "criteria and transformational operations of its own, especially those of a technico-practical nature, the professional code, however, operates *within* the hegemony of the dominant code. Indeed, it serves to reproduce the dominant definitions precisely by bracketing their hegemonic quality and operating instead with displaced professional codings which foreground . . . apparently neutral-technical questions" (Hall 1996, 136).

During my research, it was common for people supportive of the expansion proposals to refer to the work of either the consultant at the time—Program Administration and Results, Inc. (PARI) during the justice campus proceedings and Victoria Krause during the Youth Services Bureau (YSB) process—or a previous consultant to support their contention that the county needed to expand its institutional capacities. Indeed, references to decades of research supporting expansion, such as the remarks by Judge Randall's remarks early in the previous chapter, were fairly common. Some respondents did offer important criticisms of PARI, but most of those were made after the company submitted a report to the county that contained both numerous grammatical errors and highly expensive estimates for construction. Otherwise, my informants who were officials praised the work of consultants. In particular, they spoke highly of two of the more recent advisors, Krause and Amy Chandler and Associates, whose comprehensive 2004 report on juvenile justice, referred to colloquially as "The Chandler Report," laid the groundwork for the justice campus. Officials endorsed their visions for the community and their professional analyses.

Perhaps the most important if unsurprising finding I made in conducting a brief history of local consultancy was that, without exception, all of the county's consultants were established in state and national corrections networks and practices. As county officials imagined local facilities that would reflect a unique county ethos and capability, they sought out and indeed paid for expertise that came straight from mainstream professional bodies such as the American Correctional Association and the National Juvenile Detention Association.

Amy Chandler, a consultant based in Chicago whose study many of my informants mentioned in their endorsements of the more recent PARI and Krause plans for juvenile justice facilities, had "run a couple of juvenile facilities herself and says she has been involved in planning more than 70."[4] Krause was a past president of both the Indiana Juvenile Detention Association and the National Juvenile Detention Association. Chandler and Krause had worked in youth facilities and emphasized the importance of treatment, but PARI made no attempt to hide the fact that it was in the business of corrections construction. Its three principal employees all featured on their résumés their backgrounds in corrections construction and cited professional membership in organizations such as the American Corrections Association, Indiana Correctional Association, American Jail Association, and the National Association of Juvenile Administrators.

Although local officials often touted the objectivity of consultants, mentioning both their vantage points from outside of the community and their allegiance to the positivist language of technocrats, it was clear that these consultants were anything but objective, as their livelihoods depended on the service they provided and the buildings they hoped to plan and construct. By hiring consultants year after year who all came from corrections backgrounds, the county guaranteed that a need for expansion would be found as it also supported the consultants' particular forms of knowledge. Table 6.1 presents a synopsis of the studies conducted or contracted by the county between 1989 and 2009.

Representing County Knowledge: PARI

Until PARI released its report, the company appeared to be supported by county officials. PARI officials sat in privileged locations in the two rooms in which the four public hearings about the justice campus occurred. Three of the hearings took place in the official meeting room of the county government, located in the county courthouse in the downtown square. In the room in which official county policy was made, PARI representatives sat at the front, alongside the criminal justice

TABLE 6.1. Twenty Years of Studies

Source of the study	Purpose or recommendation of the study	Year of the study (and cost information)
Monroe County Judge Geraldine Lane chairs an ad hoc committee	To study juvenile justice and make recommendations about building a new facility	1989
The county hires Evansville-based firm Waal Investments	Proposes a 200-bed "campus-like facility" for juveniles	1990
The county forms a task force on juvenile justice	"To study the possibility of creating secure detention facility"	1995
The county hires South Carolina firm Chinn Planning Partnership	Recommends construction of new juvenile facility	1997 (consultancy cost: $62,000)
County officials	Proposes expansion of existing youth shelter and construction of new facility	1998
The county contracts and uses on an ongoing basis design consultant Gibraltar Inc. and program consultant Al Bennett and Associates	Proposes new jail and other office construction	1998 (proposed cost of construction: $34 million)
Greater Bloomington Chamber of Commerce	Formally asks county commissioners to commit to build a juvenile facility	2000
Committee appointed by the county commissioners	Formally proposes facility	2001
The county hires Amy Chandler and Associates	To study, prepare, and issue a report regarding a youth facility	2002 (consultancy cost: $131,292)
Gibraltar, Inc. and Bennett and Associates	Proposes a new adult jail, juvenile center, and community corrections on the Thomson site, the first proposal for a justice campus	2003 (proposed cost of construction: $58 million)
The county contracts PARI	To study and propose a comprehensive justice campus	2008 (consultancy cost: $181,000; proposed cost of construction: approximately $75 million)
The county contracts Victoria Krause	"To review program and service descriptions, job descriptions, the shelter's annual reports and local juvenile justice, child welfare and other data. She'll also look at existing programs and services, as well as talk about the potential for new program development" (Nolan 2009c).	2009 (consultancy cost: $20,800)

Sources: Beaven 1989a and 1989b; Editorial 1998 and 2009d; Nolan 2009a; "Region Briefs" 1996; Van der Dussen 1998, 2003a, 2003b, and 2003c.

official overseeing the department under discussion on that particular day. For example, at the first meeting about juvenile justice, PARI's Richard Kemp sat next to Randall, facing a podium from which community members asked questions. There was a strong sense of solidarity among local government representatives, criminal justice officials, and PARI representatives. Rather than officials joining county residents to interrogate the plan and role of the consultants, officials often attempted to insulate Kemp from criticism, a point I expand on in the next chapter.

After the consulting firm released its report to the public, the once cozy relationship between county officials and PARI soured. Rife with misspellings (including "Recomedations" in the header of each page) and offering projected costs based on the highest estimates of growth possible, the report elicited derision from local officials, who claimed that it misrepresented the county and its interests.

But the report also reflected the suggestions of local "providers" whom PARI representatives had consulted during their data-gathering phase. Despite the extreme figures and the grammatical and spelling mistakes, the report certainly integrated much of what local officials had expressed to the consultants. Indeed, Donnelly complained to me during an interview that much of PARI's final report had been plagiarized from the probation department's annual report. Her frustration with the company's process and delivery had a broader implication: that consultant knowledge can at times represent local, dominant perspectives.[5]

The PARI report helps explain the production of carceral knowledge in the county. While PARI was not transparent about the degree to which it may have plagiarized reports of the Probation Department, the company did note throughout its report the objectives and organizing principles the county commissioners had asked it to follow. Below, I include the seven objectives that PARI defined for the justice campus as they appeared in the report's executive summary. Considering the report as a form of cultural production with political intentions, I interrogate each objective to better parse how PARI attempted to create particular representations of the county, its carceral needs, and the suitability of the Thomson site. In my analysis following each item, I rely in part on the ways PARI representatives discussed the report during county meetings prior to its release, employing the kind of ethnographic content analysis advocated by David Altheide (1987).

1. The Plan Must Be Comprehensive: The plan must address the needs of the entire system. Past studies and evaluations generally addressed a single user and the Commissioners recognized that the Criminal Justice System is complex and no single user can be isolated. The actions of one department effects [sic] all departments and trying to fix one's needs without considering the whole system will have unintended consequences of [sic] other users. (Program Administration and Results, Inc. 2009, 1)

PARI argued that the system operates as an organism, with changes in one department or agency invariably affecting others, and used this rationale to argue for the systemwide expansion embodied in the justice campus. However, PARI plainly ignored the fact that the proposal massively changed and expanded facilities and even created new ones—thus conflating substantial overall growth with comprehensiveness.

2. The Plan Must Be Flexible: The Commission also recognized that the Criminal Justice System responds to laws and directives established by the General Assembly and Courts outside of Monroe County. Laws and directives are always undergoing changes that the County and local Justice Services leaves [sic] [the County] no choice but to comply [with]. These constant changes demand that the system and facilities have the ability to respond effectively and swiftly and as cost efficiently as possible. (ibid.)

This point was consistent with a larger local strategy to use state policy as an alibi for local growth. In this equation, local carceral policy was at the mercy of the state, and local actors were relatively powerless to innovate, except that they had the flexibility to expand existing facilities or build new ones to accommodate the future growth that they saw as inevitable. Indeed, during the final MCCJCC hearing about the justice campus, Richard Kemp noted that the room to expand denoted in the plan was to accommodate the county mandate for "flexibility," indicating that plans for expansion were coded in the more nuanced and accommodating terminology of being prepared for change.

3. The Plan Must Provide for Future Growth: The plan must provide for future growth and needs. Monroe County's plan must anticipate growth and change. The facilities must have the capability to be expanded to respond to

those changes effectively. System growth has historically and consistently forced Monroe County into costly renovations to their [sic] facilities, which has also caused disruptions in the day-to-day systemic operations in order to meet these demands. (ibid., 1-2)

Here PARI explicitly connected the concept of "flexibility" to the imperative of anticipating future carceral growth. PARI noted that the facilities must "anticipate growth and change," connecting complex phenomena like fluctuations of incarcerated populations, changes in laws, and dynamic cultural norms regarding behavior and punishment only to growth, with no acknowledgment of the potential for reducing incarcerated populations. This was one explicit instance in which national hegemonic carceral logic directly inscribed the county imagination with the belief that expansion was an inevitable part of the evolution of the community.

4. The Plan Must Optimize the Use of Staff and Operations: Staffing is the largest yearly cost to Monroe County. The facilities must address both growth and staff efficiencies by improving the use of technology, the improvement of site [sic] lines and the minimization of in-custody movement. These improvements will reduce operating costs and make a much safer facility for the public, the staff and those in custody. (ibid., 2)

Here PARI and the county referred to strict neoliberal governance, with concerns about economizing mobility and increasing visibility. Using terms like "efficiency," "site [sic] lines," and "the minimization of in-custody movement," PARI invoked a panoptic facility that could at once technologize control, reduce costs of employment, and render the incarcerated population more visible to their captors. In the final MCCJCC meeting about the justice campus, PARI's representative added to this "optimization" by explaining that the jail would use new video technologies in visitation and arraignments, foreshadowing subsequent developments in the county.

5. The Plan Must Incorporate Programming to Reduce the Rate of Recidivism: Because Monroe County has a passion for providing opportunities to adults and juveniles who's [sic] lives are in crisis a chance to improve

their quality of life and to enhance their chances of success, the plan must provide staff and volunteer programming spaces that are adequate to achieve these goals. (ibid.)

PARI committed to provide space for programs in the justice campus, reflecting county officials' invocations of therapy and rehabilitation during their comments at hearings and in interviews. No doubt PARI integrated programming into its proposal because of local enthusiasm for it. But absent from both the report and the official discourse was any understanding of the historical context of programs being cut because of funding constraints and/or crowding, and thus no commitment was made to any kind of accountability process to require that program space not be used for other purposes.[6] Of course, the larger point is that these conversations only imagined developing and implementing programs insofar as the justice campus would be built to house them; there was no discussion of programming outside of the institutional context.

6. The Plan Must Include the Development of Community Support and Consensus: The Monroe County Commissioners wanted the opportunity for the community to be heard and their input incorporated into the planning in order to develop public support and consensus. Monroe County has a unique constituency and their [sic] input and concerns are critical to an effective Criminal Justice System. (ibid.)

The language of consensus and support concealed the very limited range of decisions over which the community might have had some control. Although officials frequently invoked a discourse of community participation and consensus, nowhere in the report or during the presentations at the MCCJCC meetings did anyone from PARI or the county government suggest that the community had a say in whether the justice campus should even be built. In the next chapter, I explore some of the ways in which local politics acted to steer the discourse of possibilities to a limited range of options. Officials appeared genuinely interested in the public's ideas about what the facility should look like and what programs it should house, but wary of putting the actual concept of the justice campus up for informal public debate or a formal ballot-based referendum.

7. The Plan Is to Include Facility and Site Development at the "Thomson Site": The plan is to minimally include facility and site planning for a Juvenile Center, a Community Corrections (including a Work Release Center) and the County Sheriff's Department and Jail at the Thomson Site located on South Rogers Street in Bloomington, Indiana. (ibid.)

By stipulating that the plan must include at least the three facilities discussed and that the Thomson property was the only site under consideration, PARI and the county were able to limit the range of the public discussion. The four public meetings reinforced this limit, as they were structured around the three facilities and the comprehensive site plan, which was rendered by local architectural firm Smith and Vance at the Thomson site. As I argued in chapter 1, the desire to make surplus land productive was apparently guiding carceral policy.

Each of the seven points listed above had been raised during the hearings and helped construct the situated meaning of the justice campus in the county. The PARI report notes that the county commissioners communicated the principles to the company to guide the justice campus process. Following the path of the principles reveals important ways that the knowledge production process produced layers of legitimacy to try to insulate the guiding logics of the campus. Moving from the commissioners to PARI to the public hearing process, the principles could appear simultaneously as bearing the mark of official political endorsement, as the product of objective consultant analysis, and as having been vetted through a public process.

Following PARI's release of the report, there was substantial opposition from county politicians. Donnelly criticized the report for lacking content, plagiarizing material from the probation department, containing errors in math and spelling, and presenting an oversimplified and yet grossly expanded version of what county officials had requested. She mentioned to me that the idea for the campus was originally for a youth complex. During a closed meeting at which officials looked at blueprints of the Thomson site, one county official—whom she refused to name but whom another respondent identified as Bill Rusch, a former judge—asked "What if we put the adult jail here?" and indicated a place on the blueprints for the construction of a new adult facility. With that, Donnelly said, the plan became entirely different, involving the construction of the three facilities and new sheriff's offices and containing more room for expansion. Donnelly clarified that she was not opposed to the possibility of further expansion at a later date, but that she was frustrated by the way PARI had presented the expansion as a necessary and beneficial part of the overall package. In the way PARI had presented the report, she insisted, community residents were not given options; the justice campus was to include all of the buildings, a drastic expansion of county criminal justice.

Olivia Krasny—as noted in chapter 5, a long-time community activist, nonprofit executive, small business owner, and one of the citizen appointees to the MCCJCC—confirmed Donnelly's comments. In fact, Krasny claimed in an interview with me, that "no one really wanted the justice campus." When I expressed incredulity at this idea, given that the proposal had had broad popular support among officials long before the release of PARI's report, Krasny offered as an explanation a concept she called "the power of tangibility." Once Rusch suggested that the entire county criminal justice apparatus could be located on the eighty-five-acre site in a way that alleviated current overcrowding problems and accommodated future growth, that vision became hegemonic. Krasny argued that any reservations expressed by the group of people working on the issue were integrated into the plan for the expanded justice campus. Krasny's comments, in conjunction with Donnelly's claims, reinforced the idea that the justice campus concept originally had only tepid support, despite the fact that later criminal justice practitioners and other officials presented a seemingly united front on the concept. The political process conformed to Pierre Bourdieu's observation that "every established order tends to produce . . . the naturalization of its own arbitrariness" (1977, 164). This reality raises important questions about the momentum of bureaucracy, the power of tangibility, and the relative acceptance of institutional expansion, even among informed critics of incarceration.

These opinions, communicated to me in interviews, also are reflected in the public statements released by county politicians after PARI submitted its report to the county. In a *Herald-Times* article from May 2009, county council member Colin Franklin stated that the report "is in no way representative of what the council said it was looking for. What ends up happening is we have a design proposed that's maybe three times as much as anybody on the council ever proposed for any facility, with a price tag that's around twice as much as any of us thought. I feel the project suffers from such a bloated report" (quoted in Nolan 2009a). The article quotes other county council members as saying that they were "absolutely disappointed" and that PARI's report was a "monstrosity . . . out of touch with community values." The anger and frustration of these responses is curious, given the appearance of close collaboration between the consultants and county officials, and especially in consideration of the information shared at the MCCJCC hearings at the end of the previous fall.

Representing County Knowledge: Victoria Krause

In contrast to PARI, Krause, the county's consultant for the transfer of the YSB to the board of judges, was more easily locatable within the framework and discourse of Monroe County liberalism. As discussed in chapter 4, one of the first comments she made to me when we met was that she hated incarceration, so much that she dropped out of a PhD program in criminal justice because she couldn't commit to studying a system that she despised. Yet when the conversation turned toward juvenile justice and the facility she had developed and directed in Bartholomew County, her tone changed dramatically. She repeatedly observed that she was "passionate about that facility" and the potential of similar facilities to make positive therapeutic interventions in the lives of young people. The facility was a mixed juvenile detention and residential shelter complex that many local officials cited as a model for Monroe County and as at least one reason why the county hired Krause as a consultant. Krause noted during our interview that her main interest was in youth development and its capacity to empower young people. Of particular importance was her belief that youth development "can be provided in any environment, outside or on the 'inside.'" Despite her rhetorical condemnation of incarceration and her passionate embrace of the term "youth development," Krause's presence in the county as a consultant raises important questions about her role in constructing local knowledge.

Krause was deeply involved in criminal justice, despite her outwardly critical view of incarceration. She spent several years as a police officer and served as president of the National Juvenile Detention Association and state bodies concerned with juvenile justice. Her philosophical orientation to treatment and her passion for youth development certainly did not exclude detention. Indeed, for Krause, detention was an opportunity for positive intervention into the lives of youth.

As I have mentioned above, the studies of juvenile and adult corrections conducted during the previous two decades offered county officials a significant rhetorical and semiotic resource for their support for various expansion proposals. Many officials saw the knowledge produced by these studies as pointing to essential truths about expansion needs. Yet these studies, produced as they were by consultants positioned as objective experts, created a very narrow bank of knowledge from which the community could draw. Indeed, Krause's final report to the county about the YSB and the future of youth detention and treatment provides insights into how carceral knowledge was produced and how it achieved symbolic capital.

When I interviewed her, Krause prided herself on providing Monroe County "with the 10,000-foot view of juvenile services," indicating her belief in her capacity to stand far removed from, and provide an objective analysis of, the operations and needs of the local juvenile justice system. But examining Krause's report in detail challenges her claims to objectivity and comprehensiveness. In one of the attachments to her report, she listed the "stakeholders" she interviewed during data collection in three categories: YSB employees, "Monroe County elected officials, department heads, and other government employees," and "representatives of key community stakeholders" (Krause 2009). Breaking down these three groups further demonstrates that Krause used county officials' perspectives in her report, in the process constructing a narrow slice of knowledge from the position of a committed subject.

In interviewing YSB staff members, Krause could certainly claim that her report provided some sense of the complaints and reservations about the integration of juvenile probation and the transfer of the YSB to the board of judges. But Krause stopped there with her examination of criticisms about the changes. She interviewed no one from among the hundreds of community members—youth and families—who had used YSB services, although staff members had urged her to talk to people with such intimate perspectives on the YSB and the potential changes.

Moreover, one-third of her respondents were the very "elected officials" who had agitated for the change and contracted her services. Included by name in the group Krause interviewed were Randall; Donnelly; Robin Trotter, the juvenile probation supervisor, and her staff (who, it should be noted, were the very people who stood to retain their jobs if the YSB was transferred); and numerous county council and commission members who had been involved in contracting Krause's services.

Finally, the existence of Krause's third group of respondents—community stakeholders—could conceivably assuage some concerns about her sample being skewed. But, again, Krause opted for exclusively interviewing executive-level administrators of other agencies, including the directors and CEOs of different mental health providers, members of the county school system, the director of the county's Department of Child Services, and a former attorney in the prosecutor's office. Thus, in addition to not speaking with clients of the YSB, Krause did not interview a single teacher, guidance counselor, athletic coach, mentor, clergy member, or other youth worker in her "10,000-foot view of juvenile services."

It is important to note here that I am not arguing that the presence of consultants, Krause included, indicates an uncontested hegemony. Indeed, there were moments during my time in the field when community residents directly challenged the presence of consultants and the knowledge that they produced. In the story from the *Herald-Times* announcing the submission of Krause's report, the reporter included critical comments from Jim Tyler, the YSB's former director. The article, titled "Report Cites 'Dysfunctional, Unhealthy Culture' at Youth Services Bureau," included some excerpts from the report but also noted that:

Tyler has spoken publicly about his concerns about changes at the YSB, telling the *Herald-Times* back in October he believed the proposed changes were about money, not improving the quality or number of services for children. In addition, he and others have expressed concern that children in need wouldn't seek out the shelter for help if it were perceived as an "arm" of probation or the legal system after county officials opted to move three juvenile probation officers there. Chief probation officer Carrie Donnelly said earlier this week that two of those three officers have made the move to the South Adams Street site. . . . On Friday, Tyler said via e-mail that he was amazed [that Victoria] Krause "came up with all those conclusions without consulting me," adding, "Vicki has a law enforcement/probation background, and I'm confident she gave the commissioners what they were looking for." (Nolan 2010)

Despite the tendency of the *Herald-Times* to print editorials supportive of carceral expansion projects, this article featured a trenchant critique from Tyler. He pointed out the role of money in fostering a dubious change, the potential for actually deterring youth in need from seeking services because of the presence of probation officials, and the predictability of the study's findings given the consultant's background in criminal justice.

Other informants' comments confirmed that Krause's report and framing of the issue did not assert an uncontestable narrative. Many people spoke out at meetings against the reliance on consultants and their knowledge, including the observation by Ian Ozymandias, a member of DMC, that the county was "outsourcing community decision making." When I interviewed Tony Daniels, the clinical director at the YSB, the conversation turned to his incredulity about the problems with Krause's report:

When I talked to [Judge] Pat Randall the other day when he was over [at the YSB], I asked who is going to select the new director, and he said, "Me." And I said, "You!? Nobody else?" I would hope that there would be a panel, like across the board, consumers, teachers, social workers, not people like Steve Halpern [the local director of the Department of Child Services], who I have never met and who was a "stakeholder" according to Vicki Krause but who didn't know what the hell we do. He thought they referred to us; I thought, Mr. Halpern, we refer to you! We refer kids to you when we have abuse cases! Other people [who were interviewed by Krause], like the principal of this middle school, they didn't know what we do. The social workers and the teachers know us, but Krause never talked to them. She never talked to any parents. She never talked to any kids! She came in one day to the YSB and asked to talk to some kids that moment, but the logistics of it—the paperwork for confidentiality, getting the kids out of their programs—it didn't happen. So she never talked to any kids!

The problems with the report that I have mentioned were clearly not lost on local people involved with the changes to the YSB. Indeed, it is through the analyses of my respondents that I have arrived at some of the critical positions I present in these pages. For Daniels, Krause's report had larger implications than a skewed presentation of facts. In response to a question from me about whether county carceral practices and treatment of youth were exceptional, he noted that the whole process of Krause's consultant work for the county, from her hiring to the delivery of her report, confirmed the unexceptional nature of the county:

> Why would we be any better [than other communities]? My interactions with people in county government—I think [to myself], "What is so special about them?" I had been impressed with some people, but I think when it got down to really getting things done, they didn't really do much, so I'm not really optimistic. I mean the fact that they chose Vicki Krause to do this [evaluate the county's needs regarding a youth facility]—it's like, are you kidding? She was a police officer at one time! She ran a locked facility and [the report] was so skewed and her perspective is so narrow, it's almost insulting. She didn't give a crap about our backgrounds or how we got here, and she bullied people and argued about their opinion . . . Like really, are you kidding? So that's evidence of their poor decision making. Who made that decision to get her? People are saying it's Gail Zane. Gail Zane?! She's a nightmare. She's a county council member who keeps getting reelected off of one issue, no taxes: "I'm gonna lower your taxes." She's a Republican on the council. So is that the best we can do?

Interestingly, Daniels identified Krause and the report with the lone Republican on the county council, Gail Zane. Although Krause strongly identified herself as a liberal and had the support of many politicians who also considered themselves liberals, Daniels noted her alignment with the lone outspoken conservative in county government.

The criticisms of Tyler and Daniels proved prescient. Despite the critical voices in the community—challenging everything from the final report, through the premise that Krause could provide an objective analysis, and to the idea that a shelter for youth should house probation officers and should be supervised by the board of judges—the changes to the YSB happened quickly and rather quietly. Indeed, officials attended meetings during the fall of 2009 at which community members, including YSB staff members and family clients, raised significant concerns, but at the same time the officials were moving forward with the planned changes. By the time I visited the YSB in early March of 2010 to meet with Daniels, probation officers already had moved into the building, occupying the offices next to his and across the hall.

An Instructive Moment

A particularly telling moment in my fieldwork illustrates the narrow knowledge production possible in the county and, at the same time, points to the centrality of the carceral apparatus in local governance. At a meeting of the MCCJCC that I attended in the late fall of 2009, Mulvaney announced the creation of a $1.3 million juvenile services fund to be administered by the county council. The money had been in use in other places, and it was up to the council to spend it elsewhere or absorb it into a youth services fund. The council chose the latter option and required that the money be allocated to prevention services and could not be used to fund detention. After making this announcement in the meeting, Mulvaney turned to Randall and encouraged the judge and council to communicate directly on how to spend the money. I have broken down Randall's reply into the four points it contained. Randall argued that (1) the money should first fund a "day reporting program," (2) the council should confer with Krause, their juvenile justice consultant, on how to spend the funds, (3) he and the juvenile court "could spend it all," and finally (4) he would research "best practices" to bring to the county council. Mulvaney thanked Randall, noting that one of the requirements that the council placed on the distribution of the monies was that the recipient programs be "evidence-based."

Working through Randall's comments reveals the constitutive nature of knowledge production. Technocratic discourse and provider and consultant expertise constructed and supported one another. In Randall's and Mulvaney's comments about "evidence-based" and "best practices," one can see the already limited continuum of possible destinations for the money. By making funding contingent on that designation, the council immediately restricted what could be imaginable for county youth to a set of programs already closely aligned with detention and supervision. Indeed, despite the mandate that the monies not support detention, Randall's first suggestion was to fund a day reporting program, an "alternative" sanction that would undoubtedly widen the carceral net through increased surveillance and scrutiny. The designation of "evidence-based" carried enough political capital among social service and criminal justice officials to preclude any discussion of its definition or of what worthwhile programs or projects might not qualify for the label.

Implicit in Randall's comment that he could "spend it all" was both the accepted logic that the money would go through his office and, perhaps more cynically, that the judicial and carceral system consumed enormous sums of money. In the suggestion to consult Krause, Randall and the council seemingly ignored the diverse and vibrant organizations and youth-oriented workers in the community. With $1.3 million in funding available and a discussion occurring among a group of people convened precisely to foster interagency collaboration and community partnerships, there was no mention of consulting social service practitioners, youth workers, parents, teachers, community organizations, or—the most glaring absence—young people themselves. The only people assumed to be able to provide leadership and expertise in deciding how to disseminate the funds were criminal justice practitioners and a consultant from outside of the county.

Conclusion

The focus in chapters 5 and 6 delineates the centrality of knowledge production to the local struggle for and against carceral expansion. DMC had to make difficult decisions about whether and how to engage on an uneven terrain that favored those who were fluent in the circulating discourse of technocrats. Organizers risked marginalization by speaking uneasily in the language of "evidence-based practices" but also risked dismissal by invoking the potentially incompatible language of prison activism. Yet participation in the YSB meetings by mothers of sheltered and detained youth (as well as other moments described in chapter 8 and the conclusion) demonstrate that knowledge production in the county was always a contested process. People in the community resisted not only the idea of carceral expansion but also the construction of knowledge that viewed expansion as the result of a calculus of evidence-based practices, tax bases, efficiency of movement, and economy of future planning. It was up to community organizers and the families of people involved in the juvenile and adult systems to deploy a counterhegemonic knowledge about the issues central to the contest over expansion. First, however, they had to negotiate a political geography in the community that at once promoted accessible and accountable government and seemed to orchestrate political spaces and public processes that insulated dominant narratives against substantive disruption.

7

Governing through Expansion

I sat with three other members of Decarcerate Monroe County (DMC) in a row of chairs behind a large wooden table in the main meeting room of the county government. Around the table sat the members of the Monroe County Criminal Justice Coordinating Council (MCCJCC). It was very early in my fieldwork: the four hearings about the justice campus had yet to occur, but the justice campus idea had been circulating in the local media and representatives of Program Administration and Results, Inc. (PARI) were in Bloomington, speaking with local officials. Along with my three fellow organizers, I had been invited to this internal meeting of the advisory body by county council member Bridget Markham—who, while herself a supporter of the campus, believed DMC had important testimony to provide. Markham had put us on the agenda to make a public comment at the end of the meeting.

When the group's official business was concluded, Tom Grady, the MCCJCC chairman, turned to us, smiled, and invited us to speak. I stood up and read a prepared statement, which focused on three points of agreement within DMC: unequivocal opposition to new jail construction, an embrace of alternatives to incarceration, and advocacy for a ballot referendum that would put the justice campus issue to a countywide vote. When I finished, Grady thanked the DMC members for their presence and statement and then formally ended the meeting. As the MCCJCC members stood up and began speaking informally, Grady got up from his seat at the head of the table and approached the four of us. He crouched down between me and another DMC member and, extending his hand to each of us in turn, thanked us for our presence and the statement. Next he said, "I agree completely with you that we lock up far too many people in this country." Then, looking squarely into my eyes, he proceeded to tell me that the justice campus should be built and if the county was to decide to go ahead with it, DMC should "not get in our way." After that he stood up and walked away.

This encounter occurred close to six years ago as of this writing. Elapsed time and distance has dulled my memory of how it felt to be threatened. I vaguely remember brushing off Grady's comment but also being quite shaken by it. I know that the four of us quickly gathered our belongings and left the room. I have spent considerable time trying to understand what about our presence and comments that evening might have elicited a hostile and defensive response from a man who otherwise came across as rather genteel. The MCCJCC does not take official positions on policy, but Grady was one of many of its members who were ardent defenders of the justice campus proposal. His somewhat bizarre and out of character hostility suggested that, for him, the justice campus was so important that dissent and critique needed to be managed, contained, and neutralized. Taken in the context of the ensuing years of contest over carceral expansion, I understand Grady's threat as operating within what Stuart Hall and coauthors have called "repertoires of domination," or actions taken when elites perceive a "crisis of hegemony" (2013, 214). In warning us to stay out of the way of the progress toward the justice campus, Grady sensed in this first interaction with DMC the possibility of a future crisis of hegemony, in which "the basis of political leadership and cultural authority becomes exposed and contested" (ibid., 217).

Grady's perception of a threat to consent about carceral expansion led him to try and preempt political organizing. While his directive to us might have been unique in its explicit nature, it would only be the first of many contradictions between the rhetoric and practice of local political process.

To complement the earlier examinations of knowledge production and its role in shaping the carceral politics of the county, this chapter explores that carceral politics to understand its role in shaping the discourse. It examines the political processes and forums in which conversations about carceral expansion occurred. Of course, the production and articulation of knowledge and the structuring of spaces to promote and insulate that knowledge are two aspects of the same phenomenon of symbolic power (Bourdieu 1991; Wacquant 2005). I consider some of the primary scholarly goals of this book to be a critical examination of the veneer of benevolent objectivity and to attempt to show the committed subjectivities that constructed the discourse and politics of carceral expansion. This chapter focuses on the structuring of political spaces and processes so that narratives of expansion were affirmed and protected from critique while appearing to be open to contestation.

I have structured this chapter to examine closely the construct of accessibility in county politics. In certain ways, the nature of the justice campus and the Youth Services Bureau (YSB) as municipal-level projects rendered civic participation in the political processes more accessible than, say, participation in decision making about a new facility of the Indiana Department of Corrections. I briefly explore the nature of local government and its particular political configuration during the time of my fieldwork. I move quickly to a critical interrogation of the idea of accessible government, pointing to the ways that political processes—including public meetings—marginalized voices and proscribed conversations. Within this analysis of local governance, I explore how different sectors of the community, including different levels of political, civic, and nonprofit leaders, at times blurred their roles and collaborated to insulate the county narrative of carceral expansion from challenges by dissenting community members. The discussion of accessibility raises questions about the contested meaning of political accountability, an issue that this chapter examines in the context of carceral expansion.

Pierre Bourdieu's work is instructive for a critical exploration of the assumption that public meetings offered a democratic space for the discussion of the justice campus. His work on language and power offers a helpful transition from the last two chapters' discussion of what is said and who says it to a focus on the ability of the forums in which language is used to influence representation and meaning. Bourdieu challenges the traditional linguistic theory of the universality of language, instead arguing:

> Access to legitimate language is quite unequal, and the theoretically universal competence liberally granted to all by linguists is in reality monopolized by some. Certain categories of interlocutors are deprived of the capacity to speak in certain situations. . . . Inequalities of linguistic competence constantly reveal themselves in the market of daily interactions, that is, in the chatter between two persons, in a public meeting, a seminar, a job interview, and on the radio or television. Competence effectively functions differentially, and there are monopolies on the mar-

ket of linguistic goods, just as on the market of economic goods. This is perhaps most visible in politics, where spokespersons, being granted a monopoly over the legitimate political expression of the will of a collective, speak not only in favor of those whom they represent but also very often in their place. (Bourdieu and Wacquant 1992, 146–47)

Officials hosting and speaking at the four MCCJCC hearings about the justice campus advertised and framed the space as signifying the county's commitment to public input into the process. Indeed, during the introductions to all four meetings, Grady and Richard Kemp, PARI's cofounder and director, repeatedly referred to the meetings as demonstrating the county's commitment to transparency and public input.

The intentions of Grady, Kemp, and local politicians notwithstanding, the assertion that public hearings equaled an open and transparent process belied the fact that they proved to, at times, be exclusionary and marginalizing. The choice of location, time of the meeting, physical structure of the space, order of speaking, tone employed by officials, and ground rules all at times constructed the process in ways that privileged the dominant narrative of the justice campus. In the process, officials engaged in a variety of "neutralization techniques" (Mathiesen 2006, 44), which often and effectively destabilized resistant critiques. These "softer" forms of control could avoid the more confrontational exercises of power (such as Grady's threat in a private meeting) and "neutralize fresh ideas and initiatives" (ibid.). While there was a range of these techniques, they were often employed through the process of what Thomas Mathiesen calls "absorption" (ibid., 45). As this chapter describes, officials often strategically absorbed ideas totally resistant to expansion into their proposals, neutralizing their disruptive potential by attempting to make radical visions of decarceration commensurate with liberal expansion.

Incommensurability implies more than incompatibility: two phenomena are beyond comparison rather than a bad fit. In the case of the justice campus, this may seem to be a conceptual stretch. After all, as I have emphasized throughout, campus supporters were also critics of mass incarceration. But evidence from my fieldwork suggests that carceral habitus and abolitionist politics were irreconcilable, one grounded in the necessity of increased carceral capacities and the other insistent on decarceration as a starting point for reform. In her theoretical review of the scholarship of incommensurability and inconceivability, Elizabeth Povinelli discusses the importance of considering commensuration in analyses of liberal ideology:

> What seems to be at stake then is how we come to characterize moments of social repression and social violence directed at left and right radical worlds as moving forward a nonviolent shared horizon, as the peaceful proceduralism of communicative reason, rather than as violent intolerance, i.e., the pragmatic aspects of communication. To do this we have to shift our perspective. We do not ask how a multicultural or plural nation (or world) is sutured at the end of some horizon of liberal, institutionally embedded, communication. We ask instead how the incommensurateness of liberal ideology and practice is made to appear commensurate. (2001, 327–28)

Locally, Povinelli might observe that officials worked hard to make liberal carceral practices commensurate with abolition. As this chapter examines, officials at the justice campus hearings and other meetings would attempt to neutralize decarceration politics through rhetorical maneuvers that absorbed critique into dominant liberal narratives of expansion.[1] The manipulation of incomparable carceral politics—expansionist and abolitionist reforms—into a measurable social distance was an attempt by officials to pacify activists and gain important support for expansion.

Proximate Politics

Throughout my research, I was consistently struck by the accessibility of local politicians. In my previous experiences doing nonprofit and community work in large cities, politicians and other officials seemed to operate on an alternative plane of time and space: often meetings had to be set up through schedulers months in advance and at times didn't feature the officials in question but rather a legislative aide or assistant. In contrast, many Monroe County officials made themselves available, attended both official and community-based meetings, and could be found and approached at routine community gatherings and locales. It was not unusual to see several of the people featured in this book at the local food cooperative, the farmers market, and any number of local restaurants.

Some members of DMC saw this accessibility as an important potential instrument to be used and were optimistic about their ability to influence local officials because of the relatively little social and geographical distance between residents and representatives. One activist, a cofounder of DMC named James Nagle, spoke poignantly with me about how the relative proximity between activists and the political power structure factored into his decision to move back to the community after a year in New York City.

We sat down at the Bakehouse, a local coffee shop and restaurant, to catch up after his return from New York and to speak more formally for this project. I updated Nagle on recent DMC projects, concluding with some news about a county commissioner trying to schedule a debate between DMC members and the jail commander. Nagle shook his head in disbelief. "Could you imagine us trying to speak to the superintendent of Riker's Island to try to get him to change policy?" he asked rhetorically, referring to the infamous New York City jail, home to 14,000 inmates on any given day. He clarified that he had no illusions about the actual opportunity to influence local politicians, but that he found the ability to communicate the organization's points, to meet officials face to face, and to at least have the opportunity to affect change at the top refreshing after a year of frustration doing anarchist and abolitionist organizing in New York City. To illustrate his point, Nagle joked that you could be sitting in a booth at a coffee shop (as we were) discussing jail issues, and the person to speak to about that particular issue could be just across the café. In fact, during one of the first interviews I conducted for this project, I had been sitting in that same booth with Brian Mulvaney, a member of the county council, when a second member, Reuben Davison, entered the café. Mulvaney had called Davison over to our table and introduced us. Both men were active in local attempts at carceral expansion, and their political orientations would shape my research in important ways. I would later interview Davison for this book.

The concept that Nagle raised—the sociopolitical and spatial proximity between radical activists and liberal politicians—is crucial for understanding the potential that DMC members believed existed for radical reform of the system and their frustration with the county's continued reliance on traditional paradigms. In Nagle's excitement about the possibilities of organizing in Bloomington, I sensed that his experience organizing in New York City had left him discouraged by the consolidated, amorphous, and intangible nature of municipal state power there. Monroe County and Bloomington politics were remarkable for their seeming accessibility but were also highly predictable in their partisanship: they were reliably Democratic.

Carceral expansion would prove, however, that political alliances on the Left are unpredictable. It would be easy to assume that Democratic politicians were hesitant or unable to embrace radical changes in incarceration because of either political differences with activists or the political compromises required to remain in office. But the facts on the ground reveal some fallacies in this logic. First, there is important truth to the notion that there were political differences of consequence between Democrats, even leftist ones, and local activists involved with DMC. Many DMC organizers, for example, identified with and were involved in various radical political movements, including prison abolition and anarchism. But on many issues, including national incarceration, local politicians expressed political agreement with DMC members. Moreover, many people who spoke out against components of the justice campus and who expressed reservations about the YSB changes were not associated with DMC but were organizationally unaffiliated community residents, members of social service organizations, or people who had been in adult or youth detention. That is, their opposition to the changes was not explicitly couched in a larger radical politics.

Second, Democrats dominated the major governing bodies of the county and city. Of the nineteen people leading the three major bodies of local government—eight members each of the county and city councils and three county commissioners—there were two Republicans and seventeen Democrats as of January 1, 2009. In addition, major figures in municipal criminal justice, including the sheriff, the prosecutor, and most judges, were Democrats. Many of these individuals proudly advertised their liberal and progressive affiliations and even their activist pasts. The idea that local officials were forced to compromise on various issues to achieve consensus between the Democratic and Republican Parties is misleading at best. Rather, as Davison pointed out when

TABLE 7.1. Combined Democrat and Republican representation on the Monroe County Council, Monroe County Commission, and Bloomington City Council

Date	Democrats	Republicans
January 1, 2000	13	6
January 1, 2001	13	6
January 1, 2002	13	6
January 1, 2003	10	9
January 1, 2004	10	9
January 1, 2005	12	7
January 1, 2006	13	6
January 1, 2007	15	4
January 1, 2008	16	3
January 1, 2009	17	2

Source: Malik 2010

I interviewed him, the previous county government (before the 2008 elections, when there were sixteen Democrats and three Republicans on these county and city government bodies) had achieved consensus in favor of building the justice campus.

Despite some alliances between activists and county politicians on other issues, such as climate change, fighting anti-immigrant legislation, and support for local food politics, any belief by activists that Democratic political dominance would lead to significant jail reform would prove to be erroneous. Moreover, as the remainder of this chapter examines, local political processes were framed as enabling and embodying accessibility and accountability even as they worked to insulate a hegemonic narrative about expansion and neutralize the circulation of alternative and abolitionist ideas.

Accessibility, Accountability, and Deliberation

Amidst a constant stream of technocratic and budgetary discussion, pleasantries and mutual acknowledgments of hard work and sacrifice between county council members and heads of county departments, I also got to witness a revealing encounter between Jail Commander [Doug] Dobson and a colleague of his. During a break in the proceedings, he [Dobson] asked a suit who sat to [Sheriff] Frank Sullivan's left if he was planning on going to the Decarcerate Monroe County meeting on Saturday. When the suit had trouble remembering who DMC was, Dobson said, "You know, that fine group of citizens who protest us," to which this man snorted, cracked his knuckles, and said that he'd be there with all of his rings on his fingers and bells on his toes.

Regardless of what this might reveal about Dobson's perspectives on DMC activism, it perhaps illuminates his assumptions about space and place. Given that he spoke audibly and in earshot of people he didn't know, he clearly had identified the space within the courthouse as non-DMC space. Considering DMC is a public group, I wonder if he also sees the space of a budget hearing as nonpublic and as a sequestered site for bureaucratic functioning of government away from the eyes and voices of those who may be critical?

—My field notes from a Monroe County budget meeting,
    September 8, 2009

Open meetings, public input, visible politicians, and an active cable television station that filmed all county meetings suggest that residents had important and valued roles in the operations of county government. Indeed, local officials emphasized the important role of the citizenry in shaping criminal justice policy and in the deliberative processes of local government more generally.[2] For local officials, deliberation through public process ensured government accountability.

Yet a close analysis of conversations at public meetings and with current and former politicians complicates the appearance of open and vibrant democratic process. Not only were alternative forms of knowledge marginalized, but also the opportunities through which criticism and articulation of alternative visions could be expressed were limited. Indeed, in a rare moment of criticism from the inside, Markham, by then no longer a member of the county council, suggested to me that the entire public process component of the justice campus, including all four hearings dedicated to public input, had been just a façade. In her words, the four meetings were "token attempts to 'checklist' public process," a stinging indictment of a process that most local politicians defended, and one that invokes Anthony Platt's insights into the political process of a century earlier: "Many intellectuals in the Progressive movement were interested in creating a system of government which would allow the people to rule only at a carefully kept distance and at infrequent intervals, reserving most real power and planning to a corps of experts and professionals" (2009, xxvi). Markham's claims, along with the disaffection that activists and others felt about official processes, requires interrogating local deliberations and parsing claims of deliberative political process from claims of political accountability. Without paying much attention to detail or examining meeting discourse closely, one might perceive the public process to be deliberative. Yet in the course of reviewing my transcripts of meetings and looking at archival footage, it became clear to me that the structure and content of the meetings served to effectively limit the range of what was said, undermining claims about the deliberative nature of county process.[3]

The justice campus hearings operated to give the impression and appearance of deliberation. As people critical of the process suggested, and as Markham confirmed, the county promoted the public process related to the justice campus to legitimate decisions that had already been made before the hearings occurred. Deliberation occurred to the extent that county officials created space for the public to voice criticism and discuss possible alternatives to the construction of the justice campus. Ultimately, these conversations followed substantial work by county officials to shape the narrative of the justice campus. Moreover, public discussions did not assuage concerns about the narrow nature of the deliberative field—that is, who was left out of the conversation and the decision making.

Indeed, in the hearings about the justice campus, there was a noticeable absence of people directly affected by the criminal justice policies in question. Few officials spoke of this absence as a problem; none spoke of making any effort to broaden the conversation to include people such as the family members of the currently incarcerated or the formerly incarcerated themselves. The absence of these segments of the community, and the conspicuous silence surrounding it, contrasted sharply with the rhetoric officials used to argue for local carceral growth, particularly for the youth facility. Officials such as Judges Patrick Randall and Geraldine Lane, Chief Probation Officer Carrie Donnelly, Mulvaney, county commissioner John Tierney, and city council president Rose Halverson all made every effort to link the lack of a local youth facility with the social and spatial marginalization of county youth. They argued that the justice campus, and the subsequent proposal for the expansion and carceralization of the YSB, would render local youth more visible through providing local custody. Crucially, none of these officials ever mentioned the importance of youth visibility to the actual processes of making decisions about the justice campus and the YSB. That is, no one in favor of either the justice campus or the YSB spoke of the importance of young people or adults having a say in conversations about what should happen to them, and no one lamented their lack of participation in the process.

There were moments, however, when youth workers, activists, and the occasional dissident politician raised the problem of this lack of accountability to the people most affected by criminal justice policy. DMC members frequently discussed the importance of privileging the perspectives of people most affected by policies. One member, Shawn Ryland, who worked professionally with youth in the high schools as part of a Christian organization, commented at the first MCCJCC hearing, about the youth facility, that the conversation occurring was of critical importance and that it was "very disheartening that there are no teenagers here." Ryland was correct. Except for the younger members of DMC, who were in their early twenties, not a single young person was in the room, and none had been invited to attend by the hearing's organizers.

At times, county officials spoke up in ways that cut across the divide I often observed between officials and activists. During the public comment period at the first MCCJCC meeting when Ryland spoke, Tom Redmond, a county council member, was harshly critical of the process employed during the meetings:

> I'm concerned about what I heard about who has been involved in this in the past. Where are the lay youth consumers? Out at Stone Belt,[4] there are consumers that try to participate in the governance of that organization. At the Youth Services Bureau, they have consumers on their board. I haven't heard of where there have been consumers, young people who have gone through the system, who have participated in this [process]. There's been some very valid young people's views here this evening. I feel

they have views that need to be considered and as good [*sic*] as adults and leaders in the community like to think they know what's best, they haven't led the same life as the people experiencing what [they] will be subjected to . . . in the future.

While expressing a sentiment that DMC members certainly appreciated—that young people have legitimate views and could serve in a leadership or other decision-making capacity regarding issues that affect them—Redmond nonetheless made two familiar and instructive rhetorical moves. First, he referred to local "consumers" of youth services, a common term in the county, but one that no doubt points to the circulation of neoliberal constructs that view the recipients of social assistance as engaged in obtaining a market-produced service.[5] Second, his lumping county youth served by the YSB and the "young people" of DMC into the same category revealed a paternalism common among officials, many of whom continually emphasized the number of DMC members who were young adults, even though some of them were in their thirties or forties. This wasn't inherently derogatory, but it often seemed to imply naïveté and idealism. Coupled with county officials' insistence that they knew what was best, that critics of incarceration were passionate but misinformed, and that DMC members were too ideological, the comments about the organization's youthful nature seemed to refer less to age and more to a perceived lack of awareness that accompanies experience working in the system.

While DMC attempted (and often failed) to model the idea of accountability to people most affected by criminal justice in their own campaigns and structure, the group consistently pressured the local governments to do the same. DMC members suggested to county officials that public debates and conversations about carceral expansion were in fact occurring in segments of the community who were marginalized from the official process. DMC members frequented the alley outside of the local jail, where family members gathered for visitation hours, to speak informally with the people the group considered to be most affected by local criminal justice policies. Several of DMC's campaigns actively tried to use the voices and perspectives of people in the alley to contribute to and complicate the official conversations occurring in the local halls of power. DMC also lobbied, unsuccessfully, for public meetings to be scheduled in locations and at times that accommodated the schedules of working people.

DMC members recognized that the unequal system of currency—political capital—meant that what deliberation did occur had minimal impact. That is, DMC members and others critical of carceral expansion could speak at public meetings until they were blue in the face—and frequently DMC and its allies did dominate public comment periods—but they had little impact on decision making.

Still, politicians clearly went to great lengths to demonstrate that a deliberative process was occurring. Two officials—Halverson and Emily Hutton, a member of the county council—hosted monthly "citizens' breakfasts," designed to facilitate communication between residents and politicians. At one of these meetings, in February 2009, the focus was juvenile justice issues, specifically the recent transfer of control of the YSB from the county commissioners to the board of judges. The deliberative mission of the breakfasts failed to overcome the structure that I had come to expect from any meeting run by officials.

The explicit purpose of the breakfast meetings was to make the two elected officials and their expert guests accessible and accountable to constituents interested in the issues. But rather than a conversation facilitating community dialogue, or an open forum where citizens asked questions of officials, the meeting I attended served mainly as another forum in which officials could state their perspectives and initiatives regarding youth services and juvenile justice. With the two hosts and guests Randall and Mulvaney, the meeting seemed more of a coordinated and united front to present the disciplined, official perspective on the YSB: changes at the YSB needed to happen, they were going well, the transition was proceeding smoothly, and the current arrangement served the best interests of county youth. Moreover, the issues were presented in such a way as to allow these officials the space to advocate for what they saw as the true need of the community—a juvenile facility.

Because of the structure and content of the forum, these breakfast meetings offered distinctly different interpretations of participatory democracy. For people concerned with citizen-official relations, the monthly breakfasts would seem to be an initiative worthy of praise. At the breakfast meeting about the YSB, four elected officials and between ten and fifteen citizens attended, with everyone sitting around a table together at a local restaurant. Yet the very structure of the meeting and the constitutive place of the elected officials as both those offering the expertise and as the main generators of questions made the meeting just a token attempt at engaging citizens in sharing insights and concerns. Indeed, rather than officials facilitating the meeting or asking citizens for input, they offered their initiatives, frameworks, and understandings of local issues as the way to proceed.

Problematic public meeting processes were productive reminders for activists about the importance of space, tone, language, and framing. DMC members held their own internal and public meetings, used spaces that felt more neutral and friendly than county chambers, and asked parties to facilitate the public meetings who were either sympathetic to DMC's perspective or entirely removed from the political debates about expansion. DMC realized that the deliberative process of official public meetings did not mean that county officials were any more likely to consider dissenting opinions and had the added effect of granting legitimacy to the county's process and perspective.

"To 'Checklist' Public Process": The MCCJCC

The county had created the MCCJCC as an advisory body designed to facilitate communication between agencies. After the county contracted with PARI, the commissioners asked the MCCJCC to host and facilitate the four public hearings about the justice campus. It was clear from the hearings, however, that the MCCJCC had certain subjective views, despite its mission to remain objective. One of the more explicit expressions of the body's commitment to the justice campus came from Kemp at the beginning of one of the hearings. He observed that "the MCCJCC has done a great job of keeping things moving," thanking them for their role in pushing the process forward—a revealing testimony to the relationship between the MCCJCC and the justice campus but an indictment of the MCCJCC's claims to objectivity. Grady and Olivia Krasny, the citizen appointees to the MCCJCC, routinely insisted that they were separate from the criminal justice system. But the support Kemp felt from the MCCJCC and the collaborative relationship between PARI and the advisory body as was indicated through the four hearings testifies to the MCCJCC's role in lubricating the political process for carceral expansion. Moreover, the existence of the MCCJCC enabled the criminal justice system to advocate on its own behalf under the appearance of an outside body.

In addition to the two citizen appointees, the MCCJCC's members were politicians, practitioners, or providers, most of who worked in administrative positions at their agencies. The group included judges; members of the county council and county commission; and representatives from the offices of the police, sheriff, jail, prosecutor, public defender, hospital, and mental health services. Its internal meetings focused on technocratic and managerial concerns, an understandable focus for a body designed to facilitate interagency collaboration, but one that also constrained their ability to envision options outside of the network of agencies they represented. One example of this effect occurred when the MCCJCC met to discuss ways to keep the jail population down in the context of newly disseminated population caps imposed on the jail by a federal judge following a lawsuit by the American Civil Liberties Union (ACLU). As a county attorney explained to the members of the MCCJCC, the new requirements of the jail included a cap at 278 inmates, which included 30 in a setting like a dormitory, leaving 248 secure beds. The sheriff was obligated to notify the county council and commissioners and criminal court judges if the population reached 244, notify the attorney for the ACLU if the population reached 248, and contact other jails for placement if the population reached 258.

The response from the MCCJCC primarily concerned per diem costs of incarcerating adults and youth in other counties. Significantly, not a single person at the meeting raised the possibility of not incarcerating people in the first place or taking the possible costs of per diem payments and investing an equivalent sum locally in alternatives to incarceration. The shared language and tasks of managing bureaucracies lubricated the conversation, but it also narrowly shaped the possible outcomes.

Grady's warning that DMC should stay out of the way of the justice campus was one indication that the MCCJCC and its members communicated their positions to the public in both subtle and explicit ways, despite not taking official positions on criminal justice issues. In fact, the MCCJCC framed the public hearings about the justice campus as ways to make county government both accessible and accountable to the public. The formal mission of the meetings as housing a deliberative and consensus-building process partially succeeded in masking the fact that the meetings also offered the official county narrative additional forums for articulation—now, of course, under the guise of a transparent public process.

Additional examples support this rather devastating claim that the democratic process actually worked to limit the possibilities of what could be said and, in so doing, granted official county perspectives significant space and legitimacy. Grady offers one important window into this phenomenon. His citizen appointment to the MCCJCC implied that, on a body composed of administrators from all criminal justice offices in the city and county as well as from important political offices, Grady was removed from power and sat on the council to represent county citizens. Throughout the four hearings on the justice campus—including at the beginning of each one, when Grady introduced himself and the MCCJCC as facilitators of the process—he claimed: "I'm just moderating, I'm not making any decisions." He also made other statements professing objectivity and distance, which perhaps offered him some insulation from criticism. But a deeper engagement with the language and semiotics of the meetings makes it clear that Grady's claims to objectivity were contradicted by the many instances in which he displayed his allegiances, imbuing the process with his subjectivity and promoting the official narrative of the county. As chair of the MCCJCC and facilitator of the hearings, Grady gave judges priority during comment time, occasionally cut off critical comments, and often reframed such comments to fit the dominant narrative of expansion.

The MCCJCC-hosted justice campus hearings and Grady's role call into question notions of objectivity, deliberation, and fair process. The very functioning of the democratic process effectively limited democratic decision making about the justice campus, neutralizing critical perspectives and attempting to harmonize abolitionist critique with expansionist reform, a phenomenon that some theorists point to as requiring a radical reorientation to democracy.[6]

One clear example of this occurred during the first MCCJCC hearing about the justice campus, which focused on the youth facility. Ryland, the DMC member mentioned above who worked with youth in the high schools through a Christian organization, argued passionately for the importance of building trustworthy relationships with youth. In the course of his comments, he explicitly positioned community programs that enabled building those relationships in contrast to the justice campus. His comments followed on the heels of Randall's admission that "studies show that if you keep children in secure detention for more than ten days it can be counterproductive." Following this acknowledgment that there was scant social scientific evidence to support the efficacy of juvenile detention, Ryland said:

> My first question is if it becomes counterproductive after ten days, is it really good to have them there in the first place? I think the key here is . . . relationships. Relationships with kids are never counterproductive after any number of days. When kids have adults who invest in their lives and who want to know them and know what their problems are, that's never counterproductive, and that's something that's going to affect them for the rest of their lives and will break [intergenerational cycles of incarceration].

Ryland's comments implicitly challenged both the content of and epistemology behind the justice campus. According to Randall's own statement, there was meager scientific evidence—the discursive currency used to justify the expansion of programming—to support the practice of detention. Positive relationships, in contrast, retained their effects indefinitely. Indeed, Ryland's comments inspired many people in the audience, whose subsequent comments built on his juxtaposition of investing in relationships with investing in the justice campus.

Grady's direct response attempted to mitigate the severity of Ryland's critique. When Ryland finished, Grady thanked him and said that his analysis should serve as an important reminder that PARI's mandate was "not just to build a facility, but to have programs. And programs need to be housed somewhere, even if that's not the best place for them, some of the programs need to have a place and that needs to be taken into consideration." With this rhetorical maneuver, Grady translated the radical reformulation of the issues in Ryland's comments into terms that fit within the expansionist narrative of the campus. In Grady's reformulation, youth in need of noncoercive and empowering relationships became youth in need of programs, which themselves were in need of the justice campus as a home.

Ryland's comments are one of many examples of DMC activists, formerly incarcerated people, and other concerned residents publicly criticizing carceral expansion during official proceedings. To be sure, my point is not to suggest that dissenting opinions were silenced. But the objections made during the public comment period did little to disrupt the discursive trajectory of the meetings. Rather, Grady and other officials attempted to translate "radical worlds" into the language of liberal policy.[7]

Two other examples of the use of this discursive power occurred at the beginning of the first and second hearings. All four began with a designated local official and Kemp telling the audience what they had heard thus far from stakeholders and how that information informed their analysis. Yet these exercises in transparency actually masked how, as processes of documentation and codification, they served to both reward and reinforce official perspectives, while also marginalizing the perspectives of those not deemed to be stakeholders, which frequently also meant those in dissent.

At the first hearing, Grady made brief remarks and then turned the meeting over to Randall. As mentioned in chapters 4 and 5, Randall introduced the need for a youth facility by way of shaming the public into supporting the campus. He relied on the cultural capital afforded to "twenty years of studies" as well as invoking local progressive politics to claim that the county's lack of a local juvenile facility was reprehensible. He concluded his comments by inviting public discussion regarding what such a facility should look like. In this savvy move, the judge shamed the county for its lack of a facility and indicated that building one was necessary, but he also stated that public input was of paramount importance, insofar as it could help determine what programs were appropriate for the facility. Randall solicited ideas that were in alignment with expansion while attempting to preempt those challenging it.

At the second hearing, an especially egregious detour from the stated goal of public input occurred. Grady opened the meeting by introducing the process and the recent history that had resulted in the hiring of PARI. Despite his repeated claims of objectivity, Grady again spoke of the thorough work of the company before saying how the process that night would work:

Representatives of PARI have worked diligently to gather that information over the last few months and to interview and talk with many of
the people involved in the criminal justice system and the stakeholders.
However, the commissioners directed that a significant component of the
review was to include input from the public. This is the second of four forums to collect input from the public. The first was about juvenile justice.
Tonight's forum will be regarding probation and community corrections
and work release issues. People in the audience are encouraged to write
down questions or ask [them] at the microphone once that part of the
evening begins. First we'll have a brief presentation from Richard Kemp,
then the Honorable Allan Barrett will give a slightly longer presentation,
which I think will be very helpful to frame the issues and provide the
education we all need to have a good discussion of these issues.

At the beginning of the meeting, Grady outlined a very rigid process whereby the corporate representative and the conservative judge
were given time to provide the appropriate "education" and "framing"
that they believed to be lacking among members of the public in attendance. It would become clear that for Grady and Barrett, the public
was unknowledgeable if it did not have the knowledge that the state
and the law could provide. It is worth briefly restating Mark Neocleous's
treatment of state knowledge here. He writes that "sovereignty asserts
itself in the sphere of knowledge" in two ways: "first, through the way
the state has been imagined as an institution of and for knowledge and,
second, through the way this *power-knowledge nexus has legitimized
state practices over and through civil society*" (2003, 49). The two actions
performed that night by Barrett and announced by Grady—education
and framing—exercised this power-knowledge nexus over and through
something as seemingly democratic as a public meeting.

In his opening remarks that evening, Barrett noted that he had observed "misunderstandings and a lack of information among the public"
during the first justice campus hearing. Because of that, he concluded
that he should open the second meeting: "With your patience I'd like to
spend some time addressing these things so that you have some information as a backdrop for the discussion so that you can make the discussion
more productive." With that, and at the invitation of the MCCJCC, Barrett, one of the most powerful public figures in the county, took control

of the meeting. He spoke for an hour, leaving only about fifty minutes for public comment, which had been the point of the two-hour meeting, thus effectively limiting both the time for and the scope of critique.

Examples of subtler stifling of alternative visions and analyses occurred throughout the process of deliberation. At the beginning of each meeting about the justice campus, for example, Kemp opened with PARI's standard PowerPoint presentation. One of the initial slides was titled "The Following Guiding Principles Have Been Identified for the Monroe County Criminal Justice Complex" and listed all of the recurring themes found in PARI's research. But the title itself offers an insight into the process and the importance of framing. For PARI, the MCCJCC, and county officials, the meetings were not designed to discuss and debate the proposed facilities but rather to generate ideas for programs and other constitutive components of carceral institutions that were already a given. Despite DMC members' consistent opposition at each meeting to the very premise of new institutions and their proposing of various ideas to alleviate overcrowding without creating the justice campus, each successive meeting began with the MCCJCC and PARI framing the conversation by using the justice campus as a starting point.

The hearings, officially called to solicit public input, appear in retrospect as a way for the commissioners to "checklist" that they had interacted with the public before officially endorsing this model. As Markham noted in our interview, the decisions about the justice campus were made by politicians, criminal justice officials, the MCCJCC, and PARI and were subsequently marketed to the public. Through referring to the consultant's time spent conducting research in the community with providers and through the public hearing process, county officials attempted to convince the public that the justice campus was in fact both a consensus-based decision and one in which they had participated.

The nature of the process and the circulation of official discourse positioned the justice campus favorably in the struggle for hegemony. First, officials endeavored to create a limited universe of possible outcomes of the process. They frequently made concerted efforts to neutralize expressions of resistance by appropriating them into the dominant narrative of expansion. Second, officials placed carceral expansion as an inevitable development on an imagined evolutionary trajectory of criminal justice policy, a position affirmed time and again by experts (Hall 1996, 136).

Official Frustrations: Elections, Deliberation, and Analysis Paralysis

At times, officials were incredulous at and frustrated by what they perceived as the excessive degree of deliberation about policies of carceral expansion. For them, the long history of community discussions suggested the moral righteousness of carceral expansion. Moreover, as several of them would state, their status as elected officials reserved for them the political authority to act regardless of the lack of consensus; accountability to the community came through the ballot. This proved frustrating for community organizers who saw such positions as attempts to limiting both the democratic process and the scope of organizing. Two examples from a DMC-hosted community meeting about the changes at the YSB reveal the tensions between differing notions of political accountability and deliberation.[8]

The meeting occurred at the public library. The thirty chairs that DMC members had placed in a large semicircle were filled, and almost ten latecomers stood somewhat awkwardly by the door. This group included county commissioner Dorothy Fisher, a longtime local politician and an active and vocal supporter of both the justice campus and the YSB initiatives. She was silent during the meeting, although quite visible in her support of the changes under discussion; nods and shakes of her head and occasional sighs of exasperation with activists made her position clear. During a short silence in the discussion, she raised her hand and started moving toward the door as she spoke. "I'm sorry," she said, "but I need to leave. I have to say, though, that I am a grandmother. Of course, I have the best interests of the children of this community at heart. Just trust me: I will make the right decision for them."

Fisher expressed support for jail expansion in moral terms (she was a loving grandmother) rather than political ones (she was an elected member of the county's executive political body). At the same time, however, she also implied a belief that elections meant that local residents should simply place their faith in officials. She left, after all, not inviting further discussion but rather with the bald attempt to pacify activists—"just trust me."

This same meeting, which was the final of the three that DMC organized to generate discussion about and opposition to the changes at the

YSB, grew contentious rather quickly. Officials present at the meeting, including Randall, Donnelly, Robin Trotter, and Mulvaney, confirmed new rumors that probation officers were moving into the YSB, and the county was making preparations to transfer control to the board of judges. This was especially concerning to the DMC activists and YSB employees present at the meeting, since all of them had left the second meeting a month earlier feeling that there had been consistent and vocal opposition and near consensus that the move into the YSB by probation officers was problematic and deserved much more discussion. Indeed, Mulvaney had gone out of his way to communicate to DMC at that meeting that he believed the organization was going to get what they wanted—no probation officers at the YSB—due to the outpouring of concern over the proposed changes. The news that probation officers had been trying to move into the YSB at the end of the preceding week caused confusion and incredulity among people who had thought that the move had at least been postponed until further community discussion could occur.

During the third meeting, Tony Daniels, the YSB clinical director, raised doubts about whether the issue could be resolved. Donnelly tried to convince him that "everything's gonna be fine" and asked him to place his trust in her. After Daniels and others rejected her attempt at appeasement, Donnelly became agitated and argued that her election, and the elections of Randall and the county commissioners and council members, meant that they had full discretion—and a mandate—to do what they wanted. "We are *elected* officials," she stressed, finishing her remarks by saying that she and others were responsible to the community. Daniels challenged Donnelly, arguing that no elected officials had run on a platform of changing the YSB—"*No one even mentioned it!*" Daniels emphasized—and thus it was patently false to claim that the electorate had endorsed the idea through electing officials.

The claim by Fisher and the exchange between Daniels and Donnelly demonstrates a narrow local definition of democracy. In asserting that democracy essentially meant voting, Fisher's and Donnelly's comments reaffirmed the power of elected officials to act autonomously, or at least to only think about the implications of their actions on a subsequent election, rather than whether their actions accurately reflected the desires of their constituents. More distressing, no one at the third meeting raised the question of whether a series of community meetings in which local residents raised fundamental concerns with a political project counted as democracy in action. Instead, officials, activists, youth workers, and families all relied on a limited definition of democracy to rationalize and resist the actions of elected officials.

Multiple DMC members told me after the third meeting that they felt defeated and counted it as a "loss." This loss occurred on multiple grounds, most obviously in terms of challenging the actual policy being debated: as I mentioned above, probation officials were already moving in to the YSB by the time of the meeting. But DMC members also felt defeated in their inability to dictate the framing and content of the meeting. Frequently, meeting attendees deferred to the officials in the room to set the tone and "clarify misunderstandings." This had the effect of allowing technocratic discourses of policy and budget to dominate much of the conversation. Moreover, DMC did not achieve its goal of intervening in the normative usage of certain concepts like "safety" and "locality." DMC had planned to disrupt notions that local juvenile institutions provided safety and that the change at the YSB marked the only way to "keep local kids local." The trajectory and discourse of the meeting insulated the hegemonic narrative of the county.

Many officials spoke with disdain of a phenomenon in the community they described as "analysis paralysis," or the endless community discussions they perceived as derailing the necessary expansion projects. Indeed, the phrase popped up so often in my observations and interviews with county leaders that I assumed it was disseminated as a political "talking point." Randall and Barrett, probation officials, county politicians, and civic leaders all noted that they were "tired of talking" or otherwise fed up with the public process. For them, deliberation was simply a means to the necessary end of expansion and could be abused or even hijack progress if it resulted, as it had, in a stalemate. The changes to the YSB occurred in spite of the deliberative process. Even as the move had material consequences—the retention of probation officers via creative financing through the YSB, their stationing at the site, and the jurisdictional change to the board of judges—many local people involved in the issue saw the move as a symbolic gesture of political power.

Interestingly, some local officials blamed their colleagues for "analysis paralysis." In one particularly memorable interview, Bill Rusch—an outspoken and belligerent former judge who put a lot of effort during his time on the county bench into generating support for a local youth facility—decried the "cowardice" that he saw on the part of county politicians in their indecision and subjection of the issue to an ongoing process. In this fascinating and disturbing interview, the judge used profane and highly gendered language when referring to the politicians and criminal justice officials who just years before were his colleagues and partners in designing the justice campus. According to Rusch, current politicians and officials (most of whom, it should be noted, were outspoken supporters of the justice campus) "don't have the balls to build a detention facility!" During a conversation about the changes at the YSB, Rusch noted of current officials, "all they want to do is talk and study!" He then employed a military metaphor to describe what he saw as officials' incompetence and failure to act: "If we were to go to war and the enemy was on our doorstep, these people would be dead before they were out the door." Employing a mock wonkish tone to imitate a composite county politician, he sneered: "Oh, war is possibly immoral, should we fight back? It's probably not the greenest response"—mocking the degree to which he believed the politicians would not act, even when faced with imminent death. In an especially vitriolic moment, he enforced this thought by hitting the table with his fist and spitting out that he was "disgusted by these heartless, spineless, gutless politicians."

In contrast to other informants who considered elected officials as emblematic of the exceptional nature of the community, Rusch endorsed the same mythology in spite of county leaders. He was incredulous that the community had not figured out a way to build its own detention center: "You can't tell me that we are less of a community than Jackson County? Or Vincennes? This community is stronger, better, smarter than these places—we just lack the leadership." For Rusch, true leaders would have bypassed community meetings and democratic process and simply acted on behalf of what officials believed was in the community's best interest: increased carceral space.

Nonprofit Organizations and the "Bloomington Face"

Bourdieu wrote of habitus that it "generates all the 'reasonable,' 'common sense,' behaviors which are possible within the limits of . . .

regularities, and which are likely to be positively sanctioned because they are objectively adjusted to the logic characteristic of a particular field, whose objective future they anticipate" (1990, 55–56). In the context of the justice campus, habitus structured the range of possibilities, legitimized what was proposed, and marginalized proposals that were not adequately adjusted to or made within it. Thus, because progressive politicians and civic leaders on the one hand and county criminal justice officials on the other hand operated within the same carceral habitus, they served to both strengthen the dominant narrative and insulate it from institutional criticism.

In the third MCCJCC hearing about the justice campus, organized around the jail component, Robert Cantor, the radical clergyman and cofounder of Begin Again (BA) and Monroe County Justice (MCJ), devoted time during public comment to praising the jail administration. Interestingly and perhaps strategically, he and other BA and MCJ members frequently invoked the benevolence and cooperation of the jail staff, at times to offer appreciation and at other times seemingly to insulate the staff from criticism. At the meeting, Cantor spoke up in support of the jail commander's narrative about the need for a new and larger facility: "What you have just heard [from the jail commander] is true. . . . I want to affirm everything that's been said here. This is not propaganda that you're hearing. . . . I can tell you that very often my sympathies are with the people in the jail and not the system itself. However, everything said about the system and its problems here is true."

Taken on its own or out of context, this quote simply could indicate points of agreement between Cantor and the jail administration, or it could signify a strategic attempt on Cantor's part to mitigate any tension between BA, MCJ, and the jail administration. Indeed, this and similar comments might have served both functions. Yet in a broader and historicized examination of the justice campus and carceral expansion, this quote takes on added significance because it points to a pattern of cooperation between the jail administration and reformers, including examples of co-optation of those reformers by the administration. Specifically, Cantor's comments should be understood in the historical context of county activists abandoning organizing outside of the system for significant reform and accountability so they could institutionalize their position inside it. In the process, these groups sacrificed the freedom of critique afforded them when they had no institutional constraints in exchange for better access to the jail and jail population.[9]

BA and MCJ descended from a group established in the 1980s called Jail Reform Now (JRN), which was organized outside of the criminal justice system to monitor jail conditions and advocate for reforms. MCJ was created to investigate the death of a jail prisoner who was Tasered and killed while in custody in the early 2000s. Members of JRN formed MCJ; its service-oriented cousin, BA; and a third group, Bloomington Restorative Practices (BRP), which provided several restorative justice-based programs to the community for issues ranging from civil disputes among neighbors to nonviolent criminal offenses. In DMC's attempts to present local officials with substantive and yet paradigmatically alternative options to the formal justice system, the group's members frequently invoked BRP's work as an example of the direction that the county should move in. Yet DMC's faith in BRP's status as a noninstitutional and potentially radical alternative to county criminal justice was oversimplified. While providing substantively different services than those offered by the county criminal justice system, BRP nonetheless aligned its work with the system, positioning itself as an integral option on the continuum of official sanctions.

In an internal meeting of the MCCJCC that I attended in the spring of 2010, the director of BRP gave a presentation about the nature of his group's services. One of the more compelling themes to emerge during his half-hour presentation was his continued emphasis that BRP took no official position on criminal justice policy and that the local system was exceptional. He noted: "BRP believes in the criminal justice system of Monroe County, especially this community. This could be a model community of criminal justice." He went on to emphasize BRP's service to the criminal justice system: "We're a piece of your puzzle. We're here to help you."

DMC was always quick to endorse BRP because of the organization's firm commitment to restorative justice through the provision of services, including community mediation services and victim-offender reconciliation. Some members of DMC were volunteer mediators. At the same time, BRP was wholly dependent on the courts and counted several judges and local politicians as current or former members of its board. Moreover, perhaps because of this contingent relationship, BRP was quick to endorse local criminal justice policies even as the organization strategically claimed to stay out of the fray.

The same support for the county jail administration was evident in the statements of Halverson, a member of BA and MCJ, a volunteer with and board member of multiple local nonprofits, as well as an outspoken member of the city council. She offered public comments at several of the MCCJCC hearings about the justice campus. Chapter 4 included her statement at the first hearing, when she endorsed youth detention to prevent adult incarceration. She made the following comment during the third hearing, which focused on jail overcrowding and the new jail component of the justice campus:

> I've been a volunteer with Begin Again for two years. I want to be part of the solution. I so appreciate the work of Sheriff Sullivan and [Jail] Commander Dobson. They have shown us the utmost respect and we know the challenges. When I come into the jail every Saturday to lead classes as a Begin Again volunteer, I'm extremely respectful of the fact that we're a strain on your staff. Getting us up and down and cleared and through the locked doors . . . sometimes I conduct my class in the multipurpose room, sometimes that classroom is used for other programs, and I have to go right into the block to work with the inmates. . . . And I would close by asking that everyone that comes up that has an opinion today to [sic] be respectful of the fact that we have different ideas of what to do and what not to do, but that the system is doing the best it can. Can we do better as a community? Yes, of course we can, and I'm here to be a part of the solution.

Halverson used much of her allotted time to attempt to shield the panelists from criticism. She went out of her way to praise the sheriff and jail commander and asked the audience to be respectful, arguing that the system is "doing the best it can," a disputable assertion that positioned her in solidarity with the local administration of justice and in opposition to activists. Moreover, her emphasis on being "part of the solution" was a coded message to hearing attendees: it was both a dig at activists, claiming that critique and analysis were impediments to progress, and a nod to officials that she was with them. In a later interview with Halverson, it would become evident to me that she was critical of incarceration and believed strongly in noninstitutional alternatives and prevention through investing in health care and education. Yet at this hearing she chose both to endorse the justice campus as meeting the need for program space and to rhetorically protect the jail administration.

Halverson's role in the proceedings about the justice campus points to the intimacy between local officials and local nonprofits. Organizations like BA, MCJ, and BRP were dependent on the jail administration for access to prisoners or for referrals, so members of those groups tiptoed around issues of policy or publicly supported official positions. In addition, there was a substantial overlap in personnel among local governments, advisory bodies like the MCCJCC, and nonprofit organizations. Halverson wore two hats: that of the politician (although she told me she preferred the term "public servant") and that of the nonprofit volunteer. This was not uncommon, as some nonprofit executives were former politicians, and several politicians besides Halverson were volunteers with or board members of nonprofits.

Halverson presented her efforts to protect county and city politicians from criticism using a discourse of consensus building, compromise, and dialogue. During our interview, she went out of her way to praise the efforts of the chief of police, the prosecutor, and members of the jail administration, invoking their "good guy" personalities and Democratic politics. Halverson also spoke multiple times of the important ideological differences between Republicans and Democrats, referring to the cognitive scientist and linguist George Lakoff's (2002) metaphor of the stern father in contrast to the nurturing mother. Halverson proudly identified herself as a nurturing maternal figure and insisted on the distinct differences in values, outlook, and beliefs about human nature that mapped onto the political differences between the two parties. For her, being a Democratic politician meant "leading with my values," which included "rehabilitation versus confinement."

The dichotomies of Republican versus Democrat and confinement versus rehabilitation may speak to qualitative differences in political positions, including incarceration, although history suggests otherwise.[10] Moreover, whatever distinctions may exist rhetorically should not obscure the fact that rehabilitation and "confinement," which I define as incapacitation for its own sake, were both predicated on the carceral institution in the local context. Halverson lambasted the "law and order types" who existed within the community, particularly in the more conservative county rather than the progressive city, but carceral expansion during her tenure originated among, gained traction with, and was ultimately implemented by a group whose members were almost all Democrats, and many of whom shared Halverson's liberal orientation.

Halverson's faith in local incarceration, her efforts to disrupt organizing against the justice campus, and her attempts to protect officials from critique reveal a commitment to a phenomenon that Daniels labeled "the Bloomington face." His analysis of the YSB debacle—including both the transfer of jurisdiction and the premature move of probation officers on site—was that it was largely a product of the use of heavy-handed measures to avoid conflict, an attempt to harmonize differences, and paternalism—all tactics adopted to compromise and even appropriate political resistance to expansion, but in the name of building consensus. In discussing the processes through which officials implemented changes at the YSB, he said:

> It's such an Indiana thing: nonconfrontational, this "Bloomington face" of not talking about the conflict. You know, I told Randall that they could have just come in and said, "Probation is moving in, they need the money." Flat out. [They could have said,] "There's nothing wrong with YSB, don't worry, your jobs are OK." But no, they make these comments about "changing things up" and "dysfunctional culture"—what are people supposed to think? Lack of transparency, it sucks. And the probation officers, they say the same thing [about the lack of transparency]! 'Cause they're the ones that have to deal with us. You know, someone told the probation officers that I was going to be a problem. Everyone said it at those town hall meetings, "The community perception of probation will have the effect at YSB"—not me. I didn't say that the probation people were assholes, or anything like that! Never said that! What I said is that "this is the way the community perceives you!" And none of them, not Carrie Donnelly, Robin [Trotter], or Judge Randall acknowledged that there could be a problem or that confidentiality could be a problem—like that's Psychology 101.

As discussed above, Donnelly and Trotter went out of their way after heated exchanges to relieve Daniels's worries about the changes. Daniels read these gestures as both genuine and as presenting the friendly face of social control in an attempt to avoid conflict and reconcile differences. Considering these efforts by officials as a kind of cultural performance makes it possible to understand the "Bloomington face" as a form of pacification. By quelling conflict and coding hegemonic discourses in the local rhetoric of consensus, officials tried to win the hearts and minds of local critics through convincing them that their concerns would, in fact, be taken into consideration in the expansion they opposed.

Conclusion

The participation of many county government representatives in both official and community forums and other actions by that government suggested that local politics was accessible and accountable. Yet the openness of the process and the rhetoric of consensus belied operations of power and knowledge that could circumvent, preempt, and otherwise neutralize radical political opposition. Public comment periods at official meetings were infringed on by comments from the very officials who were supposedly soliciting public input. When activists and others challenged carceral expansion, officials were forced to listen but could have the final word, often adjusting the critique to fit within the vision of expansion. The presence of politicians at DMC meetings signified their willingness to meet on more neutral territory but also altered the tenor and content of the meetings. Activists lost control of meetings and found themselves deferring to local officials, thus ceding framing, tone, and discourse to them. Unsurprisingly, then, these meetings were opportune times for officials to try to assuage anxieties, respond to critiques, and shift the discussion onto a technocratic discursive terrain that other meeting attendees found difficult to navigate.

These examples also point to the relationships—which at times seemed very fluid—among county and city government bodies, criminal justice institutions, civic leaders, and the nonprofit sector. Frequently, all of them worked together with the mission of making policy and practice more humane and efficient, yet their collaboration had the consequence, whether intended or not, of ensuring that their voices remained dominant in the meaning-making processes of county discourse and the decision-making processes of county politics.

Contesting the Carceral

The story I have told in these pages has mapped out some of the contours of Monroe County's carceral habitus as it animated continued efforts to expand the criminal justice system. Focusing my efforts mostly on examining the circulation of dominant discourses of incarceration, I have offered only glimpses into how the terrain of habitus was contested and only briefly discussed those moments when people intervened in and disrupted the would-be hegemonic discourses of carceral expansion. In the final chapter and the conclusion, I step away from my analysis of liberal carceral habitus to provide a more robust examination of local resistance and conduct a more theoretical and political treatment of it. In chapter 8, I look primarily at one group, Decarcerate Monroe County (DMC), and the resistance its members articulated and engendered among other community members. The conclusion then considers the contested landscape of alternatives in the county. This ends the book with an analysis of some practical and radical interventions into both political decision-making processes and justice practices.

This part of the study addresses the most difficult terrain for me as a scholar, given my involvement with DMC. I remain confident that committed subjectivity is not a ground for the dismissal of scholarship but rather can offer important detailed, in-depth and complex accounts of social phenomena. That said, committed subjectivity requires of the scholar-activist a commitment to transparency and reflexivity as well as the ability to write through the complexities of both being an activist and being in the field.

PART 4

Contesting the Carceral

8

Organizing against Expansion

Decarcerate Monroe County (DMC) was formed in the summer of 2008 after several months of conversations among a growing group of concerned residents. Beginning in the early spring of that year, people had met with growing regularity to discuss interventions into the justice campus conversation in the community. The initial conversations among four activists, including me, quickly became larger meetings. In May of 2008, a small group organized a day of popular education about the prison-industrial complex and the justice campus that drew over seventy participants, including several politicians and judges.

DMC included people with varying experiences of community organizing and activism and with different political orientations, albeit a shared skepticism of liberalism. Several people involved with DMC were concurrently engaged in ecological defense work against the construction of Interstate 69, known as the NAFTA superhighway because it connected the countries involved in the North American Free Trade Agreement. To an extent, some of these activists attended DMC meetings to gain a better understanding of the linkages between antijail and antiglobalization work. One DMC activist, Michaela Davis, astutely noted to me that "incarceration is the common denominator linking struggles. It is a plane of contestation on its own, but also the site at which seemingly disparate struggles converge because it is a locus of repression and control."

Other people involved with DMC had longer histories of prison activism, most notably with Critical Resistance (CR), a national organization dedicated to the abolition of the prison-industrial complex. CR had arisen out of conversations and collaborations among activists challenging the idea that police and prisons were solutions to social problems deeply embedded in the structural conditions of the United States. The group organized major conferences in Berkeley in 1998, New York City in 2001 (which I attended as a college student), New Orleans in 2003, and Oakland in 2008, drawing thousands of people to each gathering. CR is a chapter-based organization, which means that groups develop region-specific campaigns and projects that both inform and are informed by CR's analysis.[1]

DMC's connection to CR would prove important for a number of reasons. CR at times served as a conduit for DMC's articulation of the justice campus as one site among many in the diverse manifestations of the prison-industrial complex. CR also fostered DMC's understanding of itself as part of a broader, even transnational, network of resistance. Moreover, CR's explicitly abolitionist politics would prove invaluable for DMC's formation of its own identity and its development of a local alternative framework through which to criticize the justice campus.

DMC coalesced around the goal of stopping the justice campus as a solution to the human rights crisis of overcrowding at the adult jail and the absence of a local youth facility. But that focus was located in a broader discursive and political context of challenging the narrative that carceral expansion imbued with the right values would be in line with the progressive identity of the community. DMC strategically couched much of its practical critique in a larger abolitionist vision of reducing Monroe County's reliance on what DMC members called "cages, coercion, and confinement." This broader context would prove crucial to DMC's remaining an active voice in community discussions of social control, as the tabling of the justice campus proposal simply meant that new initiatives surfaced, such as the changes to the Youth Services Bureau (YSB).

Yet for DMC to focus on abolition brought with it various internal and external challenges. The group had to negotiate strategic and political differences in its members' orientations to radical politics, consistently struggled to prioritize the voices and needs of the people most affected by incarceration, and had to navigate through the largely uncharted territory of organizing against incarceration when its advocates were primarily members of the local community's liberal and progressive establishment. Indeed, officials' embrace of therapeutic justice and rehabilitation and active critique of punishment presented a formidable challenge to organizers against jail expansion. Organizers had to refine their analysis of the state and punishment to articulate a coherent critique of allegedly benevolent municipal criminal justice.

Moreover, organizers encountered discursive and strategic challenges when county officials spoke not only of rehabilitation and human rights but also of debate, consensus, and public opinion. Thus, community organizers faced campaigns that relied on liberal discourses of incarceration to envision carceral expansion and the rhetoric of democratic process and community consensus to legitimate them.

The success of carceral habitus—the degree to which a belief in carceral expansion through institutions and supposed alternatives was often unshakeable—raises important questions related to a theoretically informed understanding of resistance to it. Pierre Bourdieu argued that within habitus are different dispositions: heterodoxy, orthodoxy, and doxa. According to him, doxa refers to the self-evidentiary appearance of the social world; in contrast to orthodox or heterodox beliefs that involve different or antagonistic belief structures, doxa is the unquestioned and unquestionable adherence to a "world of tradition experienced as a 'natural world' and taken for granted" (1977, 164). Were persistent attempts at carceral expansion in Bloomington an example of doxa? That is, did the possibility of radically reducing reliance on carceral institutions operate outside of the boundaries of available discourse? Or did carceral habitus operate through a form of orthodoxy, in which officials and others in the community who supported carceral expansion understood it as the best choice among other options, including shrinking community reliance on incarceration?

I argue that aspects of carceral habitus in the local context operated as both orthodoxy and doxa. Officials in favor of carceral expansion certainly understood that they had choices when it came to planning for the future of incarceration and youth detention. Indeed, by positioning the justice campus in contrast to mass incarceration, officials demonstrated their understanding of the diverse iterations of and beliefs about institutions. Crucially, however, my fieldwork also suggests that the universe of discourse operating among county officials and civic leaders would have included only carceral responses to the perceived carceral crises of jail overcrowding and lack of local youth detention had it not been for DMC's insistence on reducing community reliance on incarceration and detention.

It was the work of DMC, then, to bring the undiscussable into the discussion. In certain periods of time, the group succeeded in enacting counterhegemonic understandings of key issues. In making abolitionist change discussable, DMC contributed to what Bourdieu sees as nothing short of the beginning of political consciousness. He writes that if one accepts Karl Marx's position in *The German Ideology* (Marx and Engels 1970) that "language is real, practical consciousness," then "it can be seen that the boundary between the universe of (orthodox or heterodox) discourse and the universe of doxa, in the twofold sense of what goes without saying and what cannot be said for lack of an available discourse, represents the dividing-line between the most radical form of misrecognition and the awakening of political consciousness" (Bourdieu 1977, 170).

I have broken down the constitutive moments of DMC's intervention into three categories, an analytical tactic that runs the risk of damaging the distinct and indeed mutually constitutive nature of the ideas expressed within the categories I have created. Where relevant, I try to point to the moments where DMC's actions and discursive interventions traverse these analytic categories. Nevertheless, looking through transcripts and my field notes revealed that critical interventions into the carceral discourse occurred through three thematic means. First, DMC directly challenged liberal logics of benevolent carcerality, including offering counternarratives about decarceration. Second, activists contested county processes of knowledge production and political decision making. In addition to offering direct criticisms of these processes at county events, activists attempted to embody the structures of decision making and knowledge production that they wished to see more broadly. For example, internal DMC meetings used a consensus approach to decision making and followed a number of guidelines to facilitate the use of processes that relied neither on hierarchy nor on oppression. DMC used similar approaches at the larger, community forums that the group organized, including orchestrating the geography of the meeting room to reflect egalitarian principles. In contrast to county-organized meetings, in which there was always some demarcation between officials and the public, DMC intentionally constructed circles at most meetings.[2] Third, DMC strategically engaged in the practice of reframing issues otherwise central to the success of carceral expansion. This practice at times succeeded in injecting counterhegemonic understanding into the circulating discourse.

Challenging Liberal Logics

Official meetings about carceral expansion afforded local leaders important privileges. The justice campus hearings included officials at the front of county chambers who played the role of host and facilitator. Other officials also lined the benches that were set aside for members of the public in the audience, which allowed officials to offer public comment. The spatial distribution of official bodies throughout the room and the strategic distribution of official perspectives throughout the proceedings allowed dominant narratives of expansion to flourish. Officials at the front of the room could frame meeting agendas at the beginning but rely on other officials to make public comments to neutralize perspectives that were not aligned with expansion.

Activists and other community residents described the hearings as "farcical" and "scripted." Interestingly, despite this acknowledgment of the meetings' nature and their imposing and formal spatial arrangements, some of DMC's more powerful interventions occurred during public comments at the meetings. In these moments, activists often used personal stories to explicitly criticize the county's perspective. In leveling devastating critiques through narrative accounts, activists no doubt found meaning in sharing their personal stories but also expressed an epistemological challenge to what DMC saw as a depersonalized and disembodied official narrative.

One of DMC's tactics was to respond to the rhetoric of treatment, rehabilitation, and programming with the rhetoric of detention and incarceration, challenging the assertions of justice campus supporters that there were large and important distinctions between treatment on the one hand and incarceration on the other hand.[3] In chapter 7, I discussed Shawn Ryland's comments at the first justice campus hearing, about relationships with youth. With those comments, Ryland began to articulate a second approach that DMC would continue to use in later meetings: the question of why programming must be tied to an institutional context.

Ryland framed his comments by his experiences of working with youth at one of the local high schools. At the third hearing about the justice campus, which focused on the jail, DMC member Emily Collins recited a history of alcoholism, wealth, and incarceration in her family to illustrate the linkages between jail, poverty, and addiction:

My name is Emily Collins, and I'm a member of a group called DMC. I joined that group for a number of reasons. My family has a long history of generational recidivism. My great-grandfather was an alcoholic, but a wealthy alcoholic, so he spent very little time in jail. My grandfather, his son, was a middle-class alcoholic and spent increasingly more time in jail. My uncles, his sons, were alcoholics and drug addicts, but they were very poor so they spent years and years in jail. My cousins and brothers are already spending time in jail. I've witnessed firsthand that the fastest way to ensure that somebody is going to spend time in jail is to send them there in the first place or send their parents to jail. And I've seen this happen. It seems like the longer the problem goes down the generational line without somebody treating it, the younger it starts in the next generation. I've noticed that jail doesn't work, yet other programs are not as heavily funded as jails are. . . . . You don't sentence people to treatment, you sentence them to jail time. That doesn't work. I've noticed firsthand it's not effective. And the reason I've joined this group that is trying to stop this jail from happening is that I strongly believe in one of the demands: that we must treat drug addiction, not criminalize it. I'm not talking about simply reducing recidivism, but about not sending sick people to jail in the first place.

Collins's personal account of addiction and incarceration across generations made important arguments about the criminalization and targeting of the poor.[4] Crucially, she positioned her account in contrast to the prevailing narrative that offered the justice campus as precisely the place where people like her relatives should be treated. In what seemed to be an anticipation of that response from the panel, Collins closed her statements by saying that treating addiction must mean not sending people to jail in the first place.

Most advocates of the justice campus pointed to poverty's overwhelming role in incarceration through softly pathologizing poor people, a process Khalil Muhammad has called "writing crime into class" (2010, 229). This construction of poverty had the added bonus of granting legitimacy to the curative and benevolent facility that advocates imagined as having a role in poor people's rehabilitation. In contrast, DMC activists like Collins worked hard to problematize normative definitions of crime, to delink criminality from poverty, push for noninstitutional and nonpunitive ways to approach social problems, and demonstrate the ways that the criminal justice system targeted poor people.

During the same meeting, DMC's cofounder, Michaela Davis, commented on the problematic structure of probation fees:

> Currently, the fees of people who are on probation pay the salaries of probation officers. This creates a perverse incentive structure so that probation officers need to maintain high amounts of people on probation in order to be sure their salaries are paid. I think it's broadly recognized that this is a bad incentive structure, but there's no other funding that is coming through, and if we can't provide the funding to change that kind of incentive structure, I'm curious how we will have the funding available after we build a larger jail. I think changing that probation funding is one of those small institutional steps that we could take to change the causes of overcrowding. I think there are lots of other ones.

In this statement, Davis revealed an insidious material arrangement within the system: probationer fees funded the probation department's personnel costs. As Davis pointed out, this incentivized the system's growth.[5] She made her comments to subvert the very foundation of the justice campus: to accommodate the size of the system. Davis pointed out how the system's structure produced the problems that required expansion. In proposing real, practical, and small steps to shrink the system and thus alleviate those problems, she artfully framed an abolitionist analysis to fit the reformist context of the meeting.

Problematizing Process: Invisibility

In addition to direct challenges to the articulation of liberal carcerality, DMC members also confronted what they perceived to be the problematic process by which the county operated. One way they challenged the dominant subjectivity of spaces and the committed epistemologies of practitioners and consultants was by hosting their own meetings and privileging the voices of counterexperts: the people and families most affected by carceral policies. Another way, perhaps just as important to their contestation, was to directly challenge the process—namely, officials' claims that there was a community consensus in favor of building the campus and the obvious absence of people most affected by carceral practices.

John Thompson's study of ideology, in particular his claim that "to study ideology is to study the ways in which meaning (signification) serves to sustain relations of domination" (1984, 131), provides an important theoretical context for understanding DMC's passionate attempts to challenge official process. He writes: "What may have seemed like a sphere of effective *consensus* must in many cases be seen as a realm of actual or potential *conflict*. Hence the meaning of what is said—what is asserted in spoken or written discourse as well as that *about which* one speaks or writes—is infused with forms of power; different individuals or groups have a differential capacity *to make a meaning stick*" (ibid., 132). Thompson's claim that ideology attaches meaning to relations of domination points out the importance of local contests to Monroe County's political process. As earlier chapters showed, there can be no doubt that different local individuals and groups had differentiated ability to shape the discourse. But absent DMC's interventions into and through official processes, the expansionist narrative would likely have enjoyed an uncontested hegemony.

Julia Paley's work offers empirical support to Thompson's claims. In her study of postdictatorship Chile, Paley notes the difficulties communities faced in articulating and achieving their goals when the language and process of democracy was used to limit the range of what could be said: "Citizens and community organizations were thereby faced with the strategic question of how to achieve their goals when the practice of discussion and debate and a language of consensus were used to deter them; they faced the challenge, that is, of determining what sorts of actions to take when the limits of discussion's effectiveness had been reached" (2004, 498).

DMC faced a similar dilemma, and comments in the pages that follow clearly indicate that challenging the decision-making processes occupied a position of importance in the group's overall campaign to defeat carceral expansion. At times, it appeared that DMC was just as concerned with ensuring the integration into the discussion, and even privileging, of voices of those county residents most affected by county criminal justice policies—that is, the county's most marginalized residents—as the group was with articulating a particular abolitionist vision. In criticizing the processes of the justice campus and the YSB, activists poignantly contrasted the inclusion of outside consultants and the exclusion of the local community.

Although the Monroe County Criminal Justice Coordinating Council (MCCJCC) facilitated the justice campus process with the cooperation of a number of different individuals and agencies, DMC directed much of its criticism at Program Administration and Results, Inc. (PARI), the corrections consultant. This made some sense on both emotional and political grounds, with a prison and jail construction firm from outside of the community being a rather easy target for activists' derision. But while criticizing PARI and the process in a public meeting served the important purpose of intervening in a narrative that suggested the justice campus was the product of community consensus, it was not necessarily the shrewdest strategy. As the history of carceral expansion in the county demonstrates, consultants came and went, but the county habitus that made the justice campus possible persisted. Had DMC challenged the naturalized local logics that made the hiring of PARI common sense, the group might have been more effective in destabilizing the habitus.

At the MCCJCC hearing about the juvenile facility, DMC member Helen Bishop, who later would run for city council, challenged those defending the justice campus:

> I don't know why we have a company here that makes money from building these facilities. Why don't we have people who build YMCAs and youth centers at the table, too—different perspectives from people who don't benefit from building the kinds of facilities that we're going to build? And really to get youth at the table, too—why don't we have youth who have been through the system, that [sic] can present the challenges that they had? What are their ideas? What do they want to see? What do they see as important? I'd really be interested in knowing what the next step is. Can we move this forward and instead of politicians making these decisions [have] more of the community members? I know you guys said you've been working on this for years, but whom [sic] are you including in the conversation? Are you including leaders in the community? People from different walks of life? How can we change this conversation to include everybody? And what's the next step? Can we keep talking about this? Are you guys just having these meetings as a write-off: "OK, we've

talked to the public, now let's go build a facility"? What's your plan, what's [*sic*] your thoughts about where [the conversation] is gonna go?

In her suggestions that PARI should not even be at the meetings and that other entities that build recreational facilities should be present instead, Bishop made a powerful rhetorical move that destabilized the popular narrative that jails and detention had to serve as the institutional homes for programs. Moreover, she questioned the officials present about who they considered to be an important part of the process and who was and should have been included in the conversation. Toward the end of her remarks, where she explicitly asked if the public process was a façade, Bishop touched on a potentially sensitive and controversial issue, but she may have put her finger on the truth. As I mentioned in the last chapter, Bridget Markham, a disaffected former member of the county council, said to me in an interview that she was sure what Bishop called a "write-off" had occurred.

At the third MCCJCC hearing, which focused on the jail, DMC member Ruth Laurel addressed Richard Kemp, PARI's cofounder and codirector, directly:

> I heard you speaking a lot tonight about what "we" have told you that we want. You've said over and over "you want this" and "you want that." but I and a lot of people that I know have not talked to you and have not had an opportunity to have our interests known, and it really bothers me to have someone tell me what I want when they have not talked to me. So that goes for a lot of people in Bloomington and a lot of the people that those people know. It's not clear to me who in the community—regular citizens—has been a part of that process.

Laurel pointed out that the "you" to whom PARI referred constituted a narrow segment of the local population, largely members of the business, political, and criminal justice professional class. Thus, the consensus to which Kemp referred existed among members of the county criminal justice establishment. Themes that emerged from Kemp's conversations with people were of a limited nature by design and certainly did not reflect—at least, not necessarily so—the wishes or analyses of the larger community.

In a similar comment, Dave Santiago, a member of DMC, questioned the premise that PARI should have conversations with anyone, regardless of how limited or inclusive they might have been: "I don't think it's appropriate either that when someone [comments to the panel] 'we want to have dialogue with all these different kinds of people' then the response is 'well, the PARI corporate representative who profits off of prisons and jails has talked to those people, so you know, rest easy.' *We* need to talk to those people; we don't need to talk to [Kemp]. He shouldn't even be in the room until we, as a community, have decided what we want." The county commissioners, the county's political executives, hired PARI. Given the integral role that PARI played in the official public meetings about the justice campus, it is clear that local officials saw the company as part of the community's decision-making process. For Santiago and other DMC activists, the presence of consultants delegitimized any claim of objectivity by the county. Moreover, the use of consultants who profited off of jail expansion supported DMC's attempts to situate county carceral expansion as part of the prison-industrial complex.

One final example provides an especially poignant illustration of the difference in orientations to county decision-making processes. DMC member Haley Ralston spoke after Laurel at the third MCCJCC meeting. Ralston was speaking about the ways in which the jail acted like a debtor's prison when she mentioned, almost offhandedly, that people most affected by jail policies were not part of the process. Tom Grady, the MCCJCC chair and hearing facilitator, interrupted to ask her to clarify what she meant:

> GRADY: And by that do you mean the inmates or the people who get
> arrested, or . . . what do you mean by the people most affected?
> RALSTON: Yes and yes and the people on probation and the people
> who deal with day reporting and the people who have families who
> deal with those things and who are so obviously underrepresented
> in these forums that the focus of the questions about who knows
> anything about jail is phrased as a question of "who has been on a
> tour?" That's a problem for me. 'Cause that really speaks to the fact
> that we aren't representative of the voices of the people who will be
> affected by the systems you all are creating. However, those systems

are being created with my money and all of our money and all of
our resources and space and our energy, but that also comes from
those people we are hoping to affect, so if we don't know who they
even are—other than a one-day snapshot from 2007—who's in jail,
what for, how long, and we're not making room for people to tell us
themselves, then I'm not gonna be able to feel OK about any proposal
for any changes to the correctional system other than letting people
go until we have communication and you all can demonstrate that
you've really done your research about who you have in your hands
and whose lives you're taking apart.

Ralston astutely noted the expressed assumptions of the hearing's
organizers: that attendees would know the jail only through tours, as
opposed to having been incarcerated or having a family member incarcerated there. In their considerations of who had access to community
meetings, who wanted to attend, and who should care, officials excluded
those people most affected by criminal justice policies. Moreover, in that
exclusion, officials also made marginal other ways of experiencing jail,
including as a prisoner or a prisoner's loved one. According to officials'
construction of who should be and who was in the room for the discussion of the jail, the only way one could know the jail was through being
a practitioner or a volunteer, or by going on a tour.[6]

Problematizing Process: Knowledge Claims

Ralston's critical intervention into the notion that hearing attendees
would know the jail only through a tour suggests another plane of
contest on which DMC engaged: challenging official epistemologies.
The group offered confounding and contradictory examples, demonstrating differences of opinion within the group about official county
knowledge and perhaps different orientations to the concept of criticizing epistemology. In short, DMC's contesting of knowledge claims was
uncoordinated and, to a certain extent, unplanned. Crucially, according to some scholarship on resistance—particularly on New Social
Movement theory—the diversity of views and different articulations
of politics within and between groups is not necessarily a liability, but
rather an indication of "radical democracy."[7]

One recurring critique interrogated the statistics on which the county based much of its official positions on the existing jail and the justice campus. These data were called "the one-day snapshot" (mentioned by Ralston above) and provided a glance at the composition of the jail on a single day during the summer of 2007. This information served as the backdrop for a number of meetings I attended during my time in the field, including the second MCCJCC justice campus hearing, where Judge Allan Barrett made an hour-long statement "educating the public." During the second hour of that hearing, a number of commentators focused on Barrett and the assumptions behind and implications of his data. I include first a short exchange that broke up the comments by Chris Schuyler. Although seemingly insignificant, this DMC activist's refusal to give his name illustrated a symbolic rejection on the part of some radical organizers to recognize the public record:

CHRIS SCHUYLER: First, I'd like to start—and I hope you'll join me in thanking the people from Community Access Television Services for being here because, unlike this person sitting next to Judge Barrett who was back there yelling at them at the beginning of the meeting, I think you're doing a great job and thanks for being here. The second comment is about the nature of these meetings in general.

TOM GRADY: Excuse me, could you give your name?

SCHUYLER: No. The second comment is these meetings are farcical. These are not meetings to gain public opinion. PARI obviously already has these plans drawn up. They presented to us tonight not what *we* think but what *they* think and what they want *us* to think about criminal justice in Monroe County. If they actually cared what we think, then we'd have a public referendum, which they're completely unwilling to do because they know that the average citizen of Monroe County won't stand for this kind of crap. The third comment is for Judge Barrett. In sociology departments all over the world there is required reading, a book called *How to Lie with Statistics*. And I would urge Judge Barrett to read that book because what he did tonight was not an objective presentation of facts, but rather a subjective analysis of a minuscule amount of data that he was trying to prove to us was the general trend of all of Monroe County all of the time. It was one day, it was his analysis of the facts, and it's not what's actually going on.

This excerpt demonstrates layers of interventionist critique embedded in a single, minute-long testimony. Schuyler acutely deconstructed Judge Barrett's misuse of statistics, claiming that Barrett was simply wielding what little data he had to support the project of carceral expansion. In refusing to provide his name, Schuyler stole a moment of power from hearing organizers, rejecting the air of legitimacy that granting his name to the official record would have provided.

The following speaker was a long-time local activist named Matthew Harrison. He also addressed Barrett's misuse of statistics and its implication for local knowledge. In contrast to Schuyler's approach, Harrison challenged Barrett on his own epistemological turf:

> First of all, Barrett's statistics . . . are very incomplete, and I'm embarrassed to live in a county that spends tens and tens of millions of dollars on its criminal justice system and civil justice system that still can't generate statistics that our county was able to generate back in the 1940s. So if your computer system isn't up to snuff, how about hiring a work study, how about letting somebody from one of the local organizations that's interested in this topic as they have for years and years and years volunteer to access this information, how about opening up the public records and the jail log so that people can analyze it? We have people who can scan that data and generate the data that Judge Barrett says that we don't have the technological advance to generate. It's embarrassing to hear that every year, year after year, and decade after decade. I do not believe that the county or the criminal justice system has any business coming to the citizenry of Monroe County without those statistics, because there is no possibility for a rational, or evidence-based, scientific analysis [to be] generated without those facts.

With this last sentence, between "rational" and "evidenced-based, scientific analysis," Harrison paused briefly and turned to Barrett, holding his hand out to indicate that his usage of this language was specifically aimed at Barrett's own reliance on such concepts. While the ultimate point of Harrison's criticism was similar to Schuyler's point—namely, that the statistics on which the county relied were misleading and inhibited any kind of informed discussion—Harrison diverged sharply from Schuyler's dismissal of the proceedings as farcical and stopped short of implying malicious intent on the part of Barrett. Rather, Harrison endorsed the need for more robust and sophisticated statistical techniques, which he argued could provide more complex and reliable understandings of the county's needs.

In directly confronting both the invisibility of certain populations during official proceedings and official knowledge claims, activists called attention to the symbolic power of place and language, an important plane of contestation.[8]

Visibility and Epistemology: The Free Voices Project

DMC tried to model the visibility and accountability that the group found lacking in official processes. This commitment took on various forms. DMC held meetings in locations and at times its members thought would be more convenient for those whose voices were underrepresented in official proceedings; used consensus processes and horizontal decision making, an attempt to embody a nonhierarchical structure;[9] and conducted community canvassing to encourage people to attend community meetings. While the group had inconsistent successes with these attempts, it did formalize some of its concerns about process into a formal campaign, called the Free Voices Project.

The Free Voices Project began early in DMC's life, during the summer of 2008. The group modeled the Free Voices Project on a composite of storytelling projects in various cities and the work of other incarceration-related organizations that used media to present the narratives of prisoners and their families.[10] Based on a series of meetings focused on developing the project, DMC identified the following goals:

1. *Content*: Creating a community counternarrative of the prison-industrial complex in Bloomington through a process that prioritizes people's experiences, articulates those experiences in people's own words, and facilitates connections between folks traditionally separated by race and class barriers.
2. *Process*: Pursuing these goals through an organizing process that empowers participants; doesn't replicate traditional, hierarchical power dynamics; and that undermines problematic representations of people's voices and experiences.
3. *Political*: Remaining committed to a larger political vision that opposes jail construction, challenges problematic figures in the

criminal justice system, promotes community decarceration, and advocates for alternative models of conflict resolution.

DMC members active in the Free Voices Project primarily attended the twice-a-week all-cellblock visiting hours at the jail. There, family members would gather in an alley on the west side of the building to sign in and then wait, sometimes for many hours, for the cellblock of their loved one to be called for visitation. As chapter 3 describes, this spatial and temporal liminality would become a contested issue following the jail commander's proposal to shift from in-person visitation to videoconferencing as part of a larger renovation to the jail.

The time in the alley proved beneficial to the Free Voices Project. DMC members would spend hours talking with people waiting to visit jail inmates. At various times, DMC members administered surveys and conducted in-depth interviews, using audio recorders when possible and when people consented. The time spent in the alley also served to complicate, and alter, DMC's campaigns. Frequently, people in the alley cited police practices, arbitrary probation policies, and drug and alcohol problems, including the absence of diverse programming, as their central concerns. While DMC kept its overall focus on challenging jail expansion and promoting decarceration, conversations in the alley ultimately diversified the group's focus. By recording visitors' testimonies, DMC could relay their perspectives directly to people in power, challenging both official content and epistemology and in the process making "visible" those who official processes had ignored.[11] As discussed in a previous chapter, one especially powerful recording occurred when DMC members Dave Santiago and Victor Whitney recorded testimonies about the changes to jail visitation practices. As noted above, a local community radio station gave DMC digital audio recorders and then broadcast the edited recording. DMC members also went to county commission meetings and read excerpts of the testimonies to the commissioners.

Radical Reframing

In its attempt to bring into the discussion the previously undiscussable, DMC had to disrupt hegemonic definitions of concepts and situations central to expansion. In forcing community members, including politicians, to reflect on what brought about individual and community safety, for example, DMC successfully disrupted a rather narrow linear narrative that connected safety to a robust criminal justice system.

In moving from the direct confrontational approach that I profiled in the previous sections to this section's focus on DMC's counterhegemonic articulation of key concepts, I see a mapping out of the distinction between what the social theorists Ernesto Laclau and Chantal Mouffe call the "strategy of opposition" and the "strategy of construction of a new order" (2001, 189). The authors write:

> In the case of the first, the element of negation of a certain social or political order predominates, but this element of negativity is not accompanied by any real attempt to establish different nodal points from which a process of different and positive reconstruction of the social fabric could be instituted—and as a result the strategy is condemned to marginality. . . . In the case of the strategy of construction of a new order, in contrast, the element of social positivity predominates, but this very fact creates an unstable balance and a constant tension with the subversive logic of democracy. (Ibid.)

DMC's first official event, on May 3, 2008, brought together over seventy people, including older activists from Begin Again and Monroe County Justice, activists involved in ecological defense work, leaders of local nonprofits, and several politicians and criminal justice officials. DMC framed the day as one of popular education about the prison-industrial complex and the local justice campus. Not coincidentally, the county primary elections were only days away, and the group had compiled a list of candidates' perspectives on the issues of carceral expansion. Sitting in chairs and on the floor in the back room of a local independent and radical bookstore, DMC organizers led attendees through several different exercises designed both to educate them about local and national histories of incarceration and to foster an open but radically situated discussion— one not confined by official discourses but instead opening realms of possibilities beyond the immediately and bureaucratically practical.

One of the day's first events was a short exercise that I facilitated. The question that DMC posed to attendees was, "What makes our community, and us as individuals, safe?" The response was rapid and enthusiastic, with comments ranging from liberal concerns about equality to radical challenges to liberal categories of sociality. Below is a partial list of what was said during the course of the exercise:

> Knowing neighbors; keeping police out of my neighborhood; food access; green spaces; places to sleep; good paying jobs; social and economic equality; [having] basic needs met; race, gender, and sexual orientation equality; mutuality; no culture of violence; reduce the realm of unknown and unpredictable; communication between conflicting parties; transparency in government; well-lit communities; presumption of innocence; accountability; doing away with the callousness of systems; intentional communities; access to ombudsmen-type resources; strong families; challenging the concept of nuclear family and invisible violence; protection from harmful individuals; community conflict resolution; legal control over one's body; fewer weapons; community autonomy; strong infrastructure; intelligent organization of communities for bikes and walkers; access to clean water.

This exercise, and the context in which it occurred, offers a number of insights into local resistance. First, as would become increasingly clear in the following years, the nature of place and the frame matter. The following fall, when the MCCJCC hosted the four justice campus hearings in official county chambers, DMC members were forced to speak in limited amounts of time, often in response to questions posed by county officials, and had to cede both the opening and closing of each meeting, and thus its framing, to the officials in charge. In contrast, the May 3 event occurred in a radical community space already aligned with community organizing and activism and followed the agenda and framing of its activist organizers. That is, conversations about what kept people safe did not become a rhetorical game of budgets and evidence-based practices. Instead, when officials and civic leaders participated, it was on the rhetorical terrain laid down by DMC.

Second, the framing and content of the conversation that day disturbed what had been fixed ideas for at least a couple of the attendees. As Brian Mulvaney, the county council member, confirmed to me over a year later during our interview, it was that very conversation about

safety that he credited with disrupting his own understandings of policing and incarceration. He found himself asking critical questions about
whether and how the police bring safety and about whether more cells
and more police necessarily equal a safer community. Mulvaney would
remain supportive of the justice campus, but he credited DMC's organizing with forcing him to reevaluate his logic and ultimately leading
him to publicly deride PARI's report.

Embedded in Mulvaney's and others' testimonies about the power of
that exercise is a valuable lesson for the articulation of radical positions
in spaces where there is potential for liberal co-optation of them. DMC
did not focus its work that day on convincing attendees about the need
to abolish the prison-industrial complex, at least not directly. The word
"abolition" was not mentioned until an evening presentation by a member of CR before a smaller group of people, most of whom were activists.
Rather, the day focused on problematizing the constitutive elements of
the justice campus and thinking about creative alternatives to expansion. In this way, DMC followed the advice of Sarah Rubin—a member
of both DMC and CR—to "describe the ingredients of the *kreplach* without mentioning the *kreplach*," invoking a timeless Yiddish joke about
reducing fear of the unknown.[12]

Third, this exercise and the conversation it fostered connected DMC
and the local community to national and even transnational networks
of activists. The idea of reframing issues of safety to disrupt the narrative that equated safety with more police and prisons came from activist
trainings that some DMC members had participated in with CR, the
Prison Moratorium Project, and other national groups. Realizing that
fighting jail expansion in a Midwestern and liberal community didn't
isolate DMC's members, but rather connected them to communities
around the country and beyond, proved to be a motivating and energiz-
ing factor for the group. On the night of May 3, after a full day of work-
shops, a national organizer with CR spoke to the remaining attendees.
Large pieces of paper from the day's discussions still lined the walls of
the back room. During the organizer's talk that evening, she glanced
around the room, silently taking in the content that the workshop had
produced, and noted: "I've been to Argentina, Brazil, and everywhere
these conversations [about safety] are the same." Four months later, in
September 2008, ten DMC members traveled together to CR's tenth

anniversary in Oakland, California, to speak on a panel with groups from other communities about their respective campaigns against jail expansion.

Radical reframing of issues was not confined to DMC-hosted meetings. Indeed, the YSB meetings during the fall of 2009 discussed in previous chapters demonstrated that even activist-hosted meetings could be dominated by official discourses and narratives. Similarly, in formal meeting spaces DMC was successful in challenging some of the premises of the justice campus and calling attention to problematic processes. But there were also moments when a single comment disrupted the trajectory of a meeting, intervening in and subsequently reshaping the overall discourse. This occurred at the first MCCJCC meeting, with Ryland's discussion about the importance of relationships (quoted in part above). Ryland went on to say:

> Is it a fifteen-year-old's fault when their [*sic*] parents leave their liquor on the counter and the kids get into it? They're fifteen years old, they have access to alcohol, they're curious, they see it on television, they know what goes on down at IU [Indiana University] Bloomington, and so they get into the liquor cabinet, right? So now they're a case, they're no longer a kid. I think that the building of relationships is key—I can't stress that enough. I have volunteers that I work with who spend ridiculous amounts of time with teenagers. We go on trips, we have large group meetings, I go to the schools and I'm in the lunchrooms and I see the world, the culture, of teens today and I'm speaking from my experience. This is what I live, fifty to sixty hours a week. These kids, their relationships are broken. They probably come from homes where their parents' relationships are broken, and they come to school and it's pretty easy for kids to get lost in the shuffle at the local high schools. It's really easy, actually. And if you're not an athlete, and you're not a musician, and you don't have something to do after school, you go home and Mom and Dad are at work, then you've got a couple of hours to kill all by yourself. And what if there are cigarettes in Mom's top drawer, alcohol laying around on the countertop? What if you live in a neighborhood where there are adults out on the porch, and they're making drug deals? Our kids are surrounded by opportunities for failure; they're not surrounded by opportunities for success, they're not surrounded by relationships with positive adults. You have to pay to go

to Rhino's [an all-ages music venue], you have to pay to go to a football game at Bloomington North or Bloomington South, they have to pay to hang out at their school on a Friday night. You have to pay to go to band concerts. What if I don't have any money? What if I'm a kid and I don't have any money, and I want to do something on Friday night 'cause I desperately want to get out of the trailer park? Where am I gonna go? Again, if I don't have any money there's not that many options for me. Bowling alleys, movie theaters, these places where kids can go and be kids, be social and develop relationships, make their mistakes and learn from them. There isn't a space, a quality space for them to do that. And I believe the best space for them to do that in is within the space of a relationship with an adult. So that's what I'm doing. I'm working real hard to build more relationships with kids so they can make their mistakes, they can learn, they can grow, they can stay out of institutions that after ten days become counterproductive.

I include Ryland's comments at length in this section for several reasons. Interestingly, his comments are not necessarily politically radical. In fact, his focus on opportunities for deviance in the household ("liquor on the counter"), the absence of parental controls ("Mom and Dad are at work . . . cigarettes in Mom's top drawer"), social disorganization of the community and learning from deviants ("What if you live in a neighborhood where there are adults out on the porch, and they're making drug deals?"), and lack of money and the resulting aimlessness ("What if I'm a kid and I don't have any money, and I want to do something on Friday night 'cause I desperately want to get out of the trailer park?") invoked several of the more traditional theories of crime and delinquency of the twentieth century.[13] Although Ryland's comments did not offer a radical political intervention into the narrative of youth crime, they did destabilize the conventional discussion of how to respond to it. Rather than focusing on challenging the justice campus or suggesting alternative institutions or programs, Ryland proposed a wholly different sense of what young people need. Moreover, his comments clearly resonated with many people in attendance and offered an alternative point of reference and departure. For the rest of the evening, many subsequent speakers invoked his comments to ground their own articulations of resistance to the justice campus.

There were also moments during county meetings when DMC's work to disrupt the county narrative bore fruit in the words and actions of former justice campus supporters. One such moment, which also occurred at the first justice campus hearing, may have a larger significance in the historical context of carceral expansion and resistance in the county. The MCCJCC justice campus hearings occurred in the fall of 2008, which followed DMC's work in the spring and summer that included organizing community meetings and speaking out about alternatives to building a justice campus. One local community activist already engaged in the issue was Olivia Krasny, the civic leader and a citizen appointee to the MCCJCC, who for decades had been a primary supporter of the construction of a youth facility. In fact, people in the community who opposed construction of the jail that was built in 1986 referred to it as "Olivia's jail" because of the energy she had expended to see it built and the conviction with which she had participated in the discourse of rehabilitation and human rights. At the first MCCJCC hearing in the fall of 2008, after various people made comments offering support for or resistance to the proposal, Krasny approached the podium. After she described her history of work on the issue and the primacy of providing programming, the following exchange occurred:

> OLIVIA KRASNY: How many young people really do we need to detain, who in your opinion need to be in secure facilities?
> PATRICK RANDALL: We averaged just over seven [detained youth] last year, and that figure I don't think will be exceeded this year.
> KRASNY (*speaking slowly and deliberately*): Do we really need to build a facility to detain seven people?
> (*Applause*)

This would seem to be a highly significant moment of disjuncture in the overarching history of carceral expansion in the county. Here was a civic leader who at various times had been involved in local business, politics, and nonprofit administration, and who perhaps more than anyone had been the face of liberal carceral expansionism for the past three decades in the county, asking in front of critics and on television why the community needed a secure facility for such a small number of young people in need of secure placement.

In reflecting on this moment, Michaela Davis attributed Krasny's analysis and courage to speak out to the ways DMC had consistently placed the campus in the broader context of mass incarceration. In doing so, Davis argued, "we made it possible for some officials [who previously had been ardent expansion supporters] to break from the narrative of community exceptionalism in which the justice campus was a logical outcome." In her experiences in county meetings, Davis commented to me, "the ways that people justified policy and the rhetoric that they feel like they have to fit into in order to support a policy really seems to have this intense Bloomington pride and sense of exceptionalism and also doesn't allow for analysis of power or oppression." Moreover, Davis said that some of this support must stem from people like Krasny, who had been part of social movements and the counterculture and who now occupied political office and other positions of civic leadership. In centering power and oppression in its critique, DMC tried to offer a counterdiscourse of the justice campus, which at times succeeded in replacing the discourse of exceptionalism.

Indeed, after an exchange in which Randall and Grady tried to convince Krasny of the need for the justice campus, and in particular the juvenile facility, Krasny continued her remarks, which seemed to confirm Davis's analysis:

> While we say that we are youth oriented in this community, I actually don't think we are. We don't think much about youth and children in this community, and we don't have the [recreational and social] facilities for them that we need. So I think perhaps we can lead not with this discussion today, but in the community we should revisit [the recreational and social facilities] because that is an unfilled need here and it leads directly to the problems that we have. And finally we have to address the issue, and we can't talk about it as if it's really irrelevant, except that the economic development of this community has never taken into consideration the kinds of people were talking about—people in the jail—the types of jobs to be available, the training available for people. We just don't think about people with fewer capacities who can learn and can develop. We write them off, and it's unfortunate. So we have three conversations going on here, and I hope we don't get too far carried away with the juvenile facility without remembering that we have all those other things to consider as well.

This testimony demonstrates the success of DMC's work as well as the instability of local politics and relations of power. As a member of the MCCJCC and as someone intimately involved in local criminal justice policies for three decades, Krasny had played a significant role in the historical accumulation of local knowledge. She was unquestionably one of the iconic figures in Monroe County civic history (her portrait hangs in Bloomington's City Hall) and had established herself as one of the central players in policy making related to criminal justice, reliably taking the perspective of liberal expansion. Yet here she not only articulated positions that questioned the logic of building a facility, but she also offered a startling analysis that departed from county exceptionalism in stating that the community was not youth oriented. Moreover, her observation about economic development creating classes of surplus workers reoriented the conversation, however fleetingly, away from institutions and to the central problems of exploitation and inequality facing the community.[14]

Insurrectionary Interlude

DMC resisted the justice campus through direct challenges to local carceral practices and processes of decision making, as well as through counterhegemonic constructions of certain key concepts on which carceral expansion was predicated. But there were other ways in which people in the community made their opposition to the discourse and the political process known, including an action that occurred while many people were attending the fourth and final justice campus hearing in the late fall of 2008.

That same evening, perhaps just as Kemp was displaying to attendees his maps of the possibilities for carceral expansion, an anonymous group of individuals calling itself the Bloomington Flat Tire Brigade flattened eight tires on vehicles belonging to the Monroe County Community Corrections Program. The timing of their strike was unmistakable: the group's act of sabotage was meant to display not only local resistance to the proposed justice campus but also defiance of the political process. While DMC members followed the scripted and prescribed ways in which the county accommodated some dissent, the Flat Tire Brigade engaged in an anonymous act of rebellion, refusing to acquiesce to a process akin to Don Mitchell and Lynn Staeheli's "permitted protests": "The tools [used to construct the contemporary landscape of permitted protest] are used not to silence dissent outright, but rather to regulate it in such a way that dissent can be fully incorporated into, and become part of, the liberal democratic state" (2005, 797).

The action by the Flat Tire Brigade communicated both resistance to carceral expansion and to the façade of democratic process embodied in the hearings. An anonymous post to *Infoshop News*, the independent and anarchist news website, relayed the events and the group's analysis:

> In the late hours of Thursday Dec. 11th, the Bloomington Flat Tire Brigade targeted a number of vehicles belonging to Monroe County Community Corrections [Program]. In all, 8 tires were left flaccid, incapacitating most of the fleet of corrections vehicles. Community Corrections in Monroe County is responsible for, among many other things, extracting upwards of $200,000 worth of slave labor out of [the] over-policed and over-incarcerated communities of Monroe County each year.
>
> This action was taken on the night that the jail building consulting firm PARI presented its master plan to the County and the public for an expanded "justice campus." The plan includes a new jail with at least double the capacity of the current one, a youth detention facility, and a community corrections facility all to be housed on the same site (incidentally, the site chosen is the former location of a[n] RCA plant, which long ago left Bloomington for warmer climates (read NAFTA).
>
> We hope that this action: a) ushered in a fun filled weekend of changing tires for the fascists at Community Corrections and b) sent a message to the county that their plans for expansion and imprisonment won't be tolerated.[15]

Through my informants whom I suspected might have relationships with people in the Flat Tire Brigade, I attempted to arrange a meeting with members of the group. Clearly, granting me an interview to talk about a criminal act of sabotage against government property would constitute a risk. Perhaps unsurprisingly, my request was denied.[16]

In targeting community corrections specifically, the group also seemed to symbolically reject the narrative in the community that positioned community corrections and a community corrections ethos at the center of plans for expansion. Indeed, even people critical of the overall justice campus plan often stated their enthusiastic support for work release and other community corrections programs. The Flat Tire Brigade's targeted resistance to "slave labor" extracted by "fascists at [Monroe County] Community Corrections [Program]" and its warning that expansion would not be "tolerated" put forward an insurrectionary and defiant envisioning of the jail and the work release center as equally repressive carceral institutions.

Although infrequent, there were periodic displays of additional confrontational resistance to incarceration. In June 2008, a march began at a gathering of activists to protest Interstate 69. Chanting, drumming, and carrying torches through the streets of downtown Bloomington without a permit, the marchers caught the attention of the police. They wound their way through downtown and ended up outside of the county jail. Another anonymous post to *Infoshop News* relayed what occurred:

> Anti-I69 activists staged a raucous torch-lit march through the streets of downtown Bloomington on Saturday evening to protest the arrest of two tree-sitters and six ground supporters at an I-69 construction site. . . . Torches lit up the night sky at the Saturday action. Activists carried banners, banged drums and set off bottle rockets. Bloomington police remained on the sidelines as activists took the streets. . . . As they passed the jail, activists taunted the police with "no more roads, no more jails," "you can't put our friends in jail, we will drive the final nail," and "we will win!"[17]

The demonstration offered a visible connection between seemingly disparate and unaffiliated campaigns. In addition, the action was notable for the ways it challenged the physical boundaries between incarcerated and nonincarcerated spaces. Both confrontational actions offer important insights into how resistance to local carceral expansion was, in some ways, a challenge to dominant articulations of geographical and cultural boundaries. In the march outside the jail, community activists breached a boundary between incarcerated and free space: according to at least two of my informants, the chanting outside the jail that night elicited noticeable noise from the inside, most likely prisoners banging on the windows—one of the few ways they could communicate to the outside. This activity across the jail boundary raises important questions about the possibilities of contesting spaces of domination and exclusivity. If DMC's presence in county chambers constituted an intervention into the discourse, one perhaps ultimately muted by the politics of the space, the action outside the jail (or, for that matter, the action against community corrections vehicles) suggested other ways (albeit riskier, more confrontational, and perhaps ultimately too decentralized) to construct or occupy counterhegemonic space.[18]

Contests over space and spatial boundaries also can challenge normative definitions of identities.[19] In the actions against community corrections vehicles, which were undeniably illegal, activists demonstrated not only resistance to the justice campus proposal and related proceedings but also contested the boundary between the criminal and the noncriminal. With this action, the Flat Tire Brigade may have articulated its members' identification with the people inside the jail, rather than the people inside the county chambers who were discussing and debating the justice campus. In the case of the march, the protesters at the jail had splintered off from a gathering in protest of Interstate 69. In moving between ecological defense and antiglobalization organizing on the one hand and resistance to the jail on the other hand, activists challenged the bounded nature of classifications and definitions as they symbolically demonstrated the interconnectedness of issues.

While I use these examples to point toward resistance that occurred outside of DMC's organizing, they also suggest a central tension: the different strategic choices groups faced when passionately wanting to disrupt a particular political trajectory. DMC largely abandoned protest and direct action, organizing very little in the way of demonstrations, protests, or civil disobedience. Instead, the group's members organized public education forums, meetings, discussions, and film screenings and attended their fair share of official meetings to challenge power directly. In the Flat Tire Brigade's action on community corrections vehicles, its members may have intended to communicate a message about the limits of DMC's chosen path.

Tensions

DMC organized around abolitionist principles although its materials did not necessarily use the word "abolition." The implications of its identity created tensions, at times productive, within the group as well as in its work in the community. In both cases, tensions often revolved around issues of commensurability. I briefly explored commensurability in chapter 7 when I examined how politicians consistently absorbed radical articulations into liberal concepts to render abolition compatible with the narrative of carceral expansion. But DMC also struggled with issues of commensurability. Often the tension existed in balancing the need to be taken seriously by the liberal public and engaging in actions and using language that placed DMC squarely in what Elizabeth Povinelli (2001) refers to as a "radical world." DMC was committed to abolition as a framework and identity but struggled with what that meant for taking positions on certain policy changes, building coalitions with people or organizations with different politics, formulating strategy and framing positions, and being accountable to the people most affected by criminal justice practices. DMC's members wanted to be true to abolitionist change without somehow making DMC seem unrelated or irrelevant to the rest of the community.

In DMC's attempt both to be accountable to local populations and to locate itself among the national network of abolitionism, there was an inevitable tension between the overall focus of national organizing and the focus of DMC on a small Midwestern city. As I argue below, in this relationship between national and local is a set of tensions that those interested in furthering abolitionist politics need to unpack.

Internal Tensions

DMC's composition changed during my time with the group. Some meetings drew three people, others twenty. Periodically, people from other organizations, most often Begin Again or Monroe County Justice, would attend DMC meetings. Most often, only core members of DMC attended them. Still, there was enough political and strategic heterogeneity that the group, however small, faced ongoing tensions, particularly over its organizational structure. Recurring questions included: Was DMC an organization or a coalition? How could DMC hold onto an abolitionist identity but build a coalition with other groups that did not have abolitionist politics? How could the structure of DMC reflect the complexity of these questions? In an eloquent essay that he wrote and distributed to DMC members during the summer of 2008, DMC cofounder James Nagle proposed a thoughtful structure that he described as "The Bike Wheel":

Diversity in Organizing (Instead of Organizing Diversity)
We are forcing a debate in our community. In the most immediate sense this debate is about building a jail. But we all know the debate is about something far greater than the current proposal. The debate is about the very idea of incarceration itself. About punishment as control. About othering; race, class, gender, or otherwise. The tangled webs weaved by the very existence of incarceration in a community, a society, the world, is [*sic*] deafeningly complex. Organizing in defiance of the status quo of incarceration must reflect this complex reality. This diversity.

No New Jail, Inc.
Often the impulse is to gather the voices and bodies of defiance in one place, give it a name, and fight a simplified ominous threat: in this case, the new jail. We must reject this impulse, as it does not reflect the complex reality. It would be us being bamboozled by the very dysfunction that enables something as archaically oppressive as incarceration. Quite bluntly, it would be mirroring the dysfunctional organizational model that defines corporations and governments.

The dysfunction comes built into the attempt to organize a large mass. If every person in a corporation (Or a country! Or even a county!) were given an equal voice and vision and equal agency, nothing but time given to talking and debate would be accomplished. Instead, pyramidal schemes are established with an individual (or small group), with all the voice, vision and agency, at the top. From there trickles down decreasing levels of importance, decision making, voice, and agency. Not unexpectedly, the incarcerated mass can be found at the bottom of these pyramid schemes that surround us. That rule us.

Small Is Beautiful (and Successful!)
The alternative? Organizing small, with critical intention. Embracing the diversity of life experience, political views, tactics, and strategies, by giving them all room to breathe. We must allow complexity and diversity to define our organizing—instead of organizing to define and confine com-

plexity and diversity. That is, it is more empowering and successful to have 20 groups of five people, with their own voices, agency, and tactics— then [sic] it is to have 1 group of 100 people attempting to act with full equality and a singular vision.

This alternative is easily enacted through communication, affinity, and definition. Communicating one's interests, politics, strategies, and goals. Finding a small group of others that share in this, that have affinity. Then defining the direction, action, and needs of the affinity group: how many people are needed to accomplish the goal(s)?, What politics and tasks define the group?, What does the group hope/plan to accomplish? etc. . . .

While definition can create exclusion, it is exclusion from a small affinity group with explicit intention. NOT exclusion from the larger task at hand (that is inspiring the various groups and acts of definition and action.)

Spokes and Coalitions
With small, defined affinity groups we are building something closer to a bike wheel then a pyramid. At the center of the wheel is the hub, the issue: incarceration in Monroe County. Coming from this center are numerous spokes on an equal plane—all plugged into the same cause, but all reaching out separately guided and defined. While this is more empowering then the large mass, trickle down organization of a pyramid, it can still benefit from communication and action on the large mass level. This is where the concepts of spokescouncils[20] and coalitions come into play. We all benefit from staying in communication, networking, and working together when a situation/strategy benefits from a large mass.

As we move forward we must buck the impulse to become No New Jail, Inc. Instead, embracing diversity and complexity, organizing groups of intention defined by goals and tasks, and based on affinity that equally empowers all involved. We can all agree that building a new jail is wrong. But we do not, and need not, all agree on why we are against the new jail and what we see needing [sic] to be done to stop it. Embracing this base level of diversity will allow for a series of blows to topple any new jail they ever imagine constructing.

Nagle's vision of "diversity in organizing" expressed in the metaphor of the bike wheel reflected his anarchist politics. Importantly, the notion of a bike-wheel structure for political organizing also reflected the essential contributions of Laclau and Mouffe (2001, especially 149–93), who argue that the hegemonic articulation between groups with diverse orientations to leftist struggles is the only way forward for a socialist politics. DMC followed Nagle's proposed structure for the majority of my time with the group. It formed smaller working groups, sometimes organized around particular campaigns and sometimes around approaches to abolition. Periodically, DMC would hold a longer strategy meeting or a series of meetings, out of which came different iterations of working groups. For example, at various times, DMC members operated working groups focused on the Free Voices Project, the YSB, popular education, politicians, communication and the media, research, and alternatives to incarceration.

Despite support for Nagle's vision, these working groups eventually stopped meeting. The tension, then, was not among competing visions of organizational structure: no one in the group advocated for a hierarchical model of organization. Rather, the tension grew out of DMC's failure to increase its membership. The bike-wheel model became unsustainable because of DMC's consistently small numbers; frequently, each member was active in multiple working groups and thus might have several weekly meetings. Following Nagle's poetic metaphor, the bike wheel periodically became flat, and the group found it difficult to effectively inflate it.

External Tensions

The tension over how to structure DMC internally related to the different priorities among group members in focusing DMC's efforts. The commitment to a decentralized and nonhierarchical group structure gave way to an outward orientation to organizing that was critical of channeling DMC campaigns through the county government. In fact, there was an ongoing conversation, which reflected the tension within the group regarding political identities, between a focus on holding elected officials accountable and a focus on extra-electoral organizing, which concentrated on popular education, community canvassing, and envisioning community accountability processes that did not rely on county officials.

Davis spoke to me about how the tension over DMC's internal structure and process related directly to the group's external focus and strategy. She used the terms "urgency" and "process" to speak about the tensions that I discuss in these pages. Referring to her earlier activism, Davis recalled an emphasis on action, a sense of urgency, and a repudiation of intellectualizing issues or group process. It was at the large antiglobalization actions against the Free Trade Agreement of the Americas in Miami where Davis first witnessed anarchist processes that particularly focused on challenging the reproduction of hierarchy within activist spaces. She connected this tension between process and urgency to local struggles within DMC: "Following legislative schedules creates its own sense of urgency," she noted. "When DMC focuses on change through county government, the county's agenda and timeline directs DMC's activism and agenda." In contrast, Davis argued, focusing on other areas of organizing could mitigate that sense of urgency and become positive and productive. She wanted DMC to focus less on the agendas, timeframes, and policies of the county and more on popular education, initiating cultural change through the media, discussions, and events and through engaging in abolitionist process development.

The tension that Davis named was evident not only during DMC meetings but also in the discourse of public meetings. One example occurred during the YSB meetings in the fall of 2009. DMC struggled with how to frame and reframe the discussions that occurred at these meetings. Politicians, the juvenile court judge, and the heads of probation and juvenile probation consistently attended, and DMC wanted those officials present so they would hear the community's concerns and be accountable for addressing them. But DMC wanted the community to articulate creative solutions that did not rely on the government or its institutions. The presence of officials had the potential to compromise this important goal, as people might be less inclined to speak freely and the more overtly radical activists in attendance were hesitant to articulate their more creative, noncoercive ideas for fear of their co-optation by the officials in attendance.

The latter concern was justified at one of the YSB meetings that fall. Although DMC members entered the meeting hoping for a forum where attendees could radically imagine noncoercive or nonpunitive responses to social harm, their plans were upset by the surprising and ongoing move of probation officers onto the YSB site. The meeting largely consisted of arguments over the practical details of the move. The conversation went on for over an hour—twice the length that DMC had originally allotted—before Victor Whitney raised his hand and said that he wanted to reframe the conversation from talking about what would be best given the current situation to "what we can dream would be best for youth in the county." Whitney proceeded to offer his dream that no young person would be put in detention and that the community would have nonpunitive, restorative places for youth. This disruption of the meeting trajectory, which until this point had essentially accepted the change and was discussing how best to accommodate it, was an interesting intervention in the overall arc of the afternoon. After Whitney's comments, the meeting unfolded along two discursive tracks. Attendees at times outlined a vision that excluded probation, judges, and detention, and at other times offered reformist ways to accommodate the integration of probation into the YSB. In one example, Robin Trotter, the juvenile probation supervisor and one of the people most responsible for the colocation of probation officers and the YSB, offered her own endorsement of male role models for youth as a contribution to Whitney's vision.

I thought that the meeting felt muddled and incoherent. Many DMC activists felt defeated after it, saying that the inability of DMC to steer the conversation and to present a coherent and united framework led to local officials taking over the conversation and setting the framework. While DMC's midmeeting attempt to reframe the meeting into a creative abolitionist brainstorming session succeeded, with many people following Whitney's lead and sharing their own visions, this process included leaders of the local juvenile justice system, who already had been very clear that their overall vision for the community included a local facility. I see the meeting as embodying the tension between working outside of government and working through it. Unresolved and therefore not integrated into the meeting's agenda, the tension played out explicitly during the conversation at the meeting.

At times, DMC was unclear about its focus and whether it wanted to pressure politicians and other officials into adopting abolitionist reforms or to build up abolitionist community awareness and practice away from potentially co-opting county officials. Whichever choice it made, however, DMC would encounter another tension: between the group's abolitionist identity and its stated priority of accountability to the people most affected by carceral policies.

Abolition and Accountability

DMC's work and identity were fraught with tensions and questions related to its mission and politics: Should the group focus on pressuring elected officials to change policies or on creating means of resolving conflict that did not rely on people in power? How much should the group promote an abolitionist agenda, since that term and those politics could alienate actors who were otherwise supportive of the group's platform and agenda? More specifically, the group was faced with the question of how it could address the structural conditions of incarceration and agitate for significant systemic change while meeting the needs and desires of local people most affected by the system. This latter tension, constantly at play during my time with DMC, came up very explicitly as my fieldwork drew to a close in the spring of 2010. I had gone to the jail during visiting hours to meet two other DMC organizers and spend time talking with people about the proposed changes to visitation. In just two visits to the jail, we gathered three pages of signatures for a petition that simply asked officials to abandon the change to video visitation. By all accounts, visitors to the jail were adamantly against the proposed change and very thankful that DMC was organizing opposition.

But despite popular support, this particular campaign raised some of the tensions within the group that I have mentioned above. Of course, DMC had coalesced around opposing the justice campus and agitating for decarceration. For an abolitionist group, this made a lot of sense, and it positioned DMC alongside national groups that ran or supported similar campaigns. While the group was successful in communicating with politicians, it was less successful in organizing families of those who were incarcerated. In spite of attending visiting hours at the jail, talking with families of the incarcerated, and attempting to organize events that meshed with the schedules of low-income working people in the county, DMC's members still failed to involve a substantial number of the people most affected in the campaign against the justice campus.

In contrast, people at the jail were enthusiastic about the endeavor to fight videoconferencing, which—in trying to stop the process of visitation from becoming even more impersonal and technological—targeted a tangible and reformist goal of simply keeping the existing visitation system.

The campaign against videoconferencing had only lukewarm support among DMC members precisely because it was reformist in nature and inconsistently framed in a larger analysis of the prison-industrial complex and abolitionist goals.[21] Certainly some DMC members did not participate in activities and meetings as a result. Other organizers prioritized engaging in campaigns that the people most affected found important. For these organizers, if the issues ultimately didn't fall under an abolitionist agenda, that was a reasonable sacrifice to make for the important priority of organizing in a manner accountable to the community.

Tensions beyond the County

As I have mentioned above, DMC had direct connections to national abolitionist organizations through overlapping memberships, most importantly with CR. DMC's campaign against the justice campus coincided with CR's tenth anniversary conference. DMC decided to send representatives and raised funds to help ten members travel together to the conference, as noted above. DMC members participated on a panel focused on campaigns against jail expansion with two other groups, one from New York City and one from New Orleans.

While the conference proved to be inspiring for the ten DMC members, some of them reported feeling disoriented. CR prioritizes work in the communities hardest hit by mass incarceration, which undeniably are urban communities of color. Moreover, in organizing to abolish the prison-industrial complex, CR had focused mostly on prisons because the majority of the US incarcerated population—the largest in the world—is in prison, rather than jail. Therefore, DMC—an organization doing community organizing in a semirural county in the Midwest to try and stop municipal carceral growth—was somewhat on the margin at the CR conference. At the same time, DMC relied heavily on CR for its invaluable support in conceptualizing and framing the local issues DMC faced. To their credit, CR organizers consistently spoke of the connections between the two groups' struggles, even if DMC members at times felt unsure of their place within the larger organization. Importantly, the focus on prisons among abolitionists has changed since the tenth anniversary conference. Since the 2008 conference, jails and immigrant detention have become increasingly important to analysts of the carceral state, following legislative reforms in many states designed to reduce prison populations. For example, in 2011 California enacted a policy of realignment that was intended to reduce the number of people incarcerated in the state's Department of Corrections and Rehabilitation and bring the agency within the requirements of a federal judicial order to reduce overcrowding in state prisons. But although California's prison system may see some modest reductions, the state's municipal jails threaten to expand dramatically, with a large majority of Californian counties indicating their intention to expand old facilities or build new ones.[22] In recent years, along with other groups such as Californians United for a Responsible Budget, CR has waged campaigns specifically designed to stop jail expansion. But during the height of DMC's organizing, my fieldwork, and CR's tenth anniversary conference, there was more of an emphasis on prisons.

The tension DMC members felt between their local fight (a municipal struggle over a county jail that occurred almost exclusively on the Left) and the national discourse of abolition (which largely focused on urban communities; state, federal, and private prisons; and right-wing politics) was potentially productive for furthering abolitionist politics. Unpacking the discourse of local carceral expansion removes the dichotomized spaces at the heart of the tension and reveals that permutations of the same patterns of capitalism, national-level racialized logics of crime, and constructs of social control were manifested in local policies and practices in Bloomington and inscribed the vision of the justice campus. The context in which DMC worked was different from that in which CR focused much of its efforts, but that distinction was a potential strength of DMC's campaigns. If the group was able to articulate the local struggle with the national context and identify the direct linkages between mass incarceration and local carceral expansion, DMC might be able to enact abolitionist change in the county, diversify the broader abolitionist movement, and make abolition relevant to other communities fighting municipal carceral expansion.

Radical Democracy or Activist Aesthetic?

The tensions involved in political organizing and activism are inevitable and potentially healthy and productive for clarifying current contradictions and furthering a radical politics. While readers will need to draw their own conclusions about how to evaluate DMC's work, the group was undoubtedly successful on multiple fronts. The proposed justice campus collapsed under the weight of its own price. But the final proposed cost, an exorbitant $75 million, was not egregiously over the initial projections of $50 million and was likely negotiable. Would county officials have responded so negatively to PARI's proposal had DMC not worked to break the narrative of exceptional carceral expansion? At least several officials indicated that DMC's efforts to conceptually link local and national carceral logics and to push for decarceration destabilized their support for the justice campus. This suggests that despite the discursive and political ground that DMC had to cede to officials and the official narrative in various meetings, the group's attempt to bring the previously undiscussable into the conversation was partly successful, and the "radical world" (Povinelli 2001) of abolitionist politics became conceivable to an otherwise liberal public. Activists not only successfully intervened in the calculus that more carceral spaces equaled more therapeutic, educational, and human rights justice, but they also introduced a counterhegemonic understanding of key issues such as safety and relationships.

But there were also defeats, both in policy campaigns and in DMC's consistent efforts to broaden its local influence. DMC failed to prevent the changes to the YSB and jail visitation practices. Probation officers moved to the YSB, and control over the shelter was moved from the county commissioners to the board of judges. Jail renovations occurred that ended all in-person visitation. Beyond those defeats, DMC also readily acknowledged its struggles to involve in its work the community members who were most targeted and affected by criminal justice policy. While DMC had a core membership of about a dozen individuals, there was also substantial variation in the number of people involved due to academic and work schedules as well as varying levels of political commitment depending on the campaign. Most of the core members were young and white, although it is important to note that there was substantial class diversity, with a number of active members from poor and working-class backgrounds. There were also core members who were people of color. But the group certainly did not succeed in bringing into the membership and leadership people who were most affected locally by the policies that DMC fought.

This failure to build the group's base beyond the core membership raises important questions about DMC's structure and composition. Did the bike-wheel approach prove to be too decentralized for the task of building a broader movement? Can a working-group model really sustain long-term activism when overall membership is so low that members consistently had multiple work-group meetings to attend in a given week? Moreover, to raise what may be a more sensitive issue, was DMC's success hampered by a problem of aesthetics? That is, did DMC allow itself to become part of the activist scene in Bloomington—or at least let itself be seen in that way? It is quite possible that the group failed to expand its membership beyond the core because it was too readily identified with, and indeed defined by, an aesthetic—in this case, young, punk, and anarchist.

At the same time, DMC's organizational structure and relationship to the abolitionist movement outside of the local community was aligned with well-known visions for social movement organizing. In DMC's attempt to organize itself internally based on the concept of the bike wheel, and in the tension the organization faced between being accountable to the needs and priorities of people most affected by incarceration and trying to maintain an abolitionist analysis, DMC's work and strategy in the community implicitly invoked the vision of radical democracy outlined by Laclau and Mouffe: "Radicalizing certain of Gramsci's concepts, we find the theoretical instruments which allows [sic] us to redimension the revolutionary act itself. The concept of a 'war of position' implies precisely the *process* character of every radical transformation—the revolutionary act is, simply, an internal moment of this process. The multiplication of political spaces and the preventing of the concentration of power in one point are, then, preconditions of every truly democratic transformation of society" (2001, 191). DMC's members seemed to implicitly recognize the importance of polyvocality, even as the inevitable diversity of voices likely undermined a comprehensive or essential abolitionist vision. Still, the group's focus on process, including marginalized people, and ensuring the existence of decentralized spaces to allow its members to challenge county practices and process again aligned DMC's vision with that of Laclau and Mouffe (2001), as well as with the visions of contemporary anarchist scholars such as David Graeber (2002 and 2007).

Importantly, an abolitionist challenge to liberal carceral expansion in a semirural county may itself constitute a hegemonic articulation with the national discourse and politics of abolition. The tension between the focus of national organizations and campaigns against the prison-industrial complex and the local work of DMC had the potential to be highly productive in diversifying—and, crucially, fortifying—a movement for abolition.

Conclusion

Nonreformist Reforms and Abolitionist Alternatives

In 1977 the National Clearinghouse for Criminal Justice Planning and Architecture (NCCJPA) released its *Technical Assistance Report for Monroe and Owen Counties*, which projected that a new jail similar in size to the one in operation at that time would meet Monroe County's needs into the new millennium. The report made recommendations about keeping jail populations down. In addition to projecting very little growth in the jail population and thus recommending little carceral expansion, the report suggested ways for the county to decarcerate. One recommendation, which is particularly poignant because of the degree to which the county ignored it, was to cease criminal justice involvement in public intoxication. Specifically, the report noted: "The National Clearinghouse, along with such bodies as the National Advisory Commission on Criminal Justice Standards and Goals, recommends that the public inebriate cease to be handled by the criminal justice system. Public intoxication is considered by many to be the classic example of a victimless crime and of the failure of the criminal justice system to recognize its inability to solve problems which are more medical than criminal" (National Clearinghouse for Criminal Justice Planning and Architecture 1977, 9). The report went on to note initiatives in various cities—San Jose and Salinas, California; Kansas City, Missouri; and Phoenix, Arizona—that had followed this approach and cut their arrest and jail numbers dramatically.

The conclusion of this book reads differently from the preceding eight chapters. While chapter 8 examined the ways that community organizers challenged the discourse of carceral expansion, the conclusion ends the book by suggesting practical ways that Bloomington—and, crucially, other communities—could restructure social relations and responses to harm, including crime, to enact abolitionist change and provide the accountability and healing measures needed when harms do occur. The conclusion is still very much rooted in and indebted to my fieldwork, but the tone may strike readers as more committed. In some ways, the conclusion is my rejoinder to and intervention in the tension I examined in chapter 2's focus on the archipelago of alternatives connected to the justice campus. I begin with the reference above to the NCCJPA to make several important points at the outset. First and most important, decriminalization of various offenses and broad decarceration ground what follows in the conclusion and should ground all community conversations and campaigns about jail and prison reform. Keeping people out of jail and prison, rather than reconfiguring jail and prison to be slightly more comfortable or humane (if this is even possible),[1] should be a central goal of community organizing to combat poverty, racism, violence, addiction, or crime.

Second, the NCCJPA recommendation demonstrates that the logic underpinning abolitionist change is not confined to the campaigns of community organizers. In discussions of decriminalizing certain offenses and of detaching alternative processes from the formal criminal justice system, diverse voices contest the logic of carceral expansion and express confidence in decarceration. Community organizers need to mobilize these voices and accumulate their knowledge to contest the knowledge-power nexus at work through the state, its consultants, and their discourses.

Third, the NCCJPA study offers an important point of departure for the remainder of this conclusion. Decarceration as a tactical policy within a larger abolitionist strategy requires thoughtful consideration of alternative political processes to make such changes discussable and doable and alternative conflict resolution processes to replace the criminal justice system. At the same time, following Angela Davis's (2003, 105–15) work on abolitionist alternatives, I want to emphasize this book's commitment to doing the ideological work to break the conceptual link between crime and punishment. In insisting on locating carceral expansion as part of the changing patterns of global capitalism and racial logics, this book also cautions against the tendency to celebrate a singular alternative to the current system. As Davis argues, if we focus our critique on the prison-industrial complex, rather than the individual institution, this "more complicated framework may yield more options than if we simply attempt to discover a single substitute for the prison system. The first step, then, would be to let go of the desire to discover one single alternative system of punishment that would occupy the same footprint as the prison system" (2003, 106).

Although I do offer concrete suggestions in the following pages, I want to begin with two cautionary statements about what follows and how to read it. First, my recommendations offer a brief and broad sketch; a detailed and informed plan for radically reshaping a given city's way of engaging with conflict, be it crime or community planning, would require a separate book. In the following pages, I err on the side of brevity—gesturing toward, rather than detailing, concrete alternatives.

Second, the recommendations that follow complicate my framing of local carcerality. For example, in a section below on local treatment, I write both that expanding treatment should be predicated on decarceration and that the community should seek alternative philosophical approaches to treatment, such as harm reduction. In seeing these suggestions, a reader might wonder how these changes would be possible given the stability of carceral habitus. Do I imagine that a shift in local habitus is a precondition for such substantive changes? If not, could the argument not be made that such changes to policy would ultimately be reformulated to fit within the carceral habitus of the county? Ultimately, this is an unresolved tension. However, my claim has always been that carceral habitus is not fully calcified and is subject to being dislodged by social movement organizing. Concrete and radical alternatives through the state are possible if they follow work that illuminates carceral habitus. DMC's insistence on locating the justice campus as part of the carceral state and the group's offering of counternarratives about what it meant to be safe successfully disrupted the hardened expansionist dispositions of several officials.

I organize this discussion of alternatives into five themes that are based largely on what I observed and participated in during my fieldwork. These themes are "Alternative Conflict Resolution Processes," "Alternative Decision-Making Processes," "The Decarceration of Treatment," "From Abstinence to Harm Reduction," and "Abolitionist Geographies: Envisioning Countercarceral Landscapes." All five are based on a vision of transformative justice, community accountability, and decarceration, a framework within which personal, community, and systemic change are all paramount. In contrast to the creation of and focus on an individuated actor in need of carceral treatment and consequence, the proposed framework recognizes the structural conditions that pose the gravest threats to the safety of communities and that produce both the harms that we call crime and the collective responsibilities that communities bear for addressing them.

The reader might be curious about how alternative community decision making and alternative approaches to resolving harm, including crime, can be contained within the same framework. These are seemingly distinct areas: the first raises questions about the narrow nature of knowledge production and political capital in the community, and the second about the hegemony of the carceral institution. The fact that community decision-making processes and responses to crime and harm appear distinct actually highlights the relevance and potential of transformative justice. Scholars and activists involved in the development of transformative justice focus on community accountability, with the community involved in handling the complex situations that beget, occur within, and arise from harm and violence.[2] A community-based approach to the harms surrounding a given act is not the same thing as, and in fact can operate wholly outside of, an approach based on police and prison. One can use the paradigm of transformative justice (or its better known cousin, restorative justice) and, in particular, the concept of the Circle,[3] to consider radically different ways of resolving conflict and achieving community consensus. Generation Five, an organization working to end sexual assaults on children by concurrently working against systems of oppression, has conducted the most thorough development of transformative justice as a "liberatory approach to violence" that "seeks safety and accountability without relying on alienation, punishment, or State or systemic violence, including incarceration and policing" (2007, 5). The organization believes that "individual justice and collective liberation are equally important, mutually supportive, and fundamentally intertwined—the achievement of one is impossible without the achievement of the other"—and that "the conditions that allow violence to occur must be transformed in order to achieve justice in individual instances of violence. Therefore, transformative justice is both a liberating politic and an approach for securing justice" (ibid). In its insistence on locating sexual assaults on children within the context of structural violence and oppression, Generation Five offers a vision of transformative justice in which alternative conflict resolution processes are part of larger struggles for social justice, rather than simply a replacement for the criminal justice system.[4]

Alternative Conflict Resolution Processes

Despite Monroe County officials' genuine support for programming, county initiatives prescribed the models available locally to cognitive-behavioral therapy and abstinence-based drug treatment. There were rhetorical endorsements of potentially paradigmatically different approaches to conflict, such as restorative justice, but they received only nominal financial and political support. Indeed, at DMC's initial event, the day of public education on May 3, 2008, group members provided attendees with a list of local organizations and their annual operating budgets to draw attention to the disparities between the $50 million proposal for the justice campus and the comparatively meager budgets of organizations that constituted the community's safety net. DMC noted on this list that a local food pantry providing free groceries to 1,500 people each week operated on an annual budget of under $300,000, while a residential drug and alcohol treatment program that had served 400 people in the previous year had an operating budget of only $900,000. Most notably, Bloomington Restorative Practices (BRP), the local organization based on restorative justice, operated on an annual budget of just $56,400, which covered various restorative processes for close to 150 people (26 in the Victim Offender Reconciliation Program, and over 100 adults and a dozen youth in the Shoplifters Alternative Program). Volunteer mediators did much of BRP's work in the community because the organization had only enough funds to pay one person full time. Indeed, in the county meetings I attended, there was almost no mention of using BRP, expanding its services, integrating it into the continuum of care, or considering it as an alternative to the court system.

The existence of a restorative justice organization in Monroe County, however underfunded it may have been, certainly offered an opportunity for decarceration activists to highlight a possible alternative to the formal system, though BRP's primary purpose for DMC may have been a heuristic one. Indeed, DMC understood that practices based on restorative and transformative justice presented a rich and vibrant alternative that it could develop. As I offer a brief sketch of how such practices could be integrated into the existing criminal justice approach, readers should be aware of the important and divergent practical and philosophical positions concerning the relationship between restorative justice and the criminal justice system.[5]

One option would be for organizations such as BRP and practices such as Victim-Offender Reconciliation, mediation, Circles of Support and Accountability, Sentencing Circles, and Re-Integration Circles to be integrated into the operations of the county criminal justice system. In other words, this recommendation is to make these processes in the community into robust options—with funding and other support—for diverting many cases from the criminal justice system. This could be done at a number of points in the criminal justice process, from arrest through sentencing. These practices also could operate entirely outside of the formal system.

There are examples of formal community processes integrating restorative justice into their responses to crime and harm.[6] Moreover, there are organizations dedicated to the conceptual and practical development of this model for communities interested in moving from retributive to restorative justice frameworks. One organization's online project, for example, uses a hypothetical community called RJ City and a case study of a robbery there to offer readers an extensive blueprint for how a restorative justice network can replace or supplement a criminal justice system.[7]

The option of supplementing or replacing the formal criminal justice system of Monroe County with restorative justice is perhaps the intuitive place to start a section on alternative processes. After all, as I mention above, restorative justice already operated within the county's existing system and received some support from both criminal justice officials and local activists. In essence, my argument here is that restorative justice should be significantly expanded in the county, replacing criminal justice processes and reliance on incarceration in many circumstances. Coupled with campaigns to unseat liberal and conservative expansionist politicians and criminal justice officials, this strategy of implementing reforms based on restorative justice through official county processes could result in significant changes.

Yet this recommendation does not alleviate certain concerns raised by informants during my time in the field. In particular, an investment in restorative justice does not necessarily reduce reliance on the existing system. In fact, there is nothing inherent in the above recommendation to prevent restorative justice from expanding the reach of the existing system and perhaps ensnaring more people. Indeed, it was BRP's intimacy with the formal criminal justice system that made DMC's support for BRP less enthusiastic than it might have been. Basic research into the state of restorative justice in the contemporary United States reveals its rather comfortable place in national conversations among federal criminal justice agencies,[8] which is precisely why national activists have pushed for the conceptual and political development of transformative justice as a distinct, if related, approach that avoids the inherent co-optation of restorative justice.[9] Moreover, concurrent with the global emergence and mainstreaming of restorative practices in Western societies with histories and present conditions characterized by colonialism, a highly important interventionist critique has emerged from indigenous and Western scholars and activists about the co-optation and appropriation of indigenous restorative justice practices.[10] Finally, as critical scholars have pointed out in their examinations of prominent restorative justice research, the practice too often relies on the same individuated logic of responsibility as the formal criminal justice system, and thus "society is viewed in terms of 'individuals,' rather than as social formations, social forces, and social structures. As such, the shaming/integration theory is ahistorical and fails to capture the deterioration of the condition of the working class, and their progressive marginalization in production, consumption, and community life" (Takagi and Shank 2004, 158).

Even as the state appropriates various indigenous restorative practices, collapses their geographical and cultural diversity into the single approach of restorative justice, and then co-opts those restorative elements by suturing them to its own criminal justice apparatus (Tauri 2009), a potentially liberating politics may still be organized through a reappropriation of restorative practices under the framework of transformative justice. Thus, a second option emerges, whose possible success is borne out by developments in the field: community-based systems of accountability and justice that exist outside of the criminal justice system and that, more importantly, reject the carceral logics of exclusion, isolation, and caging.

This second path is considerably less developed in practice and in both academic and activist literature. Its distrust and critique of the state is closely aligned with radical politics. In Monroe County, it was largely DMC members and other community activists who articulated this position. The argument this second path makes is that communities should intentionally develop decentralized and grass-roots processes for resolving conflict outside of formal social control organizations and move toward what one scholar-activist has called "noncarceral communities."[11] One model to which DMC organizers consistently referred was based in Philadelphia, where members of a radical political community developed transformative justice projects to address cases of sexual assault. These projects—Philly's Pissed, which no longer exists but which worked with survivors of assault, and Philly Stands Up, which continues to work with perpetrators—could offer Monroe County residents templates for designing community responses to harm, including violence, that intentionally operate outside of the criminal justice system.[12]

Crucially, this second path is not only the province of radical activists. Indeed, in an appendix devoted to a discussion of how to fund restorative justice processes in communities (found in Pranis, Stuart, and Wedge 2003), Barry Stuart, a former judge, discusses his "mistake" in trying to integrate restorative practices into the criminal justice system:

> I tried to discover ways to bring the community into the justice system. To a limited extent, this is a progressive step. However, the more important step is to . . . engage the justice system in responding to the needs of the community. . . . Many community justice initiatives are not community based or led. They're based within the justice system and led by the justice system. . . . In these initiatives, the values and objectives of the justice agencies prevail. . . . If community justice initiatives are based on justice system values and led by justice professionals, the community provides an alternative method for pursuing justice system objectives. . . . Circles, to be fully effective, need to be based in and led by the community. Circles offer the basis for forming a genuine partnership among all state agencies and the community, but it's a partnership that operates on community values and objectives. Many of my early initiatives were led by the court and based on our systems' values. This was my first mistake. (Stuart 2003, 251–52)

I lay out these two paths so that readers can grasp the diversity of ways in which Monroe County, and perhaps other communities, could begin to shrink reliance on the carceral paradigm. It is possible for both approaches to exist simultaneously. Indeed, underfunded and underused though it was, BRP operated both in conjunction with the existing system on the continuum of sanctions and outside of that system as a dispute resolution alternative open to the community. Community organizing could work to make options based on restorative justice more available to judges and simultaneously engage in public education to develop the kind of transformative justice analysis and approach advocated by Generation Five and others.

Framing responses to conflict through transformative justice practices and principles can make possible a radical shift away from carceral expansion, such as that found in Monroe County. In their book examining the restorative practice of Circles, Kay Pranis, Barry Stuart, and Mark Wedge note that Circles change the approach of Western criminal justice in four distinct ways: (1) from coercion to healing; (2) from solely individual to individual and collective accountability; (3) from primary dependence on the state to greater self-reliance within the community; and (4) from justice as "getting even" to justice as "getting well" (2003, 10). This kind of radical shift can destabilize parts of carceral habitus and reinscribe alternative understandings of what creates public safety and community justice.

Alternative Decision-Making Processes

As I mentioned in part 3, processes of knowledge production and political decision making were important to the emergence and robust nature of proposals for carceral expansion. Public meetings gave officials a chance to frame the relevant issues and possible responses under the guise of an open process geared toward community input and criticism. At the justice campus hearings hosted by the Monroe County Criminal Justice Coordinating Council (MCCJCC), the setup of the room and the structure of the agendas facilitated the dominance of county officials and so-called experts. The spatial privilege afforded to these people, and their appearing at the beginning of meeting agendas to present material and frame subsequent discussions, inevitably allowed them to consistently restate their positions and respond to public criticism in ways that often reframed articulations of resistance into endorsements of expansion. DMC struggled with these issues not only at official meetings but also at its own, such as the three focusing on the Youth Services Bureau (YSB). At these events, officials were often able to control the discourse and circumscribe conversations to fit expansionist policies.

For these reasons, community organizers should consider alternative methods for structuring community meetings, particularly those with the explicit purpose of facilitating community input or privileging the voices of the public. One technique of community planning that Monroe County could adopt is the Circle method, which is featured in several restorative justice processes, such as sentencing circles and circles of support and accountability.[13] Jennifer Ball, Wayne Caldwell, and Kay Pranis (2010) suggest that the frustration and marginalization of public hearings can be rectified by community investment in Circle processes. As John Forester, a leading theorist of community planning, says of public hearings in his foreword to the book by Ball and coauthors, "these overly formal and minimally interactive public hearings might be thought of as reflecting 'a political design from hell': participating community members often feel more angry, more resentful, less trusting, and more cynical about public planning processes than when they arrived" (Forester 2010, xi).

Circles would offer a chance to reclaim democracy in Monroe County from its usage as signifying political representation. Moreover, the use of Circles would mitigate the political capital attributed to distinctions of expertise that was crucial in the reproduction of power and knowledge during the justice campus and YSB processes. The Circle process is a form of radical inclusion that rejects notions of expertise as the basis of a hierarchy of experience and treats the perspectives of experts in the Circle as equal to those of all other participants. Ball and coauthors explain:

> Circles provide a structured way to have very difficult conversations. They create an atmosphere of respect that opens participants to hearing one another in new ways. . . . Circles do not try to limit the discussion or isolate an event from other related experiences. The Circle dialogue is open to anything that participants feel is relevant to discuss in order to resolve conflicts, repair harm, or change conditions. . . . It allows people to acknowledge the forces affecting their behavior that are not of their

making. And it explores ways to address these larger forces. . . . The very nature of Circles makes them highly effective in dealing with complex, systemic problems. (2010, 48)

One final point about the Circle process serves to both support the assertion by Ball and coauthors about the effectiveness of the process and to reinforce earlier cautions about romanticizing restorative justice: Circles require investments of trust and time. Monroe County officials who criticized "analysis paralysis" might be reluctant to engage in what would probably feel (at first) like discussion without progress. Other people who felt disaffected and ignored during and after official community meetings about carceral expansion might not trust that Circle processes would be more democratic or provide a more favorable outcome. Indeed, both groups might be correct. There are no guarantees that Circles would provide the quick and expansionist answers that officials wanted. Community residents would be right to remain skeptical that changing the process would automatically change the results. The point in my recommendation is that the Circle would provide a superior and democratic process through which the community—and here I mean, at the very least, the people in the room who have no official titles but who have the most to lose from carceral expansion—can decide its future. Indeed, as Pranis and coauthors note about Circle processes at a community organization working with youth in Boston, "it is not unusual for a Circle with young people to spend hours and even days discussing [values and] guidelines. . . . The guidelines involve a genuine discussion about the meaning of [values such as respect, love, and confidentiality] and the concrete implications of living those values" (2003, 34).

The Decarceration of Treatment

Many Monroe County officials and leaders expressed concern about the lack of quality treatment options for jail prisoners and detained youth. Indeed, the ability to broaden the scope of treatment programs available was a central argument for the building of a new and larger jail and a local detention facility. To the extent that jails and juvenile detention facilities remain part of community landscapes, they should most certainly operate according to principles of treatment and education.

But well-meaning officials and activists succumbed to the anxieties provoked by the narrative that jail and juvenile detention prisoners desperately needed services. The more imperative project that is obscured by such so-called crises is the decarceration of treatment.

The intense community focus on providing treatment options in the jail was due, in part, to the high numbers of community residents who were incarcerated. As the antijail activist Matthew Harrison poignantly stated at the second MCCJCC hearing on the justice campus in response to Barrett:

> [In response to] the comment that we are working with people who are broken: we are working with a *system* that's broken. Everybody in this country is now facing a time of reduced expectations. It's the wrong time to come and say, "We need more money, we need bigger buildings, we need a giant correctional campus." If the correctional figures who are now responsible for our system want to come before the county and advocate new programs and new facilities, they need to bring before us which old programs they're going to do away with.

Harrison's demand that any proposals for new facilities or program come with a commitment to dismantle old programs confronted the tendency of the local system to expand through a rhetorical commitment to programs and service.[14] He went on to address earlier comments from Barrett, who had broken with the narrative of the county bench being treatment-centric when he defiantly claimed that "the judges have a bright line of demarcation [in] dealing with repeat offenders. Crimes of personal violence, crimes involving the use of a dangerous weapon, commercial dealing in dangerous drugs: those are people we don't spend any time thinking about how we might continue working with them. They are people from whom the community needs protection." Harrison pounced on this claim, focusing his critique on the judge's admission that a majority of people held in the jail were there before their trial:

> I'm also embarrassed that we would have up on the screen that the majority of people are in pretrial and then we would have one of our local judges say that the judges have a clear line of demarcation, that people who are *accused* of these crimes, we don't deal with, we don't look to help.

These are people that under our system of government have traditionally been presumed as innocent, and it's apparent that the system is not
regarding them as presumed innocent. The statistics presented tonight
were self-justifying; they were almost entirely negative; there's almost no
input from anybody that's incarcerated. I've been incarcerated for a very
heinous crime—I would call it attempted voting—I've been held by one
of these judges [nodding at Barrett] for up to thirty days on a pretext
that I might not show up for bail. I refused to pay for my freedom. I
think that's something that needs to be addressed. Bail schedule [cost] has
crept gradually upwards, and it's not the only factor [involved in] whether
people are going to obey court orders . . . the other factor is whether
they're going to show up. We could easily release a large percentage of
people from jail. People who have lived in this county, been born in this
county, have relatives here. And yes, indeed, they may be recidivists, but
being a recidivist is not a crime. If one is convicted, then one can say that
person is guilty of a crime. But until that occurs that person has not been
[found] guilty of a crime, and it's not a crime to have been convicted,
let alone plea bargained to escape this draconian system which saddles
people with anything from work release to years of probation to lost jobs,
lost families. Almost anybody who's locked up for any period of time
loses a spouse. I'd like to say I was one of those people.

Following Harrison's logic, conversations about treatment availability
and types of programs are important, but they should follow rather
than precede conversations about reducing or expanding the number
of prisoners. As Harrison astutely noted, the most obvious place to start
the decarceration process would be with the large numbers of people
in jail awaiting trial, whose charges indicate that they are not a threat
to their community and whose histories in the community suggest that
there is no reason to believe they would abscond. The number of pretrial
jail prisoners in Monroe County is part of a nationwide phenomenon.
Reports from the Justice Policy Institute (Petteruti and Walsh 2008)
and the Vera Institute of Justice (Subramanian et al. 2015) indicate the
alarmingly large share of people who are held in American jails before
trial—62 percent of jail inmates—because they are simply too poor to
post bail. Also implicit in Harrison's testimony was the important point
that providing programs while someone is incarcerated does not offset

the harms that incarceration perpetrates; the availability of classes or drug treatment in jail does not necessarily preserve interpersonal relationships that no doubt become strained.

Alternative Paradigms: From Abstinence to Harm Reduction

While decarceration must serve as the a priori principle guiding abolitionist campaigns and movements for jail and prison reform, advocates for the justice campus in Monroe County were correct in their emphasis that the county must expand the availability of treatment, therapy, education, and other programs in the jail (and, of course, outside of it). But communities like Monroe County must also question the paradigms underlying their program provision and consider alternative models of treatment. Cognitive-behavioral therapy or abstinence-based drug treatment may be the appropriate models for some people in jail, but certainly not all of them. Frequently, DMC members would hear from families of jail inmates that their loved one's probation status had been contingent on not drinking alcohol when the original charge had nothing to do with alcohol consumption. When the person on probation was found to have been drinking, he or she was subsequently arrested for technical violations. County officials operating within abstinence paradigms may not realize that these are potentially devastating interventions into attempts at harm reduction, the process whereby people engaging in potentially harmful behavior take steps to minimize the harm that results. Moreover, Monroe County had a heavily paternalistic orientation to program provision, embodying an ethos of "doing good for people" instead of "doing good with people" that other approaches, such as peacemaking, suggest.[15]

Liberal politicians, criminal justice officials, and the *Bloomington Herald-Times* were fond of the county's drug court. But this evidence-based program offered one rather narrow approach to a problem that has diverse causes, manifestations, and even symptoms. Moreover, compliance in drug court is connected explicitly to the threat of incarceration; delving into the structural, psychological, and perhaps violent context of addiction is a complex process requiring and deserving work that occurs outside of a coercive context. Monroe County could adopt harm reduction as an official approach to drug and alcohol use, including the provision of harm reduction therapies in the jail and community.

In contrast to an abstinence-only model of drug treatment, harm reduction treatment frames its approach differently:

> Unlike traditional "quit now and forever" programs, we do not ask that clients stop all substance use, unless that is their goal, and we help families find alternatives to "tough love." The therapist helps the client to lay out, clearly and honestly, the harm being done to themselves and to others. The client, or the client and family together, choose the most urgent issues on which to focus. Together, client and therapist then work to *reduce the harm* that is being done, establishing goals and implementing gradual, realistic steps to achieve them. At the Center [for Harm Reduction Therapy], we work with the whole person. Drug and alcohol problems are addressed alongside other social, emotional, health and occupational concerns.[16]

Having existing county institutions adopt a harm reduction approach would still make abstinence programming possible, but within a larger framework that sees abstinence as one of the possible solutions and one that the user must choose to embrace. Importantly, harm reduction seems to change the question that communities, social services, and criminal justice officials ask from "Are you doing drugs?" to "Are you being safe?" and to change follow-up responses from demands for ceasing all use under threat of carceral punishment to continued work on how to increase individual and community safety.

Abolitionist Geographies: Envisioning Countercarceral Landscapes

As I hope this book has made clear, the carceral institution has occupied a central place in the cultural and political landscape of Monroe County. As I discussed in early chapters, the conceptual centrality of the institution was intimately connected to the spatial potential of the Thomson site. One argument I have made is that it was the surplus land—understood through a particular neoliberal grammar—that structured the imaginings of the justice campus.

The discursive and material reality (and their mutually constitutive nature) of the contest over county carceral expansion resonates with Don Mitchell's descriptions of "culture wars" over public spaces. Mitchell offers a helpful reflection on the connection between discourse and materiality: "Like other wars, wars over culture are territorial; they literally take place, whether that place is on the wall of a convention center, on the city streets outside, or in the print and electronic media. Culture wars are about defining what is legitimate in a society, who is an 'insider' and who is an 'outsider.' They are about determining the social boundaries that govern our lives" (2000, 5). Mitchell's use of "culture wars" as an analytic to examine contests over "social boundaries" provides an insight into efforts to destabilize the carceral habitus of Monroe County. One of the ways in which to contest the unquestioned nature of carceral institutions and to intervene in the multiple narratives that posit them as the only response to various crises is to envision, propose, and construct alternative physical landscapes to replace imagined carceral geographies.[17]

After the defeat of the justice campus proposal, members of DMC who were involved in other local campaigns related to community sustainability participated in discussions with prominent local environmental design activists to imagine an alternative future for the eighty-five-acre Thomson site. In the following e-mail message sent to DMC members, a prominent practitioner of permaculture—an ecological design practice for sustainable living—offered a preliminary analysis of the possibilities at the site to DMC members and other community activists:

> I have recently been reviewing the original map and doing tracing paper sketches of road and path access, catchment, buildings (produce warehouses, coolers/root cellars, campus/dormitories/classrooms/barns/sheds/ shelters), aquaculture, fields, orchards, forest gardens, urban forests. . . . Basically the aim is to design the 80 acres to meet many of the community's needs described in the Sustenance section of the Peak Oil Task Force [report]. Some of those targets include the training and deployment of new urban garden farmers, increasing the number and scale of community garden plots, the creation of food processing and distribution hubs, more space for year around agriculture, space for business incubation, [a] year around farmers market with roofed sales shelters, cold storage and root cellars; orchards, aquaculture, vineyards, mycoculture, seedbank and arboretum. . . . The design I'm contemplating could add more resilience to our local food economics, train more farmer/growers, help to reskill our local culture and create jobs, manage runoff and catchment of millions of

gallons of water high in the landscape (with gravity flow to growers and other users) along with a multitude of additional yields over time.

DMC members received this message almost one year to the day after the final MCCJCC hearing in December 2008, which presented the official rendering of the justice campus. Those eighty-five acres had been used for seventy-five years in the service of various capitalist, carceral, and community interests. Inscribed onto the old Thomson site was the political-economic history of industrialization, military Keynesianism, unionization, deindustrialization, and neoliberal outsourcing; the material projection of carceral habitus onto space that structured the visual and analytic registers of community members; and the resistant and productive imagining of space that had been industrial and carceral. The collaboration between DMC and the practitioner of permaculture was an inspiring development for local activists and should resonate with those committed to a radical rethinking of carceral responses to diverse community problems. Moreover, according to recent articles from the *Herald-Times*, it appears as if this countervisualization of the site has shaken the carceral habitus of the county. As of this writing, the county commissioners are entertaining several proposals for the eighty-five acres. Among the proposals are a greenhouse that would provide food and jobs for local youth and adults with autism, a disc golf course, a solar farm, a farm school, and a permaculture site (Bunn 2013a and 2013b).

The dedication of the majority of this book to an examination of carceral expansion in the county indicates a rather cynical outlook. If nothing else, this book has pointed to the hegemony of carceral logics that animate and confine our ability to think about incarceration. The total reliance on incarceration as a catchall solution to problems that the state itself has generated has limited the community's capacity to think of noncarceral responses to a variety of behaviors—including some that are not against the law, such as those that lead to technical violations of probation and parole. Moreover, this carceral imagination is not politically discriminating. That is, communities such as Monroe County that have an overall liberal orientation and boast a number of leftist political leaders also articulate what they perceive to be solutions through discursive registers and material proposals that rely on carceral logics. Thus, in Monroe County, officials used local carceral expansion as a form of resistance to state and national prison policy. This rather bleak outlook is one way that I could end this book.

I suggest a sober, if still radically hopeful, position. Persistent attempts at carceral expansion in Bloomington should give pause to reform efforts that do not centralize decarceration as the means and end of their strategy. Moreover, this book has shown how well-meaning initiatives that may purport to be decarcerative can result in further elongating the carceral continuum. Specialty courts, work release centers, and juvenile treatment—all conducted in the name of reform and humane policy—can broaden the reach of systems that in all sorts of ways enact daily violence in people's lives.

The radical hope I maintain is based on my own observations of people struggling to destabilize the logics that justify such a system. Indeed, the diffuse and hegemonic quality of carceral logic and practice is not the only lesson of this book. There were moments of resistance in Monroe County that disrupted and occasionally defeated carceral discourses and projects. These moments can occur discursively, as I illustrated through much of chapter 8's discussion of DMC's challenge to the rhetoric of the justice campus. They also can reshape understandings of issues on which carcerality has been predicated, and a changed understanding can then cause carceral projects to lose momentum and legitimacy. These moments can occur as insurrectionary acts of rebellion, risking freedom and safety to flatten the tires of the carceral machine. Resistant moments can arise through the promotion of paradigmatically alternative models of conflict resolution, decision making, and program provision.

Perhaps most devastating to carceral expansion, resistance can take the form of reimagining once-carceral space, disrupting incarceration's seeming inevitability and offering a counterhegemonic cartography. In the case of Monroe County, local activists reimagined the bricks and mortar of the justice campus as the rainwater catchment barrels, compost piles, greenhouses, education centers, green jobs, and garden beds of a sustainable and noncarceral community landscape. The insistence on this vision for the eighty-five-acre site appears to have circulated widely and upwardly, beginning among grass-roots land-use and decarceration activists and moving into the realm of official county politics as it gained momentum. In the process, the trajectory for the old Thomson site from deindustrialized surplus land to carceral development appears to have been broken.

Epilogue

As I write these final words in the early fall of 2014, I am struck by how much more relevant the book has become since I completed the majority of the research in 2010. At that time, I worried that my focus on expansions of municipal jail and juvenile detention facilities (rather than prisons) and on liberal politics and discourses might make the book marginal or even irrelevant. But in recent years we have begun to glimpse a shift in the composition of the carceral state as well as a notable change in its justifying logic and rhetoric. First, legislative and administrative changes around the country have been heralded as prison reform but have also resulted in jail expansion projects, including those that, like the justice campus in Monroe County, justify themselves through appeals to what the scholar-activist James Kilgore has recently called "carceral humanism."[1] In addition, discussions of prison reform emanate from the most conservative corners of American politics, as right-wing politicians, think tanks, media, and even private prison companies have changed their tune and now discuss reform, reentry, and rehabilitation.[2] What lessons might *Progressive Punishment* have for understanding such developments?

As the book makes clear, well-meaning efforts at reform can lead to the enhancement and enlargement of carceral logics and infrastructure. In the context of four decades of insistence on imprisonment, it is perhaps not surprising that the carceral state has developed a tendency to frame virtually any social problem in the language of punishment, correction, and social control. Neoliberal ideology, policy, and discourse have effectively naturalized carceral expansion into a new political common sense for communities facing multiple crises of deindustrialization and rising social inequalities. But jails and prisons should not be stimulus programs designed to bring jobs or infrastructure to rural and semi-rural communities; we should be organizing to close facilities, decarcerate populations, and demand just employment agendas for depressed economies. Similarly, to the extent that jails and prisons exist, they most certainly should have robust mental health, education, and treatment options, but we must resist any attachment of campaigns for programs to campaigns for expansion. The carceral state is an exercise in "official racial class war,"[3] and expanded, new or allegedly humane institutions simply enable the treatment—coercive, punitive, and encaged—of more poor people left out of labor markets, marginalized or abandoned by shrinking social services, and left to be managed by incarceration, presented as it might be in the benevolent rhetorical guise of a justice campus. The growing importance of the jail in American imprisonment, the routing of welfare state services through the carceral apparatus, and the attention being paid to reentry and rehabilitation by the Right indicate the reorganization of the carceral state around and through new discourses and initiatives. My hope is that *Progressive Punishment* can be read as a case study of one community's production and contestation of this insidious phase of the carceral state.

Rather than fighting for so-called carceral humanism, we would do well to consider the insights from a growing number of critical prison scholars whose acute analyses might hold the key to abolition of the prison-industrial complex and the structural conditions that make it possible. This field broadens scholarly inquiry beyond crime and punishment to engage more deeply, critically, and historically with the underlying logics that produce, and are reproduced by, the carceral state. This work historicizes and challenges common-sense explanations of the rise of the carceral state (Gottschalk 2006; Muhammad 2010; Murakawa 2014; Platt 2009); examines the relationships between imprisonment and immigrant detention (Loyd, Mitchelson, and Burridge 2012); illuminates the shadowy extensions of the carceral state into civil power (Beckett and Murakawa 2012) and considers it beyond the boundaries of the prison (Hannah-Moffat and Lynch 2012; Story forthcoming); reveals how the state normalizes the violence of carceral and police power in schools (Meiners 2011; Simmons 2009), as well as against the backdrop of state violence abroad (D. Rodriguez 2006a; Wall 2013); demonstrates the insidious punishment that reforms can perform (Braz 2006; Kilgore 2014a, 2014b and 2015); traces the ascendance of the carceral state back to capitalism's restructuring of the state itself (De Giorgi 2006; Gilmore 1999 and 2007; Gilmore and Gilmore 2008; Peck 2003; Stein 2014; Wacquant 2009b); maps the ways carceral practices exist in space generally (Moran 2015) and organize racialized, class-based, and gendered domestic spaces (Haley 2013; Shabazz 2010), urban neighborhoods (Alexander 2010; Beckett and Herbert 2009; Clear 2007; Story 2013; Wacquant 2001), and rural landscapes (Bonds 2009 and 2012; Huling 2002; Schept 2014) specifically; centralizes prisons and prisoners in histories of racism, capitalism, imperialism, and struggle (Berger 2014; James 2002 and 2007; D. Rodriguez 2006b); explores the intersections of carceral state violence with gender, sexuality, and ability (Ben-Moshe, Chapman, and Carey 2014; Kim 2011; Law 2011 and 2014; Musto 2013 and forthcoming; Richie 2012 and 2014; Stanley and Smith 2011); details the cultural work that penal regimes perform to legitimize—indeed, to normalize—the acceptance of their presence in our lives (Brown 2009 and 2014; Walby and Piché 2011); and considers and centers the very project of abolition itself (Critical Resistance 2000; CR10 Publications Collective 2008; Davis 2003). In this growing, interdisciplinary field of trenchant, radical, and insurrectionary work, critical prison scholars—many of whom join activists in addressing these issues on the ground—provide the intellectual tools with which to perceive, disrupt, and dismantle the next iteration of the carceral state and imagine and build a noncarceral future.

NOTES

INTRODUCTION

1 See A. Davis 2003; Hartnett 2011; Schlosser 1998; Sudbury 2005. More broadly, see Critical Resistance 2000.

2 See Alexander 2010; Austin and Irwin 2001;Bonds 2009; Brown 2009; Clear 1994 and 2007; Clear and Frost 2014; Currie 1998; De Giorgi 2006; Donziger 1996; Garland 2001; Gilmore 1999 and 2007; Hallett 2006; Hooks et al. 2010; Huling 2002; James 2002 and 2007; Loury 2008; Mauer 2000; Mauer and Chesney-Lind 2002; Muhammad 2010; Simon 2007; Western 2006.

3 Alexander (2010, 7) and Gottschalk (2006, 10) offer historical perspectives on the complicity of liberals in both opening the door for and then actively championing penal growth. L. Feldman, Schiraldi, and Ziedenberg (2001, 2) offer a particular (and particularly poignant) focus on President Bill Clinton as "the Incarceration President," a claim that Wacquant (2009a, 153 and 302) also makes compellingly. Simon (2007, 59) also recognizes Clinton's strategy to match or outdo President George W. Bush on punitiveness. See Braz 2006 and Murakawa 2014 for different perspectives on expansion that are similar to the one taken in this book.

4 National Clearinghouse for Criminal Justice Planning and Architecture 1977, 29–30 and Appendix A-4.

5 Multiple sources offered this analysis of the historical trajectory of the jail, including long-time activists who filed suit to stop its construction as well as current and former members of county government who favored and organized its construction. While activists who opposed its construction cited its immediate overcrowding as evidence of the "if you build it, they will come" principle, those in favor of its construction—all of whom were progressive Democrats—defended their choice.

6 Trevor Richardson v. Monroe County Sheriff and Monroe County Commissioners, 1:08-cv-0174-RLY-JMS (US District Court, Southern District of Indiana 2008), 2. See also Higgs 2008b and Lane 2009.

7 See BBC News n.d.

8 McLennan 2008, 3. See also Platt 2009 and Willrich 2003.

9 See Garland 1990; Murakawa 2014; Platt 2009; Prisciotta 1996; Rothman 2002.

10 See Bonds 2009 and 2012; Gilmore 2007; Hooks et al. 2010; Hooks, Mosher, Lobao, and Rotolo 2004; Huling 2002; Schept 2014. On the "common sense" of neoliberalism more broadly, see Harvey 2005.

11 For a similar observation about the relationship between economic, political, and ideological processes, see Burawoy 2012, 194.

12 See Wacquant 2009a for foundational work that traces the origins and international circulations of what he calls the "neoliberal punitive doxa" (ibid., 2).

13 Platt refers to a study from the 1960s that observed: "The control of the 'environmental causes' of crime is not simply making the basic political and economic changes that would eliminate poverty and poor living conditions in the first place. Instead, the prevention of crime meant linking up the criminal justice system with the schools, the family, and other institutions that affected the lives of the people considered likely to become criminal. In practice, then, the apparently 'humane' emphasis on the environmental causes of crime became the political reality of increased control over aspects of the lives of many people—especially poor people—that previously had been relatively neglected" (2009, xxvii).

14 Many scholars engaged in historical and contemporary excavations of the carceral state and its varying logics have made variations of this argument. For historical examinations of rehabilitation and the logics that suture it to racialization, criminalization, and punishment, see Brown 2009; Foucault 1977 and 1980, especially 37–54; Garland 1990, especially 249–76; Platt 2009; Prisciotta 1996; Rothman 2002. For work that explores this relationship in current practice, see McCorkel 2013.

15 See, for example, Coombs and Newman 2011; Gingrich and Jones 2014; Right on Crime 2015; Viguerie 2013; Zornick 2014.

16 Gilmore 2007; Gilmore and Gilmore 2008; Harvey 2005.

17 For similar considerations of hegemony and resistance, see Lazarus-Black and Hirsch 1994; Scott 1985 and 1990.

18 Other ethnographic and theoretical work attuned to the structuring of local processes and the need for multiscalar analyses influenced my approach. Perhaps most in line with the methodological approach of *Progressive Punishment*, the geographer Jamie Peck has argued that "the *realities* of state restructuring are therefore inevitably more complex than stylized readings of processes like 'deregulation', 'privatization', 'neoliberalization' and 'hollowing out' typically suggest. The task of theoretically informed research on state restructuring has to extend beyond mere reaffirmation of these received categories. . . . [C]arefully formulated empirical work is required in order to expose underlying patterns and processes, and to generate critical cases and counter-cases" (2003, 223). Writing of the mission of cultural geography, Don Mitchell argues that the discipline constitutes "the study of how particular social relations intersect with more general processes, a study grounded in the production and reproduction of actual places, spaces, and scales *and* the social structures that give those places, spaces and scales meaning" (2000, 294). The anthropologist Phillipe Bourgois has observed that the ethnographic method "allows the 'pawns' of larger structural forces to emerge as real human beings who shape their own futures" (1996, 17), but he and Jeff Schonberg have also insisted on understanding the everyday violence and suffering of homeless heroin injectors as a "politically structured phenomenon" (2009, 16). In addition, James Clifford and George Marcus

observe that "cultural analysis is always enmeshed in global movements of difference and power" and call for ethnography to "define its object of study in ways that permit detailed, local, contextual analysis and simultaneously the portrayal of global implicating forces" (1986, 22). See also Abu Lughod 1991; Gupta and Ferguson 1997.

19 Of course, ethnography is also a representation. For a discussion of representation in the context of proposing ethnography's task in a globalized world, see Appadurai 1996, 56. See also Bourgois and Schonberg 2009.

20 See Bourgois and Schonberg 2009; Graeber 2004 and 2009; Hale 2006; Kirsch 2002; Scheper-Hughes 1992 and 1995; Thomas 1993.

21 This is not to say that criminology does not have a history of activist research or a present. Indeed, the legacy of the Berkeley school of criminology, familiar as it was with radical activism of the 1960s and 1970s, continues to inspire contemporary activist scholarship. In addition, journals such as *Contemporary Justice Review*, *Radical Criminology*, and *Social Justice* feature work by activists, scholar-activists, and those whose work focuses on leftist movements. Finally, recent work advocating for an activist criminology headlined the discipline's annual meeting and subsequently appeared in the discipline's flagship journal (Belknap 2015). For an examination of the Berkeley school and its legacy, see Platt 2014. For some discussion of activist research methods, see Ferrell and Hamm 1998a and Schept 2014.

22 Quoted in Hillier and Rooksby 2005, 7.

23 Michael Burawoy takes a slightly different position on reflexive science, although his also inspires my approach in this book. He writes: "Reflexive science starts out from dialogue, virtual or real, between observer and participants, [and] embeds such dialogue within a second dialogue between local processes and extralocal forces that in turn can only be comprehended through a third, expanding dialogue of theory with itself" (1998, 5). See also Burawoy et al. 1991.

24 For a recent discussion of the complexity of conducting prison ethnography, see McCorkel 2013.

25 For example, Angela Davis identifies the prison as a "key ingredient of our common sense" (2003, 18), and Dylan Rodriguez, writing of the reaction of outrage to the photographs of abuse and torture at Abu Ghraib, calls the prison a "naturalized landscape on which the political drama of other scenes of torture and terror take place" (2006a, 10). See also Schept 2014; Wacquant 2009a and 1999.

26 Readers interested in more developed and precise analyses of this phenomenon should see M. Davis 1998; De Giorgi 2006; Gilmore 1999 and 2007.

27 On modernist discourses and state governance, see Horkheimer and Adorno 2002; Bourdieu 1977; Foucault 1980; Neocleous 2003; Said 1979; Scott 1998. In chapter 5, I rely on some of these theorists to trace the connections between state and local knowledge. Ultimately, I find that a number of processes work to transmit state knowledge into the local sphere, circumscribing through discourse the very knowledge about crime and incarceration that could be produced.

28 This includes chapters such as "Critically Applied Public Anthropology" in Bourgois and Schonberg 2009; "Prison Reform or Prison Abolition?" and "Abolitionist

Alternatives" in A. Davis 2003; "Mothers Reclaiming Our Children" and "What is to be Done?" in Gilmore 2007; "Framing Alternatives" in Wehr and Aseltine 2013; and American Friends Service Committee 1971; CR 10 Publications Collective 2008; James 2005; Loyd, Mitchelson, and Burridge 2012; Morris 1995; West and Morris 2000.

PART 1. NEOLIBERAL GEOGRAPHIES OF PROGRESSIVE PUNISHMENT

1 On planning and prison expansion, see Gilmore 2007.
2 M. Davis 1998, 416. See also Gilmore 1999 and 2007.
3 On the ideology of landscape, see Mitchell 1996; N. Smith 2008. On the instrumental and at times ideological role of prison architecture, see Evans 2011; Foucault 1977; Garland 1990, especially 258–60; Jewkes 2013; Jewkes and Moran 2014.
4 On the work of visuality, or the authorial role of the state in structuring the way it can be perceived, see Mirzoeff 2011. On the relationship between visuality and the carceral landscape, see Schept 2014.

CHAPTER 1. CAPITAL DEPARTURES AND THE ARRIVAL OF PUNISHMENT

1 Numerous scholarly, popular, and industry publications detail the history of RCA and its relationship to Bloomington. See Counts, Madison, and Sanders 2002; Cowie 1999; "RCA Handbook of Information in Bloomington" (hereafter "RCA Handbook"), 1960, 7, folder 10, box 5, O'Hara RCA Thomson Company Collection, 1900–2006, William Henry Smith Memorial Library, Indiana Historical Society, Indianapolis, IN (hereafter RCA Thomson Collection).
2 Cowie 1999, 42.
3 Counts, Madison, and Sanders 2002, 30.
4 "RCA Handbook," 7
5 "RCA in Indiana," January 1961, folder 9, box 5, RCA Thomson Collection.
6 Federal Register, Volume 42, Number 199, Friday, Oct 14, 1977, Box 87, Folder 21, RCA Thomson Collection.
7 For example, between April 1975 and July 1982, Bloomington lost 3,500 RCA positions (Cowie 1999, 129).
8 Quoted in Fabris 1985.
9 Bernard Isautier, chairman and CEO, Thomson Consumer Electronics, October 18, 1990, folder 3, box 103, RCA Thomson Collection.
10 For a more detailed analysis of RCA and the changing political economy that resulted in its series of departures from American cities, including Bloomington, see Cowie 1999.
11 On the normalizing and aestheticizing of the visual field and the available narratives in which to situate it, see Mirzoeff 2011. Considering the justice campus as an aesthetic—its name, mission, and imagined spatial contours—is especially productive in thinking through how local officials critical of incarceration could propose it and overlook its inevitable contradictions. Fredric Jameson has noted that "the aesthetic act is itself ideological, and the production of aesthetic or narrative form

is to be seen as an ideological act in its own right, with the function of inventing imaginary or formal 'solutions' to unresolvable social contradictions" (1981, 79).

12 There is substantial scholarship on the connections between job loss, persistent joblessness, and incarceration. See, for example, Currie 1987; Simon 1993; W. Wilson 1997.

13 Werth 1998a; Lane 1999.

14 Through the 1960s and 1970s, an average of 4 prisons were built in rural areas of the United States each year. During the 1980s that figure jumped to 16, and during the 1990s it jumped again to 25. In the 1990s alone, 245 prisons were constructed in rural communities, or a new prison every fifteen days. Altogether, 350 prisons have been built since the 1980s. On specific communities in various places in the United States struggling to resolve crisis through prison siting, see Bonds 2009; Huling 2002 (citing a 2001 paper by Calvin Beale); Hunter and Wagner 2008; Schept 2014; Williams 2011. Bonds (2009 and 2012) especially situates rural prison growth in the northwestern United States in the context of neoliberal economic restructuring. Other work has further explained the processes of crisis and surplus in contemporary formations of capitalism that have prompted prison growth. See De Giorgi 2007; Gilmore 1999 and 2007, especially 30–86.

15 See Editorial 2009a; Hinnefeld 1998; Morin 2003; Travis 2003a, 2003b and 2008; Werth 1998b, 2001, 2004a, and 2004b.

16 For brief histories and analyses of the foundation's financial dealings and eventual collapse, see Allen 2006; Mohrweis 2003.

17 Werth 2001. See also Travis 2003a and 2003b.

18 Werth 2001.

19 On CRED funding in Indiana, see Landers and Harmon 2012.

20 The use of a County Option Income Tax would allow Monroe County to raise income taxes by a fraction of a percent to channel the monies directly to juvenile services, including the transformation of a youth shelter into something like a youth facility.

21 Landers and Harmon 2012, 2.

22 Werth 2001. See also First Capital Group n.d.

23 M. Rodriguez 2008.

24 Editorial 2009a.

25 Van der Dussen 2002.

26 Juvenile Justice Task Force 2007.

27 Nolan 2009a.

28 For a rich discussion of urban gentrification, including its relationship to the processes of uneven development at work in Bloomington, see N. Smith 1996 and, more broadly, 2008. Smith discusses the tax incentive districting that the county deployed in the wake of Thomson's departure and locates its origins in the economic policies of President Ronald Reagan and Prime Minister Margaret Thatcher.

29 J. Wilson and Kelling 1982. For important critiques of broken windows policing, see Harcourt 2001; McArdle and Erzen 2001; Stewart 1998.

30 See City of Bloomington 2015.

31 Ibid., 8.
32 Editorial 2013.
33 City of Bloomington 2015, 8.
34 Editorial 2013.
35 Beckett and Herbert 2009, 8. See also Lynch Omori, Roussell, and Valasik 2013.
36 On moral regulation, see Hunt 1999. On the spatial logics of this policing strategy and the broader capitalist urban geographies that set the conditions for its existence, see Herbert and Brown 2006.
37 Cowie 1999, 41
38 In addition to noting the economic instability of prisons as replacements for the loss of industrial jobs, Peter Wagner (2002) has been especially vocal in pointing to the gerrymandering that has occurred in states around the country where rural prisons have been delivered to communities suffering from the loss of manufacturing jobs and small farms. Specifically, new growth in prison populations is counted toward a given rural community's population growth. Thus, new districts are created, giving these communities money and political representation. Following the trajectory of prisoners' bodies reveals that the money and political power given to prison towns comes from somewhere: prisoners' home communities, which lose both the individual who is incarcerated and the financial and political capital that comes with him or her. See Gilmore 2007; Hunter and Wagner 2008.
39 Considerable work in geography and critical social theory has made pointed observations about the productive role of capital in mobilizing very definitions of nature (Harvey 1996; N. Smith 2008) and conceptions of space (Lefebvre 1991). Karl Marx also observed that "nature becomes for the first time simply an object for mankind, purely a matter of utility; it ceases to be recognized as a power in its own right; and the theoretical knowledge of its independent laws appears only as a stratagem designed to subdue it to human requirements, whether as the object of consumption or as the means of production" (1973, 410, as quoted in Harvey 2001, 53).
40 As De Giorgi has noted of the era of Fordist capitalism during which RCA arrived and thrived in Bloomington, and under which biopolitical regimes of disciplinary control enjoyed their most universal application, "in fact, it is particularly in the first half of the twentieth century that the project of a perfect articulation between the discipline of the body and the regulation of whole populations came to completion, embodied as it was in the economic regime of the factory, in the social model of the *welfare state* and in the penal paradigm of the 'correctional' prison" (2006, x).

CHAPTER 2. CONSOLIDATIONS AND EXPANSIONS

1 On the work that landscape does to (re)produce social relations, see Mitchell 2000, especially chapters 4 and 5. This point is also taken up forcefully by Mark Neocleous, who argues (following Lefebvre 1991) that "the fabrication of *social* order is simultaneously the fabrication of *spatial* order" (Neocleous 2003, 101).
2 Beckett and Western 2001, 44. There has been considerable and compelling scholarship on the post-Keynesian withdrawal of welfare and the neoliberal state's restruc-

turing around incarceration as a solution to the crises that the state itself produced. See Gilmore 2002 and 2007; Gilmore and Gilmore 2008; Peck 2003; Wacquant 2009b.

3 Simon 2007.

4 See Garland 2001, 34. More broadly, see Garland 1990, especially chapter 6; Rothman 2002.

5 An argument could be made that much of the prison's history can be understood within a similar dynamic of reformist and even benevolent intentions eliciting brutally punitive changes. Indeed, Charles Dickens's observations of early American penality suggest that subsequent Jacksonian reforms, child saving, twentieth-century penal welfarism, and modern articulations of liberal carcerality such as the justice campus are part of a genealogy extending from the origins of the institutions. Michelle Brown has aptly observed that Dickens "foregrounds a complex and crucial tension in prison tourism by positioning the benevolent intentions of the system's implementers against the uncanny sense that something remains dreadfully wrong with the practice of punishment itself" (2009, 95). See also Dickens 1985.

6 Keith Hayward's discussion of modernist space resonates here: "On the one hand, there is the classical modernist attempt to *recapture order, re-colonise, re-condition and discipline* these emergent unruly zones—essentially to reintegrate the abandoned postindustrial spaces left in the wake of a superseded Fordism and repair the broken net of the modernist project. On the other hand, the literature points to the appearance of a new and distinctive mode of social control in which overt exclusion is precisely the crucial mechanism, *the solution not the problem*" (2004, 156). See also Beckett and Herbert 2009.

7 Indeed, Wacquant notes the legislative changes in California and at the federal level in the United States that signify the merging of welfare management into the penal realm: "in the 1980s alone, in addition to reducing public assistance, California passed nearly 1,000 laws expanding the use of prison sentences; at the federal level, the 1996 reform that 'ended welfare as we know it' was complemented by the sweeping Violent Crime Control and Law Enforcement Act of 1993 and bolstered by the No Frills Prison Act of 1995" (2010, 204). Thus, according to Wacquant, prison takes the physical, spatial, and social place of welfare and, in the process, subjects welfare to the growing punitive logics guiding incarceration. See also Wacquant 2009b, especially 55–86.

8 Other, broader critiques of Wacquant are important, if not totally germane here. See, for example, Piven 2010; Valverde 2010.

9 For a more substantive consideration of the politics of security, including their heavy reliance on liberalism, see Neocleous 2008 and 2011.

10 Lemert 2007, 96.

11 Wiest et al. 2007.

12 Truancy was already constituted as an infraction of the law and had been formally handled by the Juvenile Division of the Probation Department since 2004. Indeed,

according to the department's annual report for 2008, truancy accounted for 53 percent (140 of 267) of the status offenses referred to the department, an eight-year reign as the top referral within the status offense category. Truancy accounted for 14 percent of the total referrals to juvenile probation (146 of 999). See Monroe Circuit Court Probation Department, 2008, 75–81 and 115. The truancy court certainly did not introduce truancy as a juridical category, but it further cemented it onto the carceral continuum.

13 In *Governing through Crime*, Jonathan Simon writes that parents consume security and buy into governance through crime, yet this investment has consequences, especially for families without resources. He notes that for poorer families, "encounters are likely to be more state centered and coercive. The message to parents is that the repression of criminal conduct must take priority over any other objectives of child rearing and that parents will be expected to accomplish this largely on their own or with what they can purchase" (2007, 202).

14 This point is important methodologically, as it suggests that simply observing and analyzing patterns of speech and rhetoric is insufficient to an analysis of discourse. Rather, what is needed is an ethnographic layer to interrogate the meanings embedded in particular constitutive moments of discourse. See Altheide 1987; Ferrell, Hayward, and Young 2008, especially 176–92.

15 See also S. Cohen 1991; J. Miller 1998; Rothman 2002. For a compelling critique of the net-widening analyses offered by Austin and Krisberg (1981), see Sloop 1996, 172–84; McMahon 1990.

CHAPTER 3. "RED NECK" AND "UNSOCIALIZED," WITH "SUBCULTURAL NORMS AND VALUES"

1 False consciousness is generally associated much more with ideology and hegemony than with habitus. In spite of Pierre Bourdieu's insistence on the agentive work of habitus, I would argue that his consistent location of agency at the mercy of implicating and inscribing structures suggests a belief that our dispositions are frequently the product of forces beyond our control. He says as much when laying out his understanding of the universe of available discourses within habitus. In *Outline of a Theory of Practice*, he writes that "when there is a quasi-perfect correspondence between the objective order and the subjective principles of organization, the natural and social world appears as self-evident. This experience we shall call doxa, so as to distinguish it from an orthodox or heterodox belief implying awareness and recognition of the possibility of different or antagonistic beliefs. Schemes of thought and perception can produce the objectivity that they do produce only by producing misrecognition of the limits of the cognition that they make possible, thereby founding immediate adherence, in the doxic mode, to the world of tradition experienced as a 'natural world' and taken for granted" (1977, 164). On habitus as the embodied site of hegemony, see also Schaffer 2004, especially 119. On the doxa of carceral common sense, see also Wacquant 1999.

2 McCorkel 2013, 3 (quoting Gowan and Whetstone 2012).

3 Higgs 2008a.

4 Interestingly, and unsurprisingly, there is a strong rhetorical connection between the framing of jail intervention by local officials and civic leaders and that of the Center for Therapeutic Justice. In *American Jails*, the center praises the work of the American Jail Association and then writes: "Without a doubt jails offer an opportunity for early intervention and prevention. In a cost-effective manner, jails can be a window of opportunity for offenders to be assessed, educated, treated and trained for release into a productive life. Effective reduction of recidivism will take money and jobs away from the jail-to-prison industrial complex" (Center for Therapeutic Justice 2000). This perspective likely offered an intellectual affirmation of local orientations in Bloomington to the jail.

5 Prisciotta 1996, 52. See also Foucault 1977, especially 293–308; Rothman 2002, especially 261–89.

6 Barrett's view of a correctional justice campus resonates historically with the "liberal totalitarianism" that Erik Wright observed at the end of penal welfarism. In contrast to the purely "custodial prison," Wright observed that in the "Correctional Prison," "the totalitarianism of the structure ostensibly serves to create a setting where rehabilitation can occur. The formal goal of the prison is no longer to exact retribution, but to transform the 'antisocial criminal' into a 'responsible, law abiding citizen.' Prison officials argue that a prerequisite for accomplishing this goal is order and security within the prison. The totalitarianism of the prison regime is seen as a necessary means to that end" (1973, 154). Moreover, Barrett offers a rather striking example of changes in penality and power observed and predicted by Michel Foucault in *Discipline and Punish*. Foucault writes of the "theoretical disavowal" French judges display toward punishment: "Do not imagine that the sentences that we judges pass are activated by a desire to punish; they are intended to correct, reclaim, 'cure'" (1977, 10).

7 I spend little time covering this development because it occurred as I was drawing my data collection to a close. DMC activists working with the community radio station WFHB interviewed family members of jail prisoners to gauge their response to the changes in visitation. Many described the change as further punishing their loved ones. See WFHB 2010.

8 Brooks 2010.

9 Nolan 2009b.

10 See, for example, Garland 1990; J. Miller 1998; Platt 2009, 19; Prisciotta 1996.

11 Garland 1990, 249. See also G. Gray and Salole 2006.

12 On this point, see Wacquant 2009b, especially 287–316.

13 See Norris 2008.

14 Fields 1990, 118.

15 Murakawa 2014, 12.

16 I found that Bloomington constructions of this dual poverty were closely aligned with observations made elsewhere about broader trends in the construction of morally and intellectually inferior others (Schwalbe et al. 2000).

17 Michael Willrich has noted in reference to Foucault's work on "moral authorities, social investigators, and public officials" that "by producing authoritative knowledge of social life," those people "shaped cultural conceptions of what it meant to be a normal, healthy, fully realized person" (2003, xxviii).

18 See P. Gray 2013; Hannah-Moffat 2005; Harcourt 2010; Kramer, Rajah, and Sung 2013; Robinson 2008.

19 For example, Patricia Erickson and Steven Erickson note that "the social construction of mental illness remains an 'individuated-legal' construction and seeks to prevent criminalization of the mentally ill through programs designed to treat the person's 'mental illness.' Such an approach is consistent with how we currently frame social problems in our society. Rather than seeing them as embedded in structural inequality, we view social ills as rooted in individual pathology and rely on solutions like mental health courts to address the individuals who come to their attention" (2008, 190).

20 Bonilla-Silva 2006, 3.

21 See, for example, Foucault 1977 and 1980; Neocleous 2003, 45–61. Consider also officials' dispositions toward "jailable" individuals in light of Scott Schaffer's productive argument for understanding habitus as the embodiment of hegemony: "[Habitus] becomes the site of the dominant social order and its manifestations in the cultural, linguistic, political and economic realms, and leads the individual social actor to misrecognize the power relations manifesting themselves through interpersonal interactions, that is interactions of habituses, as arbitrary, when in fact they are a direct result of the structuring of society" (2004, 104)."

22 Gillis 2006; Piquero and Mazerolle 2001.

23 Circuit court judge Allan Barrett in the justice campus hearing hosted by the MC-CJCC, November 2008.

24 See Lane 2011, describing public defender Dan Little's characterization of one of his own clients.

25 Reuben Davison in an interview with me.

26 Ibid.

27 Brian Mulvaney, a member of the county council, and Victoria Krause, a consultant to the county on juvenile justice issues, in separate interviews with me.

28 Probably to their embarrassment, liberal and leftist officials thus endorsed some of the same constructs and conclusions as some of the more explicitly conservative criminologists. See Bennett, DiIulio, and Walters 1996.

29 Indiana Code 35–43–4–2 provides that theft is a D felony if the fair market value of the property is less than $100,000. Such theft is punishable by six months to three years in prison.

30 Indiana Code 34–47–4–2 provides for "procuring personal jurisdiction" over a person who is in violation of a court order. This is often used to jail people for failure to pay child support. Interestingly, Decarcerate Monroe County discovered substantial public opposition to this particular practice, notably from the spouses and partners of those doing time under these writs. According to them, the overdue

child support payments more often reflected low-wage employment and thus a lack of ability to pay, rather than a lack of desire to do so.

31 Indiana Code 35–42–2–1 provides that someone who knowingly or intentionally touches another person in a rude, insolent, or angry manner commits battery, which is a class B misdemeanor. However, the offense is a class A misdemeanor if it results in bodily injury to another person or is committed against a law enforcement or correctional facility officer or a firefighter who is lawfully engaged in the execution of his or her duties.

32 See, for example, the discussion of what can constitute a "violent" offense in Clear and Frost 2014, 21.

33 The institutional racism of mass incarceration has been profiled and dissected in a rich literature, including work on the criminalization of Blackness (Delgado 1994; Muhammad 2010), the contemporary disproportionate imprisonment of people of color (Clear and Frost 2014; Gilmore 2007; James 2002 and 2007; Loury, 2008; Wacquant 2001), and the collateral consequences of such racialized incarceration (Clear 2007; Mauer and Chesney-Lind 2002), including the extension of Jim Crow discrimination through incarceration (Alexander 2010).

34 Linneman and Wall 2013, 324.

35 Newitz and Wray 1997, 172. On the historical origins and broader circulations of terms such as "white trash," see Wray 2006.

36 For a short discussion of the notion of "real crime" as Black crime, see Alexander 2010, 193. For a contemporary ethnographic examination of this phenomenon in practice, see McCorkel 2013.

CHAPTER 4. "A LOCKDOWN FACILITY . . . WITH THE FEEL OF A SMALL, PRIVATE COLLEGE"

1 Simon 2010.

2 See the last note in chapter 2.

3 Crawford 1999; Myers and Goddard 2013.

4 See Crawford 1999; Lea and Stenson 2007; Meiners 2011; Rose and Miller 1992.

5 The quote is from Randall, but it was supported by testimony from other officials.

6 Foucault has written of the French juvenile reformatory Mettray that the workers there had to be "not exactly judges, or teachers, or foremen, or non-commissioned officers, or 'parents' but something of all these things in a quite specific mode of intervention. They were in a sense technicians of behavior, orthopedists of individuality. Their task was to produce bodies that were both docile and capable" (1977, 294). Writing of the "World of Juvenile Justice" during the Progressive era, the historian David Rothman observes that "the descent from the rhetoric to the reality of juvenile institutions is precipitous. The ideals that justified incarceration had little relevance to actual circumstances. No matter how frequently juvenile court judges insisted that their sentences of confinement were for treatment and not punishment, no matter how vehemently superintendents declared that their institutions were rehabilitative and not correctional, conditions at training schools belied these claims" (2002, 268).

7 This orientation of the probation department and the juvenile court is grounded in the institutions' historical development. See Platt 2009, especially 142–45; Rothman 2002.

8 Important work on youth experiences of detention has profiled the ways that youth manage and negotiate coercive programming in the context of detention. See Abrams and Anderson-Nathe 2013; Cox 2011.

9 Brown 2009; Foucault 1977; Garland 1990 and 2001.

10 Kramer, Rajah, and Sung 2013.

11 Foucault 1977, 184

12 P. Gray 2013, 520. See also Fox 1999; Kramer, Rajah, and Sung, 2013; Robinson 2008.

13 There is no shortage of scholarship that reveals the work the juvenile justice process performed in the service of instantiating class and labor relations. See Platt 2009; Prisciotta 1996; Rothman 2002. Alexander Prisciotta writes of the prison reform movement at Elmira Reformatory in New York State that its benevolent rhetoric "masked a repressive class control agenda" designed to "build docile bodies . . . and instill youthful offenders with the habits of order, discipline and self control and to mold obedient citizen-workers. The 'socialization' and 'normalization' of offenders was aimed at controlling the lower classes and, on a practical and symbolic level, contributing to the development of an orderly society" (1996, 7–8). In slightly different terms, it is perhaps appropriate to consider the juvenile reformatory's historical and contemporary role as a form of pacification, fabricating a particular social order centered around deference to accumulation and state power (Neocleous 2000 and 2011; see also Schept, Wall, and Brisman forthcoming).

14 Muhammad 2010.

15 Alexander 2010, 192–202; Delgado 1994; Wacquant 2001

16 McCorkel 2013, especially 70–93. See also Cox forthcoming.

17 See Cox forthcoming; Roberts and Mahtani 2010.

18 Muhammad 2011, 77.

19 Hall et al. 2013, 68. See also Croteau and Hoynes 2013; Foucault 1980; Hall 1982, 64; Kappeler and Potter 2004.

20 Anthony Platt observed a similar pattern of concern about the newly created juvenile court, noting that certain child savers had advocated for the creation of the court so that children "might be saved from contamination of association with older criminals" (2009, 129).

21 The organization sees its mission and vision in the following way: "Critical Resistance seeks to build an international movement to end the prison industrial complex (PIC) by challenging the belief that caging and controlling people makes us safe. We believe that basic necessities such as food, shelter, and freedom are what really make our communities secure. As such, our work is part of global struggles against inequality and powerlessness" (Critical Resistance 2014).

22 This irony raises the issue of visibility as another contested term central to the fight for hegemony. In the county narrative, the panoptic visibility of youth being detained and treated locally is paramount. For community organizers and some youth

workers like Daniels, visibility means youth playing an active—indeed, expert—role in the political process through which a facility is built or not. These issues are discussed again in part 3.

23 For a discussion of punishment and social exclusion and abandonment, see Brown 2009. For example, Brown writes that "punishment is never about inclusion . . . [rather,] punishment [is] the institution par excellence from which to consider how and when we will treat those who fall outside the frames of social inclusion, of how and under what conditions we will respond through the intentional invocation of pain to the weaknesses, violence, vulnerabilities, and suffering of others" (ibid., 35).

PART 3. CARCERAL EPISTEMOLOGY

1 Don Mitchell writes: "Culture wars are about defining what is legitimate in a society, who is an 'insider' and who is an 'outsider.' They are about determining the social boundaries that govern our lives" (2000, 5). Elsewhere, David Harvey has observed that representations of space and their contestations are "as fiercely fought and as fundamental to the activities of place construction as bricks and mortar" (1993, 23).

2 See, for example, Fanon 2004; Richards 1993; Said 1978; R. Young 2001. For an especially pertinent analysis of the relationship between colonialism and the construction of criminological knowledge, see Agozino 2003.

3 Here I mean, as I believe Foucault does, not solely the academic discipline of criminology and its discourse but also the larger, more popular and political discourse of criminology produced by media, politicians, agencies, and organizations and consumed by many. I do not necessarily see these as mutually exclusive discourses, but rather as infusing and constituting one another. Thus, Monroe County meetings about local facilities that featured lay and professional discussions of crime and criminal justice, an example of the latter discourse, used terms and concepts of the former—such as "evidenced-based practices," "criminological literature," and "accepted criminological theory"—as a form of symbolic capital to render their discourse more official.

4 For a concise explanation of these tendencies in the context of explaining the relatively slow embrace of social constructionism within academic criminal justice, see Nicole Rafter 1990. Rafter writes of the dominance of the discipline by the professional model that prioritizes agency needs and solutions to immediate and practical problems, the influence of conservative politics that "favors outcome assessment over critical inquiry," and the discipline's rather narrow scientific positivism that views social facts as "inert and independent" (ibid., 376).

5 For further critiques of the epistemological foundations of criminology, their contemporary manifestations in the discipline, and strategies for countering them, see Agozino 2003; S. Cohen 1988; J. Young 2011.

6 While compelling, this point is ultimately insufficient in explaining the county discourse. Officials often explicitly jettisoned punishment or framed it as rehabilitation, but there were important moments when it was clear that officials supported

punishment for its own sake. Crucially, this occurred in references to the populations most marginalized or othered. Judge Allan Barrett noted, for example, that there were some populations for whom the county didn't even think twice about providing services while they were incarcerated, populations subjected to what he called a "bright line of demarcation"—which, in this context, can be understood as separating those punished and treated from those solely punished (see the conclusion). Additionally, Program Administration and Results, Inc. reported that the county commissioners had instructed them that three populations of offenders shouldn't even be considered for incarceration or services in the county. Moreover, I disagree with Foucault's premise when it is applied to the discourse of punishment more broadly. Khalil Muhammad (2010), John Sloop (1996), and Geoff Ward (2009) have certainly demonstrated that discourses and practices of punishment and rehabilitation are mapped onto racialized and class-based populations in distinctive and even predictable ways. A discourse of punishment that is not mitigated by any reference to treatment and rehabilitation can certainly retain meaning and support as long as the population in question is sufficiently other.

7 See Thompson 1984, 46. While I devote part of chapter 6 to a discussion of the challenges to such knowledge production processes, here I wish to point readers to compelling scholarship that illuminates successful resistance waged through the narrative process. See Chang 1993; Ewick and Silbey 1998, 241–44; Polletta 2000. On narrative more broadly, see Ewick and Silbey 1995; Presser and Sandberg 2015.

CHAPTER 5. SEEING LIKE A JAIL, 1

1 Summarizing work by David McNeill, Marcel Danesi and Paul Perron write: "Speech and gesture constitute a single integrated referential/communication system that allows a person to get the message across effectively" (1999, 126). See also McNeill (2005, especially chapter 2), but note that he refers to this type of gesture as a "gesticulant."

2 Theo Van Leeuwen writes that semiotic resources are "signifiers, observable actions and objects that have been drawn into the domain of social communication and that have a *theoretical* semiotic potential constituted by all their past uses and all their potential uses and an *actual* semiotic potential constituted by those past uses that are known to and considered relevant by the users of the resource, and by such potential uses as might be uncovered by the users on the basis of their specific needs and interests" (2005, 4).

3 Liz Trinder offers a critical and wide-ranging examination of the growth and use of evidence-based discourse and policy across fields. Following Anthony Giddens (1993), Trinder writes that evidence-based practices embody the promise of modernity that science can assess, control and mitigate risk. In the late modern questioning of expertise and scientific objectivity, she writes, the faith placed in the evidence-based approach constitutes "sustained optimism" (2000, 10). Trinder argues, however, that this faith in the "proceduralism" of evidenced-based practices—their promise to "exclude bias and ensure accountability and transparency, through the institution of standardized, rational and neutral procedures" (ibid.)—misses

the extent to which evidence-based practices contribute to what Giddens calls the "sequestration of experience" (1993, 144). That is, the procedures of evidence-based practices "establish boundaries outside which alternative ideas and experiences are set. . . . The potential messiness of the real world—patients with multiple and complex conditions—is met by a battery of procedures designed to render the complex manageable through the procedural production of evidence" (Trinder 2000, 10).

4 Important work has examined how technological and scientific discourse operates to privilege certain forms and expressions of knowledge while marginalizing and discrediting others. Referring to Carol Cohn's (1987) work with defense intellectuals, Michael Schwalbe et al. observe: "Techno-strategic discourse strictly avoids reference to human pain and suffering and instead uses the abstract and dispassionate language of strikes, counter-strikes, megatonnage and megadeaths. Given the rules of this discourse, to speak of pain and suffering is to discredit one's self as a 'soft-headed activist instead of an expert'" (Schwalbe et al. 2000, 435). The technical discourse of military culture, in other words, renders marginal and subordinate other discourses, and thus other ways of representing the meaning of war.

5 See especially Agozino 2003; Chang 1993; Richie 2012.

6 See Hartsock 1983.

7 A number of important scholars have noted the importance of social service providers to the growing scope of the carceral state. See Garland 1990; Platt 2009; Rothman 2002.

CHAPTER 6. SEEING LIKE A JAIL, 2

1 US Census Bureau n.d.

2 See Center on Juvenile and Criminal Justice. 1999.

3 For a broader analysis of police power, media, and hegemony, see Hall et al. 2013, especially 56–80.

4 Van der Dussen 2005.

5 I use "representation" here to invoke Stuart Hall's (1997) definition of three understandings of representation: as reflection, intention, and construction. See also Jhally (1997), in which Hall eloquently observes that the word, understood as "re-presentation," implies the presence of something that was already there, perhaps the most intuitive interpretation of Donnelly's claim that PARI plagiarized her department's report. Hall continues examining the idea of representation as "standing in for," invoked frequently in the discourse of democracy and political representation. He then subverts these two ideas by examining a third understanding: representation as "the production of meaning through language. . . . Meaning is produced by the practice, the work, of representation" (1997, 28). With these definitions of representation, PARI's report can be seen to reflect already produced understandings by the county and to stand in for the county residents on whose behalf county officials contracted the report. Most poignantly, the report can be understood as the creation of meaning given to the justice campus.

6 Petersilia 2003.

CHAPTER 7. GOVERNING THROUGH EXPANSION

1 In addition to Povinelli, readers interested in the politics of incommensurability should see Espeland and Stevens 1998.

2 This emphasis on deliberation is central to theories of democratic process and republican governance. See Goodin 2008. Amy Guttman and Dennis Thompson write that "the moral authority of collective judgments about policy depends in part on the moral quality of the process by which citizens collectively reach those judgments. Deliberation is the most appropriate way for citizens collectively to resolve their moral disagreements not only about policies but also about the process by which policies should be adopted. Deliberation is not only a means to an end, but also a means for deciding what means are morally required to pursue our common ends" (1996, 4).

3 Julia Paley's ethnographic work in Chile is helpful in clarifying the distinctions between deliberative and accessible county politics and process on the one hand and accountable politics and process on the other. Paley's work with Llareta, a Chilean health organization, reveals the limitations of Jürgen Habermas's vision of deliberative democracy, positing instead that deliberation "is a necessary but insufficient condition for democracy, which must also entail the impact of public opinion on public policy and law" (2004, 497). She notes that her time in the field with Llareta encouraged this decentering of deliberation and developing a vision of accountable democracy. Paley writes of postdictatorship Chile: "The attempt to generate consensus through conversation—which, in the form of rational discussion, Habermas elevates to a communicative and democratic ideal—was, in practice, *used to forestall, rather than facilitate, the impact of public opinion on decision making. In fact, Chilean political elites used a Habermasian language of consensus and debate to exclude nonelite Chileans from influencing public policy*" (ibid., 498; my emphasis). In reconciling postdictatorship democracy with a process of deliberation that actually excluded citizen voices, Paley observed Llareta developing an alternative normative framework of accountable democracy, in which citizen perspectives directly influenced decision making.

4 A large nonprofit agency in Bloomington serving people with developmental disabilities.

5 See McLaughlin 2009.

6 Laclau and Mouffe 2001.

7 Povinelli 2001.

8 For an important discussion of the differences in deliberative and accountable democratic practices, see Guttman and Thompson 1996, especially chapter 4.

9 Readers interested in this emerging theme of the relationship between nonprofit organizations and power structures would be wise to look at Incite! Women of Color against Violence 2007. This edited volume offers a critical and unsparing analysis of the co-optation of leftist social movements and community organizing by the nonprofit model.

10 Nationally, Democrats have been just as complicit in the growth of the carceral state as Republicans and have hardly been champions of rehabilitation. See Alexander 2010, 7; L. Feldman, Schiraldi, and Ziedenberg 2001; Gottschalk 2006, 10; Simon 2007, 59; Wacquant 2009b, 153 and 302. For a historical treatment of how twentieth-century liberals "built prison America," see Murakawa 2014. Moreover, in recent years, Republicans have presented a critique of incarceration couched in notions of fiscal responsibility and Christian values of second chances and redemption. See Bauer 2014; Viguerie 2013.

CHAPTER 8. ORGANIZING AGAINST EXPANSION

1 For more on the group, see Critical Resistance 2014

2 On using circles for community planning, see Ball, Caldwell, and Pranis 2010.

3 Michel Foucault has noted of the prison revolts occurring during the 1960s and 1970s that they leveled their assaults against the very body of the prison: "What was at issue was not whether the prison environment was too harsh or too aseptic, too primitive or too efficient, but its very materiality as an instrument and vector of power; it is this whole technology of power over the body that the technology of the 'soul'—that of the educationalists, psychologists, and psychiatrists—fails either to conceal or to compensate, for the simple reason that it is one of its tools" (1977, 30).

4 For further discussions of the relationships between poverty, the war on drugs, and incarceration, see Currie 1998; Donziger 1996; Mauer 2006; Reiman and Leighton 2009; Wacquant 2009a and 2009b.

5 Randall Shelden notes that this arrangement defined jails from their beginnings: "It was ironic that the financing of local jails depended on fees paid to jailers by those confined there when the majority of jail prisoners were drawn from the poorest classes" (2010, 58). Summarizing Seán McConville (1995), Shelden continues: "Phrased another way, fees were extracted 'from misery'" (2010, 58). There is growing attention to fee structures and their impact on lives already disorganized by systems of surveillance and punishment. See Beckett and Harris 2011; Harris, Evans, and Beckett 2010 and 2011; Kilgore 2014c.

6 But framing the attainment of knowledge of a jail through participation in a tour has other implications as well. Some noted sociologists (Wacquant 2002) have embraced, and even advocated for, the carceral tour as an important tool of research and education, but others (Brown 2009; Goffman 1961; Piché and Walby 2010) have been critical of the tour's ability to produce knowledge, pointing out that its purpose may in fact be to provide specific knowledge that both protects and validates institutional practices. In the present study, the tour appeared to have a more complicated purpose. Given officials' goal of promoting the construction of a new justice campus, it seems likely that the tour, in their minds at least, would have advanced that goal, probably demonstrating the various problems with institutional capacity and overcrowding. Thus, the tour would have transparently depicted the problems with the jail while also serving as a tool to promote institutional expansion.

7 Laclau and Mouffe 2001, 149.

8 Bourdieu and Wacquant 1992, 146–47.

9 David Graeber (2002 and 2007) has made the point that these practices are perhaps best described by the analytic term "democracy," or what he defines as a "form of governance (a form of communal self- organization)" (2007, 75).

10 See, for example, Thousand Kites n.d.

11 Following Nicholas Mirzoeff, DMC could be understood, in part, as organizing for "the right to look" (2011).

12 The joke goes this way: There's a little boy who refuses to eat *kreplach*. Every time a bowl of soup with *kreplach* is put in front of him, he shrieks ,"Ew, *kreplach*!" and refuses to eat. The child's parents decide to show him exactly what goes into the *kreplach*, explain slowly and clearly that it's nothing to be afraid of, and hope that he'll be fine. So one day, one of the boy's parents takes him into the kitchen and together they begin to prepare the dumpling. The boy enthusiastically and hungrily watches his parent chop up meat and onions, roll out dough, fold it together, and cook it. Just before placing the bowl of soup in front of the boy, the parent drops in the *kreplach*. The boy takes one look at it and shrieks, "Ew, *kreplach*!" For the full joke, see ZT 2006. Rubin used this story to help DMC members strategize about how to propose abolitionist changes, which the group assumed most community members would support, without referring to abolition and sending officials "shrieking."

13 On opportunities for deviance and the absence of capable guardians, see Felson and Boba 2010. On social disorganization of neighborhoods, see Shaw and McKay 2003. On the social learning of crime, see Akers 2003; Sutherland and Cressey 2003. On the strain associated with the absence of money, see A. Cohen 2003; Merton 1938; Messner and Rosenfeld 2007. On relationships as a form of control, see Gottfredson and Hirschi 2003.

14 Important research on the relationship between incarceration, political economy, and employment provides substantial support to Krasny's observation that economic development has left behind entire segments of the population. See, for example, De Giorgi 2006 and 2007; Gilmore 2007, Kilgore 2013; Rusche 1978; Wacquant 2009b; Western and Beckett 1999; W. Wilson 1997.

15 "Bloomington, Indiana" 2008.

16 The act against community corrections and the group's refusal to talk with me about it must also be understood in the larger context of state repression of re- sistance occurring at the time. While activists in Bloomington coalesced around fighting the justice campus, elsewhere in the state there were intense confrontations between ecological defense activists who were fighting the expansion of Interstate 69 and the state police and Department of Natural Resources. There was substantial support in Bloomington for the ecological defense work, and some of the activists fighting the highway had roots in the community. According to some compelling work (see especially Potter 2011), the targeting of ecological defense activists by state and federal government agencies was comparable to the Federal Bureau of Investigation's COINTELPRO efforts in the 1960s and 1970s (see Churchill and

Vander Wall 1988). With the possibility of surveillance, recording, infiltration, and arrest raised by increased governmental focus on regional activism, particularly activism that involved direct action and sabotage, the secrecy around the Flat Tire Brigade's actions is better understood.

17 "Torch Lit March through Streets of Bloomington" 2008.

18 Dylan Rodriguez provides some insights into understanding the transgression of material and symbolic boundaries between incarcerated and free space in his moving account of an action by the New York Campaign to Free Angela Davis on the sidewalk outside the women's house of detention where Davis was incarcerated. He writes that the protest disrupted and altered the geography of the prison, an act that has implications for "subversive collective agency in the face of the U.S. gulag" (2001, 54). He continues: "While neither the women inside nor the protesters outside could pretend to harbor a determining, definitive political agency, they found in their collaboration—verbal, performative, and defiant in its simultaneous politicization of the Greenwich Avenue sidewalk and the prison looming above it—a form of resistance and radicalism that *occupied* a new political space while *constructing* it though physical and oral acts of disruption" (ibid.). Rodriguez goes on to suggest that the protest suggested possibilities for convergences and solidarities between prisoners and nonprisoners in a way that "denaturalizes" the physical space and "deconstructs the institutional integrity/authority of the prison, resulting in a fleeting formation of a strategic trench from which both imprisoned and free can sustain a Gramscian war of position *in concert with one another*" (ibid).

19 For a poignant discussion of culture, space, and identity, see Mitchell 2000, especially 57–76.

20 According to Nagle, "a spokescouncil is a collection of affinity groups and clusters (a collection of affinity groups), who meet together for a common purpose. A 'spoke' is short for a 'spokesperson,' selected by each affinity group to represent them [*sic*] in the spokescouncil. The council usually makes decisions via a consensus decision making process."

21 Recent work by activist scholars and journalists has framed the transitions from in-person visitation to videoconferencing in the kind of analysis that DMC needed at that time. See Rabuy and Wagner 2015; Schenwar 2015.

22 See Californians United for a Responsible Budget 2013. In that press release announcing a gathering in Sacramento to challenge jail construction, the organization noted that forty-two of the state's fifty-eight counties had plans to build new jails, and thirty-six were asking the state for financial support.

CONCLUSION

1 For a poignant critique of campaigns for more benevolent cages, see Braz 2006.

2 See, for example, Generation Five 2007 and 2015; Kim 2011; Morris 1995; Philly Stands Up 2015; Richie 2014.

3 I capitalize the word "Circle," following the practice of leading authors on the Circle method. Jennifer Ball, Wayne Caldwell, and Kay Pranis (2010, 44) write that they

choose to capitalize the word to signify that the Circle is not just an arrangement of chairs in the shape of a circle, but a process that is applicable in complex and diverse contexts.

4 For a more in depth consideration of Generation Five's work and the potential of transformative justice, see Tyson 2014.

5 There is a substantial literature on restorative justice, including critical work that cautions against its often-romanticized status as a magic bullet. Readers interested in an excellent and diverse collection of perspectives on and processes within restorative justice should see Sullivan and Tifft, 2008. For both the philosophical context and practical application of Circles, see Boyes-Watson 2008; Pranis, Stuart, and Wedge 2003. For pioneering work on restorative justice and shaming, see Braithwaite 1989 and 2002. Other important literature has presented compelling critiques of restorative justice, focusing on its potential to further penalize offender populations (Levrant, Cullen, Fulton, and Wozniak 1999), its oversimplified juxtaposition of retribution and restoration, and its mythologized role as an indigenous model of justice (Daly 2002; Tauri 2005, 2009, and 2014), and its failure to locate individual harms in the structural contexts in which they must be understood (Takagi and Shank 2004), including settler colonialism.

6 The National Institute of Justice (2007) offers communities information on changing local systems into restorative justice models. Additionally, some academic researchers have conducted evaluations of existing programs. For an extensive list of empirical program evaluations of restorative justice processes, see College of Education 2014. For a partial list of work that advocates for the integration of transformative justice practices into communities as an alternative to the criminal justice system, see Prison Culture 2015.

7 See Prison Fellowship International 2007–8.

8 Paul Takagi and Gregory Shank, for example, note that following Attorney General Janet Reno's call for increased investment in community justice, "the Office of Justice Programs, the National Institute of Justice, the Office for Victims of Crime, the Office of Juvenile Justice and Delinquency Prevention, the Bureau of Justice Assistance, and the National Institute of Corrections hosted a national conversation on restorative justice" (2004, 147).

9 Generation Five has observed quite poignantly: "The Restorative Justice approach has largely been co-opted by the State for use in coercive contexts in which the integrity of such a model is put into question. Some faith-based Restorative Justice projects have partnered with the State and become service providers in tandem with State-based systems of accountability. Other Restorative Justice models are offered as post-incarceration rehabilitation programs intended to 'restore' the community standing of the person or people that are abusive. To a greater or lesser extent, these models do expand the possibilities of accountability and transformation through engaging and educating members of the intimate and/or community networks in which the abuse occurs. But such models have been appropriated by the criminal legal system as a way to involve the community in punishing the

person that has been violent and then 'restoring' the conditions that already existed when the abuse originally took place" (2007, 20–21).

10 See Daly 2002; Takagi and Shank 2004; Tauri 2005, 2009 and 2014.

11 Tyson 2013.

12 See Philly Stands Up 2015.

13 For a list of the diverse contexts in which Circles have been used, see Ball, Caldwell, and Pranis 2010, 55–61 and 88–96.

14 Despite the relevance of Harrison's point and my own discussion in earlier chapters of the way alleged county alternatives broadened the scope of the carceral apparatus, there is reason to be cautious about an analysis limited to net widening. Maeve McMahon offers some compelling evidence that points to the ways in which a net-widening analysis can have the unanticipated effect of reinforcing that apparatus. She argues that the perception that "nothing works" (1990, 125) with respect to rehabilitation, which has been attributed to Robert Martinson's (1974) assessment of prison programs and to community alternatives, has led to critical scholars' abandoning reform efforts in favor of more critique and, ironically, has also led to prison administrators' justifying increased carceral infrastructure.

15 Pepinsky 1991, 324.

16 Center for Harm Reduction Therapy 2015.

17 On this point, see Ferrell 2001, 167.

EPILOGUE

1 Kilgore 2014a. On the declines in the state prison population, see Clear and Frost 2014; Pew Center On the States 2010. On the expansion of jails in California, see Californians United for a Responsible Budget 2013. For examples of "mental health jails," see Cullors-Brignac and Zuñiga 2014.

2 The Corrections Corporation of America recently announced that "reentry programs and reducing recidivism are 100 percent aligned with our business model" (quoted in Takei 2014). See also Coombs and Newman 2011; Gingrich and Jones 2014; Right on Crime 2015; Viguerie 2013; Zornick 2014.

3 Gilmore 2007, 64.

SELECTED BIBLIOGRAPHY

Abrams, Laura S., and Ben Anderson-Nathe. 2013. *Compassionate Confinement: A Year in the Life of Unit C*. New Brunswick, NJ: Rutgers University Press.

Abu Lughod, Lila. 1991. "Writing against Culture." In: *Recapturing Anthropology: Working in the Present*, edited by Richard G. Fox, 137–62. Santa Fe, NM: SAR.

Agozino, Biko. 2003. *Counter-Colonial Criminology: A Critique of Imperialist Reason*. New York: Pluto.

Akers, Ron. 2011. "A Social Learning Theory of Crime." In *Criminological Theory: Past to Present: Essential Readings*, edited and selected by Franklin T. Cullen and Robert Agnew, 130–42. 4th ed. New York: Oxford University Press.

Alexander, Michelle. 2010. *The New Jim Crow: Mass Incarceration in the Age of Colorblindness*. New York: New Press.

Allen, Bob. 2006. "Baptist Foundation of Arizona Case Has Similarities With Enron." *Ethics Daily*, January 31. http://www.ethicsdaily.com/baptist-foundation-of-arizona-case-has-similarities-with-enron-cms-6900#sthash.m8FdwAL4.dpuf. Accessed December 7, 2014.

Altheide, David. 1987. "Ethnographic Content Analysis." *Qualitative Sociology* 10 (1): 65–77.

American Friends Service Committee. 1971. *The Struggle for Justice: A Report on Crime and Punishment in America*. New York: Farrar, Straus and Giroux.

Appadurai, Arjun. 1996. *Modernity at Large: Cultural Dimensions of Globalization*. Minneapolis: University of Minnesota Press.

Associated Press. 2010. "Daniels Endorses Findings of Criminal Code Review." *Bloomington Herald-Times*, December 16.

Austin, James, and Barry Krisberg. 1981. "Wider, Stronger, and Different Nets: The Dialectics of Criminal Justice Reform." *Journal of Research in Crime and Delinquency* 18 (1): 165–96.

Austin, James, and John Irwin. 2001. *It's about Time: America's Imprisonment Binge*. Belmont, CA: Wadsworth.

Ball, Jennifer, Wayne Caldwell, and Kay Pranis. 2010. *Doing Democracy with Circles: Engaging Communities in Public Planning*. St. Paul, MN: Living Justice.

Bauer, Shane. 2014 "How Conservatives Learned to Love Prison Reform. *Mother Jones*, March–April. http://www.motherjones.com/politics/2014/02/conservatives-prison-reform-right-on-crime. Accessed December 17, 2014.

Beaven, Steven. 1989a. "Juvenile Center to Be Forum Topic." *Bloomington Herald-Times*, September 18.

———. 1989b. "Panelists Say Juvenile Plan Needs Revision." *Bloomington Herald-Times*, September 20.

BBC News. n.d. "World Prison Populations." http://news.bbc.co.uk/2/shared/spl/hi/ uk/06/prisons/html/nn2page1.stm. Accessed December 3, 2014.

Beck, Ulrich. 1992. *Risk Society: Towards a New Modernity*. Thousand Oaks, CA: Sage.

Beckett, Katherine, and Alexes Harris. 2011. "On Cash and Conviction: Monetary Sanctions as Misguided Policy." *Criminology and Public Policy* 10 (3): 505–37.

Beckett, Katherine, and Steve Herbert. 2009. *Banished: The New Social Control in Urban America*. New York: Oxford University Press.

Beckett, Katherine, and Naomi Murakawa. 2012. "Mapping the Shadow Carceral State: Towards an Institutionally Capacious Approach to Punishment." *Theoretical Criminology* 16 (2): 221–44.

Beckett, Katherine, and Bruce Western. 2001. "Governing Social Marginality: Welfare, Incarceration and the Transformation of State Policy." *Punishment and Society* 3(1): 43–59.

Belknap, Joanne. 2015. "Activist Criminology: Criminologists' Responsibility to Advocate for Social and Legal Justice." *Criminology* 53 (1): 1–22.

Ben-Moshe, Liat, Chris Chapman, and Allison C. Carey, eds. 2014. *Disability Incarcerated: Imprisonment and Disability in the United States and Canada*. New York: Palgrave Macmillan.

Bennett, William J., John J. DiIulio Jr., and John P. Walters. 1996. *Body Count: Moral Poverty—and How to Win America's War against Crime and Drugs*. New York: Simon and Schuster.

Berger, Daniel. 2014. *Captive Nation: Black Prison Organizing in the Civil Rights Era*. Chapel Hill: University of North Carolina Press.

Bishop, Donna. 2012. "Evidence-Based Practice and Juvenile Justice." *Criminology and Public Policy* 11 (3): 483–89.

"Bloomington, Indiana: Flat Tire Brigade Strikes at Community Corrections." 2008. *Infoshop News*, December 11.

Bogazianos, Dimitri. 2012. *5 Grams: Crack Cocaine, Rap Music and the War on Drugs*. New York: New York University Press.

Bonds, Anne. 2009. "Discipline and Devolution: Constructions of Poverty, Race, and Criminality in the Politics of Rural Prison Development," *Antipode* 41 (3): 416–38.

———. 2012. "Building Prisons, Building Poverty: Prison Sitings, Dispossession, and Mass Incarceration." In *Beyond Walls and Cages: Prisons, Borders, and Global Crisis*, edited by Jenna M. Loyd, Matt Mitchelson, and Andrew Burridge, 129–42. Athens: University of Georgia Press.

Bonilla-Silva, Eduardo. 2006. *Racism without Racists: Colorblind Racism and the Persistence of Racial Inequality in America*. Lanham, MD: Rowman and Littlefield.

Bourdieu, Pierre. 1977. *Outline of a Theory of Practice*. Translated by Richard Nice. New York: Cambridge University Press.

———. 1990. *The Logic of Practice*. Translated by Richard Nice. New York: Polity.

———. 1991. *Language and Symbolic Power*. Translated by Gino Raymond and Matthew Adamson. New York: Polity.

———. 1994. "Rethinking the State: On the Genesis and Structure of the Bureaucratic Field." Translated by Loïc Wacquant and Samar Farage. *Sociological Theory* 12 (1): 1–19.

———. 2000. "The Abdication of the State." In Pierre Bourdieu et al., *The Weight of the World: Social Suffering in Contemporary Society*, translated by Priscilla Parkhurst Ferguson, *181–88*. Stanford, CA: Stanford University Press.

———. 2005. "Habitus." In *Habitus: A Sense of Place*, edited by Jean Hillier and Emma Rooksby, 43–52. 2nd ed. Burlington, VT: Ashgate.

———, and Loïc Wacquant. 1992. *An Invitation to Reflexive Sociology*. Chicago: University of Chicago Press.

Bourgois, Phillipe. 1996. *In Search of Respect: Selling Crack in el Barrio*. New York: Cambridge University Press.

———, and Jeff Schonberg. 2009. *Righteous Dopefiend*. Berkeley: University of California Press.

Boyes-Watson, Carolyn. 2008. *Peacemaking Circles and Urban Youth: Bringing Justice Home*. St. Paul, MN: Living Justice.

Braithwaite, John. 1989. *Crime, Shame and Reintegration*. New York: Cambridge University Press.

———. 2002. *Restorative Justice and Responsive Regulation*. New York: Oxford University Press.

Braz, Rose. 2006. "Kindler, Gentler, Gender Responsive Cages: Prison Expansion Is Not Prison Reform." *Women, Girls & Criminal Justice*, October–November, 87–91.

Brooks, Nicole. 2010. "Staffing, Facilities Still Issues for Sheriff." *Bloomington Herald-Times*, January 4.

Brown, Michelle. 2009. *The Culture of Punishment: Prison, Society and Spectacle*. New York: New York University Press.

———. 2014. "Visual Criminology and Carceral Studies: Counter-Images in the Carceral Age." *Theoretical Criminology* 18 (2): 176–97.

Bunn, Rachel. 2013a. "County Seeking Use for 85 Empty Acres." *Bloomington Herald-Times*. July 21.

———. 2013b. "Disc Golf Course, Gardens among Proposals for Empty Monroe County Property." *Bloomington Herald-Times*, November 8.

Burawoy, Michael. 1998. "The Extended Case Method." *Sociological Theory* 16 (1): 4–33.

———. 2012. "The Roots of Domination: Beyond Bourdieu and Gramsci." *Sociology* 46 (2): 187–260.

———et al.1991. *Ethnography Unbound: Power and Resistance in the Modern Metropolis*. Berkeley: University of California Press.

Californians United for a Responsible Budget. 2013. "36 Counties Beg for Jail Construction Money." http://curbprisonspending.org/36-counties-beg-for-jail-construction-money/. Accessed December 20, 2014.

Center for Harm Reduction Therapy. 2015. "What We Do." http://harmreductionther-apy.org/helping-harm-reduction-therapy/. Accessed February 21, 2015.

Center for Therapeutic Justice. 2000. "American Jails." Gwynn, VA: Center for Thera-peutic Justice. http://www.therapeuticjustice.com/JAILS_are_not_prisons.pdf. Accessed February 21, 2015.

Center on Juvenile and Criminal Justice. 1999. "Shattering 'Broken Windows': An Analysis of San Francisco's Alternative Crime Policies." http://www.cjcj.org/up-loads/cjcj/documents/shattering.pdf. Accessed February 21 2015.

Chang, Robert S. 1993. "Toward an Asian American Legal Scholarship: Critical Race Theory, Post-Structuralism, and Narrative Space." *California Law Review* 81 (5): 1241–323.

Churchill, Ward, and Jim Vander Wall. 1988. *Agents of Repression: The FBI's Secret Wars against the Black Panther Party and the American Indian Movement.* Cambridge, MA: South End.

City of Bloomington. 2015. "Parking Meters." https://bloomington.in.gov/media/me-dia/application/pdf/15402.pdf. Accessed February 23, 2015.

Clear, Todd R. 1994. *Harm in American Penology: Offenders, Victims, and Their Com-munities.* Albany: State University of New York Press.

———. 2007. *Imprisoning Communities: How Mass Incarceration Makes Disadvantaged Neighborhoods Worse.* New York: Oxford University Press.

———, and Natasha Frost. 2014. *The Punishment Imperative: The Rise and Failure of Mass Incarceration in America.* New York: New York University Press.

Clifford, James, and George E. Marcus. 1986. *Writing Culture: The Poetics and Politics of Ethnography.* Berkeley: University of California Press.

Cohen, Albert K. 2011. "Delinquent Boys." In *Criminological Theory: Past to Present: Essential Readings,* edited and selected by Franklin T. Cullen and Robert Agnew, 173–77. 4th ed. New York: Oxford University Press.

Cohen, Stanley. 1988. *Against Criminology.* New Brunswick, NJ: Transaction.

———. 1991. *Visions of Social Control: Crime, Punishment, and Classification.* Malden, MA: Blackwell.

Cohn, Carol. 1987. "Sex and Death in the Rational Work of Defense Intellectuals." *Signs* 12 (4): 687–718.

College of Education. 2014. "Reseach Annotated Bibliography Title." Minneapolis: Uni-versity of Minnesota. http://www.cehd.umn.edu/ssw/rjp/Resources/Research_An-notated_Bibliography/AB_Title.asp. Accessed December 21, 2014.

Coombs, Robert, and Jason D. Newman. 2011. "Justice Reinvestment: Bipartisan Effort Shakes Up Justice System." *Capitol Ideas.* May–June. http://www.csg.org/pubs/capitolideas/may_june_2011/LegislativeSessionWrapUp_JusticeReinvestment.aspx. Accessed February 21, 2015.

Counts, Will, James H. Madison, and Scott Russell Sanders. 2002. *Bloomington: Past and Present.* Bloomington: Indiana University Press.

Cowie, Jefferson 1999. *Capital Moves: RCA's Seventy-Year Quest for Cheap Labor.* Ithaca, NY: Cornell University Press.

Cox, Alexandra. 2011. "Doing the Programme or Doing Me? The Pains of Youth Imprisonment." *Punishment and Society* 13 (5): 592–610.

———. Forthcoming. "Responsible Submission: The Racialized Consequences of Neoliberal Jvenile Justice Practices." *Social Justice.*

Crawford, Adam. 1999. *The Local Governance of Crime: Appeals to Community and Partnerships.* New York: Oxford University Press.

Creps, Marcela. 2007. "Five Arrested on Drug Charges; Six Children Put in State Custody." *Bloomington Herald-Times,* October 19.

Critical Resistance. 2000. "Critical Resistance to the Prison Industrial Complex." Special issue, *Social Justice* 27 (3).

———. 2014. Critical Resistance. http://criticalresistance.org/. Accessed December 17, 2014.

CR10 Publications Collective. 2008. *Abolition Now! Ten Years of Strategy and Struggle against the Prison Industrial Complex.* Oakland, CA: AK.

Croteau, David, and William Hoynes. 2013. *Media/Society: Industries, Images and Audiences.* 5th ed. Thousand Oaks, CA: Sage.

Cullors-Brignac, Patrisse, and Diana Zuñiga. 2014. "A Mental Health Jail Is an Oxymoron; Diversion Is What's Needed." *Los Angeles Daily News,* June 24

Currie, Elliot. 1987. *Confronting Crime: An American Challenge.* New York: Random House.

———. 1998. *Crime and Punishment in America: Why the Solutions to America's Most Stubborn Social Crisis Have Not Worked—and What Will.* New York: Henry Holt and Company.

Daly, Kathleen. 2002. "Restorative Justice: The Real Story." *Punishment and Society* 4 (1): 55–79.

Danesi, Marcel, and Paul Perron. 1999. *Analyzing Cultures: An Introduction and Handbook.* Bloomington: Indiana University Press.

Davis, Angela. 2003 *Are Prisons Obsolete?* New York: Seven Stories.

Davis, Mike. 1995. "Hell Factories in the Field: A Prison Industrial Complex." *Nation,* February 20, 229–34.

———. 1998. *Ecology of Fear: Los Angeles and the Imagination of Disaster.* New York: Henry Holt.

De Giorgi, Alessandro. 2006. *Re-Thinking the Political Economy of Punishment: Perspectives on Post-Fordism and Penal Politics.* Burlington, VT: Ashgate.

———. 2007. "Toward a Political Economy of Post-Fordist Punishment." *Critical Criminology* 15 (3): 243–65.

Delgado, Richard. 1994. "Rodrigo's Eighth Chronicle: Black Crime, White Fears. On the Social Construction of Threat." *Virginia Law Review* 80 (2): 503–48.

Dickens, Charles. 1985. *American Notes.* New York: St. Martin's.

Donziger, Steven R., ed. 1996. *The Real War on Crime: The Report of the National Criminal Justice Commission.* New York: Harper Perennial.

Editorial. 1998. "Space Solution Must Be Realistic." *Bloomington Herald-Times,* January 27.

———. 2009a. "Another Reason to Celebrate This Season." *Bloomington Herald-Times*, December 19.

———. 2009b. "Graffiti Not Art: It Is Vandalism." *Bloomington Herald-Times*, April 29.

———. 2009c. "Rock-Throwing Incident More Than a Harmless Prank." *Bloomington Herald-Times*, September 26.

———. 2009d. "Twenty Years of Studies Has Bought Only Frustration." *Bloomington Herald-Times*, May 10.

———. 2013. "Extra Focus in Downtown Bloomington on Public Safety Is Welcome, Cameras and All." *Bloomington Herald-Times*, November 16.

Erickson, Patricia E., and Steven E. Erickson. 2008. *Crime, Punishment and Mental Illness: Law and the Behavioral Sciences in Conflict*. New Brunswick, NJ: Rutgers University Press.

Espeland, Wendy Nelson, and Mitchell L. Stevens. 1998. "Commensuration as a Social Process." *Annual Review of Sociology* 24:313–43.

Evans, Robin. 2011. *The Fabrication of Virtue: English Prison Architecture, 1750–1840*. Reissue. New York: Cambridge University Press.

Ewick, Patricia, and Susan S. Silbey. 1995. "Subversive Stories and Hegemonic Tales: Toward a Sociology of Narrative." *Law and Society Review* 29 (2): 197–226.

———. 1998. *The Common Place of Law: Stories from Everyday Life*. Chicago: University of Chicago Press.

Fabris, John. 1985. "RCA Tax Abatement Approved by Council." *Bloomington Herald-Times*, February 14.

Fanon, Frantz. 2004. *The Wretched of the Earth*. Translated by Richard Philcox. New York: Grove.

Feeley, Malcolm, and Jonathan Simon. 1992. "The New Penology: Notes on the Emerging Strategy of Corrections and Its Implications." *Criminology* 30 (4): 449–74.

Feldman, Allan. 1991. *Formations of Violence: The Narrative of the Body and Political Terror in Northern Ireland*. Chicago: University of Chicago Press.

Feldman, Lisa, Vincent Schiraldi, and Jason Ziedenberg. 2001. *Too Little Too Late: President Clinton's Prison Legacy*. Washington: Justice Policy Institute.

Felson, Marcus, and Rachel Boba. 2010. *Crime and Everyday Life*. 4th ed. Thousand Oaks, CA: Sage.

Ferrell, Jeff 2001. "Remapping the City: Public Identity, Cultural Space, and Social Justice." *Contemporary Justice Review* 4 (2): 161–80.

———and Mark Hamm, eds. 1998a. *Ethnography at the Edge: Crime, Deviance and Field Research*. Boston: Northeastern University Press.

———. 1998b. "True Confessions: Crime, Deviance, and Field Research." In *Ethnography at the Edge: Crime, Deviance and Field Research*, edited by Jeff Ferrell and Mark Hamm, 2–19. Boston: Northeastern University Press.

Ferrell, Jeff, Keith Hayward, and Jock Young. 2008. *Cultural Criminology: An Invitation*. Thousand Oaks, CA: Sage.

Fields, Barbara. 1990. "Slavery, Race and Ideology in the United States of America." *New Left Review*, May–June, 95–118.

First Capital Group. n.d. "Investment Profile: Indiana Enterprise Center." Bloomington, IN: First Capital Group. http://firstcapitalusa.com/pdfs/FirstCapIECCaseStudy-Approved091506.pdf. Accessed December 7, 2014.

Forester, John. 2010. Foreword to Jennifer Ball, Wayne Caldwell, and Kay Pranis, *Doing Democracy with Circles: Engaging Communities in Public Planning*, xi–xii. St. Paul, MN: Living Justice.

Foucault, Michel. 1977. *Discipline and Punish: The Birth of the Prison*. Translated by Alan Sheridan. New York: Random House.

———. 1980. *Power/Knowledge: Selected Interviews and Other Writings, 1972–1977*. Edited by Colin Gordon. Translated by Colin Gordon, Leo Marshall, John Mepham, and Kate Soper. New York: Random House.

Fox, Kathryn J. 1999. "Reproducing Criminal Types: Cognitive Treatment for Violent Offenders in Prison." *Sociological Quarterly* 40 (3): 435–53.

Garland, David. 1990. *Punishment and Modern Society: A Study in Social Theory*. Chicago: University of Chicago Press.

———. 2001. *The Culture of Control: Crime and Social Order in Contemporary Society*. Chicago: University of Chicago Press.

Generation Five. 2007. "Toward Transformative Justice: A Liberatory Approach to Child Sexual Abuse and Other Forms of Intimate and Community Violence." http://www.generationfive.org/wp-content/uploads/2013/07/G5_Toward_Transformative_Justice-Document.pdf. Accessed February 20, 215.

———. 2015. *http://www.generationfive.org/*. Accessed February 20, 2015.

Giddens, Anthony. 1993. *Modernity and Self-Identity: Self and Society in the Late Modern Age*. Stanford, CA: Stanford University Press.

Gillis, Marjorie. 2006. "Hire That Reading Czar." *New York Times*, September 24.

Gilmore, Ruth Wilson. 1999. "Globalization and U.S. Prison Growth: From Military Keynesianism to Post-Keynesian Militarism." *Race and Class* 40 (2–3): 171–88.

———. 2002. "Fatal Couplings of Power and Difference: Notes on Racism and Geography." *Professional Geographer* 54 (1): 15–24.

———. 2007. *Golden Gulag: Prisons, Surplus, Crisis, and Opposition in Globalizing California*. Berkeley: University of California Press.

Gilmore, Ruth Wilson, and Craig Gilmore. 2008. "Restating the Obvious." In *Indefensible Space: The Architecture of the National Insecurity State*, edited by Michael Sorkin, 141–62. New York: Routledge.

Gingrich, Newt, and Van Jones. 2014. "Prison System Is Failing America." *CNN Crossfire*, May 22. http://www.cnn.com/2014/05/21/opinion/gingrich-jones-prison-system-fails-america/. Accessed February 22, 2015.

Glaze, Lauren E., and Erinn J. Herberman. 2012. "Correctional Populations in the United States, 2012." Washington: Bureau of Justice Statistics.

Goffman, Erving. 1961. *Asylums: Essays on the Social Situation of Mental Patients and Other Inmates*. New York: Anchor.

Goodin, Robert E. 2008. *Innovating Democracy: Democratic Theory and Practice after the Deliberative Turn*. New York: Oxford University Press.

Gordon, Avery. 2008. *Ghostly Matters: Haunting and the Sociological Imagination*. Minneapolis: University of Minnesota Press.

Gottfredson, Michael R., and Travis Hirschi. 2011 "A General Theory of Crime." In *Criminological Theory: Past to Present: Essential Readings*, edited and selected by Franklin T. Cullen and Robert Agnew, 224–32. 4th ed. New York: Oxford University Press.

Gottschalk, Marie. 2006. *The Prison and the Gallows: The Politics of Mass Incarceration in America*. New York: Cambridge University Press.

Gowan, Teresa, and Sarah Whetstone. 2012. "Making the Criminal Addict: Subjectivity and Social Control in a Strong-Arm Rehab." *Punishment and Society* 14 (1): 69–93.

Grady, Tom. 2008. "Get Involved in Decision on Criminal Justice Facility." *Bloomington Herald-Times*, December 26.

Graeber, David. 2002. "The New Anarchists." *New Left Review*, January–February, 61–73.

———. 2004. *Fragments of an Anarchist Anthropology*. Chicago: Prickly Paradigm.

———. 2007. "Democracy Emerges from the Space in Between." In *Beyond Resistance: The Future of Freedom*, edited by Robert Fletcher, 75–109. New York: Nova Science.

———. 2009. *Direct Action: An Ethnography*. Oakland, CA: AK.

Gray, Garry C., and Abigail Tsionne Salole. 2006. "The Local Culture of Punishment: An Ethnography of Criminal Justice Worker Discourse." *British Journal of Criminology* 46 (4): 661–79.

Gray, Patricia. 2013. "Assemblages of Penal Governance, Social Justice and Youth Justice Partnerships." *Theoretical Criminology* 17 (4): 517–34.

Gupta, Akhil, and James Ferguson. 1997. *Culture, Power, Place: Explorations in Critical Anthropology*. Durham, NC: Duke University Press.

Guttman, Amy, and Dennis F. Thompson. 1996. *Democracy and Disagreement: Why Moral Conflict Cannot Be Avoided in Politics and What Should Be Done about It*. Cambridge, MA: Harvard University Press.

Hale, Charles R. 2006. "Activist Research v. Cultural Critique: Indigenous Land Rights and the Contradictions of Politically Engaged Anthropology." *Cultural Anthropology* 21 (1): 96–120.

Haley, Sarah. 2013. "'Like I Was a Man': Chain Gangs, Gender and the Domestic Carceral Sphere in Jim Crow Georgia." *Signs* 39 (1): 53–77.

Hall, Stuart. 1982. "The Rediscovery of 'Ideology': Return of the Repressed in Media Studies." In *Culture, Society and the Media, edited by* Michael Gurevitch, Tony Bennett, James Curran, and Janet Woollacott, 52–86. London: Methuen.

———. 1996. "Encoding/Decoding." In *Culture, Media, Language*, edited by Stuart Hall, Dorothy Hobson, Andrew Lowe, and Paul Willis, 128–38. New York: Routledge.

———. 1997. "The Work of Representation." In *Representation: Cultural Representations and Signifying Practices*, edited by Stuart Hall, 13–74. Thousand Oaks, CA: Sage.

Hall, Stuart, et al. 2013. *Policing the Crisis: Mugging, the State, and Law and Order*. 35th anniversary ed. New York: Palgrave Macmillan.

Hallett, Michael. 2006. *Private Prisons in America: A Critical Race Perspective*. Urbana: University of Illinois Press.

Hallsworth, Simon, and John Lea. 2011. "Reconstructing Leviathan: Emerging Contours of the Security State." *Theoretical Criminology* 15 (2): 141–57.

Hannah-Moffat, Kelly. 2005. "Criminogenic Needs and the Transformative Risk Subject: Hybridizations of Risk/Need in Penality." *Punishment and Society* 7 (1): 29–51.

Hannah-Moffat, Kelly, and Mona Lynch. 2012. "Theorizing Punishment's Boundaries: An Introduction." *Theoretical Criminology* 16 (2): 119–21.

Harcourt, Bernard. 2001. *Illusion of Order: The False Promise of Broken Windows Policing*. Cambridge, MA: Harvard University Press.

———. 2010. "Neoliberal Penality: A Brief Genealogy." *Theoretical Criminology* 14 (1): 74–92.

Harris, Alexes, Heather Evans, and Katherine Beckett. 2010. "Drawing Blood from Stones: Monetary Sanctions, Punishment and Inequality in the Contemporary United States." *American Journal of Sociology* 115 (6): 1753–99.

———. 2011. "Courtesy Stigma and Monetary Sanctions: Toward a Socio-Cultural Theory of Punishment." *American Sociological Review* 76 (2): 234–64.

Hartnett, Stephen John. 2011. *Challenging the Prison Industrial Complex: Activism, Arts and Educational Alternatives*. Urbana, IL: University of Illinois Press.

Hartsock, Nancy. 1983. "The Feminist Standpoint: Developing the Ground for a Specifically Feminist Historical Materialism." In *Discovering Reality: Feminist Perspectives on Epistemology, Metaphysics, Methodology, and Philosophy of Science*, edited by Sandra Harding and Merrill B. Hintikka, 283–310. Boston: D. Riedel.

Harvey, David. 1993. "From Space to Place and Back Again: Reflections on the Condition of Postmodernity." In *Mapping the Future: Local Cultures, Global Changes*, edited by Jon Bird, et al., 3–29. New York: Routledge.

———. 1996. *Justice, Nature and the Geography of Difference*. Malden, MA: Blackwell.

———. 2001. *Spaces of Capital: Toward a Critical Geography*. New York: Routledge.

———. 2005. *A Brief History of Neoliberalism*. New York: Oxford University Press,

Hayward, Keith. 2004. *City Limits: Crime, Consumer Culture, and the Urban Experience*. Portland, OR: Cavendish.

Herbert, Steve, and Elizabeth Brown. 2006. "Conceptions of Space and Crime in the Punitive Neoliberal City." *Antipode* 38 (4): 755–77.

Higgs, Steve. 1990. "Detention Center Budget Gets Funds." *Bloomington Herald-Times*. October 10.

———. 2008a. "In Jail for no Reason at All." *Bloomington Alternative*. October 5.

———2008b. "Bigger Jail or More Prevention?" *Bloomington Alternative*. October 19.

Hillier, Jean, and Emma Rooksby, 2005. "Introduction to the Second Edition: Committed Scholarship." In *Habitus: A Sense of Place*, edited by Jean Hillier and Emma Rooksby, 3–18. 2nd ed. Burlington, VT: Ashgate.

Hinnefeld, Steve. 1998. "Displaced Workers' Options May Depend on Training." *Bloomington Herald-Times*, March 29.

Hooks, Gregory, et al. 2010. "Revisiting the Impact of Prison Building on Job Growth: Education, Incarceration, and County-Level Employment, 1976–2004." *Social Science Quarterly* 91 (1): 228–44.

Hooks, Gregory, Clayton Mosher, Linda Lobao, and Thomas Rotolo. 2004. "The Prison Industry: Carceral Expansion and Employment in U.S. Counties, 1969–1994. *Social Science Quarterly* 85(1): 37–57.

Horkheimer, Max, and Theodor Adorno. 2002. *Dialectic of Enlightenment: Philosophical Fragments.* Translated by Edmund Jephcott. Stanford, CA: Stanford University Press.

Huling, Tracy. 2002. "Building a Prison Economy in Rural America." In *Invisible Punishment: The Collateral Consequences of Mass Imprisonment,* edited by Mark Mauer and Meda Chensey-Lind, 197–213. New York: New Press.

Hunt, Alan. 1999. *Governing Morals: A Social History of Moral Regulation.* Cambridge: Cambridge University Press.

Hunter, Gary, and Peter Wagner. 2008. "Prisons, Politics and the Census." In *Prison Profiteers: Who Makes Money from Mass Incarceration,* edited by Tara Herivel and Paul Wright, 80–89. New York: New Press.

Incite! Women of Color against Violence, ed. 2007. *The Revolution Will Not Be Funded: Beyond the Non-Profit Industrial Complex.* Boston: South End.

Irwin, John.1985. *The Jail: Managing the Underclass in American Society.* Berkeley: University of California Press.

James, Joy, ed. 2002. *States of Confinement: Policing, Detention, and Prisons.* New York: Palgrave Macmillan.

———, ed. 2005. *The New Abolitionists: Neo(slave) Narratives and Contemporary Prison Writings.* Albany: State University of New York Press.

———, ed. 2007. *Warfare in the American Homeland: Policing and Prison in a Penal Democracy.* Durham, NC: Duke University Press.

Jameson, Fredric. 1981. *The Political Unconscious: Narrative as a Socially Symbolic Act.* Ithaca, NY: Cornell University Press.

Jhally, Sut, dir. 1997. *Stuart Hall: Representation and the Media.* Northampton, MA: Media Education Foundation.

Jewkes, Yvonne. 2013. "The Aesthetics and Anaesthetics of Prison Architecture." In *Architecture and Justice,* edited by Jonathan Simon, Nicholas Temple, and Renée Tobe, 9–22. Burlington, VT: Ashgate.

———, and Dominique Moran. 2014. "Should Prison Architecture Be Brutal, Bland, or Beautiful?" *Scottish Justice Matters* 2 (1): 8–11.

Juvenile Justice Task Force. 2007. "Proposal for Monroe County Juvenile Justice Center." January 11.

Kappeler, Victor E., and Gary E. Potter. 2004. *The Mythology of Crime and Criminal Justice.* Long Grove, IL: Waveland.

Kilgore, James. 2013. "A Displaced and Discarded Labor Force: The Myth of Prison Slave Labor Camps in the U.S." *Counterpunch,* August 9–11. http://www.counterpunch.org/2013/08/09/the-myth-of-prison-slave-labor-camps-in-the-u-s/. Accessed February 23, 2015.

———. 2014a. "Repackaging Mass Incarceration." *Counterpunch,* June 6–8. http://www.counterpunch.org/2014/06/06/repackaging-mass-incarceration/. Accessed February 23, 2015.

———. 2014b. "The Spread of Electronic Monitoring: No Quick Fix for Mass Incarceration." *Truthout*, July 30. http://truth-out.org/news/item/25232-the-spread-of-electronic-monitoring-no-quick-fix-for-mass-incarceration. Accessed February 23, 2015.

———. 2014c. "Tackling Debtors' Prisons: Reflecting on the Death of Eileen DiNino." *Truthout*, June 20. http://truth-out.org/news/item/24478-tackling-debtors-prisons-reflecting-on-the-death-of-eileen-dinino. Accessed February 23, 2015.

———. 2015. *Understanding and Ending Mass Incarceration: A Primer*. New York: New Press.

Kim, Mimi E. 2011. "Moving beyond Critique: Creative Interventions and Reconstructions of Community Accountability." *Social Justice* 37 (4): 14–35.

Kirsch, Stuart. 2002. "Anthropology and Advocacy: A Case Study of the Campaign against the Ok Tedi Mine." *Critique of Anthropology* 22 (2):175–200.

Kramer, Ronald, Valli Rajah, and Hung-En Sung. 2013. "Neoliberal Prisons and Cognitive Treatment: Calibrating the Subjectivity of Incarcerated Young Men to Economic Inequalities." *Theoretical Criminology* 17 (4): 535–56.

Krause, Victoria. 2009. *Monroe County Youth Services Bureau/Youth Shelter Final Report and Recommendations*. http://www.heraldtimesonline.com/stories/2010/01/17/0115_ysb_final_report_0117.pdf. Accessed February 21, 2015.

Laclau, Ernesto, and Chantal Mouffe. 2001. *Hegemony and Socialist Strategy: Towards a Radical Democratic Politics*. 2nd ed. Brooklyn, NY: Verso.

Lakoff, George. 2002. *Moral Politics: How Liberals and Conservatives Think*. Chicago: University of Chicago Press.

Landers, Jim, and Jessica Harmon. 2012. "Fiscal Issue Brief: Indiana's Geographically Targeted Development Programs: Community Revitalization Enhancement Districts." Indianapolis, IN: Indiana Legislative Services Agency, July 1. http://www.in.gov/legislative/pdf/CommunityRevitalizationEnhancementDistricts2012.pdf. Accessed December 7, 2014.

Lane, Laura. 1999. "Thomson Workers Move On in Year after Closing." *Bloomington Herald-Times*, March 28.

———. 2009. "Lawsuit Settlement: Monroe County Jail Overcrowding Must Stop." *Bloomington Herald-Times*. November 17.

———. 2011. "Bloomington Jury Hearing Case of Man Charged with Shooting at Three Women." *Bloomington Herald-Times*. January 26.

Law, Victoria. 2011. "Where Abolition Meets Action: Women Organizing gainst Gender Violence." *Contemporary Justice Review* 14 (1): 85–94.

———. 2014. "Against Carceral Feminism." *Jacobin*. October 17. https://www.jacobinmag.com/2014/10/against-carceral-feminism/. Accessed February 21, 2015.

Lazarus-Black, Mindie, and Susan Hirsch, eds. 1994. *Contested States: Law, Hegemony and Resistance*. New York: Routledge.

Lea, Jon, and Kevin Stenson. 2007. "Security, Sovereignty, and Non-State Governance 'From Below.'" *Canadian Journal of Law and Society / Revue Canadienne Droit et Société* 22 (2): 9–27.

Lefebvre, Henri. 1991. *The Production of Space*. Translated by Donald Nicholson-Smith Malden, MA: Blackwell.

Lemert, Charles. 2007. *Thinking the Unthinkable: The Riddles of Classical Sociological Theories*. Boulder, CO: Paradigm.

Levrant, Sharon, Francis T. Cullen, Betsy Fulton, and John F. Wozniak. 1999. "Reconsidering Restorative Justice: The Corruption of Benevolence Revisited?" *Crime and Delinquency* 45 (1): 3–27.

Linnemann, Travis, and Tyler Wall. 2013. "'This Is Your Face on Meth': The Punitive Spectacle of White Trash in the Rural War on Drugs." *Theoretical Criminology* 17 (3): 315–34.

Little, Dan. 2009. "It's Educationally Sound to Pay Attention to All of Life's Lessons." *Bloomington Herald-Times*, September 22.

———. 2010. "Modest Monument Deserves Attention for Those Who Have Given." *Bloomington Herald-Times*, May 4.

Loury, Glenn C. 2008. *Race, Incarceration, and American Values*. Cambridge, MA: MIT Press.

Lowman, John, Robert J. Menzies, and T. S. Palys, eds. 1987. *Transcarceration: Essays in the Sociology of Social Control*. Burlington, VT: Ashgate.

Loyd, Jenna, Matt Mitchelson, and Andrew Burridge, 2009. "Thinking (and Moving) beyond Walls and Cages: Bridging Immigrant Justice and Anti-Prison Organizing in the United States." *Social Justice* 36 (2): 85–103

———, eds. 2012. *Beyond Walls and Cages: Prisons, Borders, and Global Crisis*. Athens: University of Georgia Press.

Lynch, Mona, Marisa Omori, Aaron Roussell, and Matthew Valasik. 2013. "Policing the 'Progressive' City: The Racialized Geography of Drug Law Enforcement." *Theoretical Criminology* 17 (3): 335–57.

Malik, Michael. 2010. "Decade Saw Shift to the Left in Local Government." *Bloomington Herald-Times*, January 3.

Martinson, Robert. 1974. "What Works? Questions and Answers about Prison Reform." *Public Interest* 35 (spring):22–54.

Marx, Karl, and Friedrich Engels. 1970. *The German Ideology*. New York: Prometheus.

Mathiesen, Thomas. 2006. *Prison on Trial*. 3rd ed. Winchester, UK: Waterside.

Mauer, Marc. 2000. "The Causes and Consequences of Prison Growth in the United States." *Punishment and Society* 3 (1): 9–20.

———. 2006. *Race to Incarcerate*. New York: New Press.

Mauer, Marc, and Meda Chesney-Lind, eds. 2002. *Invisible Punishment: The Collateral Consequences of Mass Imprisonment*. New York: New Press.

McArdle, Andrea, and Tanya Erzen, eds. 2001. *Zero Tolerance: Quality of Life and the New Police Brutality in New York City*. New York: New York University Press.

McConville, Seán. 1995 "Local Justice: The Jail." In *The Oxford History of the Prison: The Practice of Punishment in Western Society*, edited by Norval Morris and David J. Rothman, 297–327. New York: Oxford University Press.

McCorkel, Jill. 2013. *Breaking Women: Gender, Race, and the New Politics of Imprisonment*. New York: New York University Press.

McLaughlin, Hugh. 2009. "What's in a Name: 'Client', 'Patient', 'Customer', 'Consumer', 'Expert by Experience', 'Service User'—What's Next?" *British Journal of Social Work* 39 (6): 1101–17.

McLennan, Rebecca M. 2008. *The Crisis of Imprisonment: Protest, Politics, and the Making of the American Penal State, 1776–1941*. New York: Cambridge University Press.

McMahon, Maeve. 1990. "'Net-Widening': Vagaries in the Use of a Concept." *British Journal of Criminology* 30 (2): 121–49.

McNeill, David 2005. *Gesture and Thought*. Chicago: University of Chicago Press.

Meiners, Erica R. 2011. "Ending the School-to-Prison Pipeline/Building Abolition Futures." *Urban Review* 43 (4): 547–65.

Merton, Robert. 1938. "Social Structure and Anomie." *American Sociological Review* 3 (5): 672–82.

Messner, Steven F., and Richard Rosenfeld. 2007. *Crime and the American Dream*. 4th ed. Belmont, CA: Wadsworth.

Miller, Jerome. 1998. *Last One over the Wall: The Massachusetts Experiment in Closing Reform Schools*. 2nd ed. Columbus: Ohio State University Press.

Miller, Reuben J. 2014. "Devolving the Carceral State: Race, Prisoner Re-Entry and the Micro-Politics of Urban Poverty Management." *Punishment and Society* 16 (3): 305–35.

Mirzoeff, Nicholas. 2011. "The Right to Look." *Critical Inquiry* 37 (3): 473–96.

Mitchell, Don. 1996. *The Lie of the Land: Migrant Workers and the California Landscape*. Minneapolis, University of Minnesota Press.

———. 2000. *Cultural Geography: A Critical Introduction*. Malden, MA: Blackwell.

———. 2003. "Dead Labor and the Political Economy of Landscape—California Living, California Dying." In *Handbook of Cultural Geography*, edited by Kay Anderson, Mona Domosh, Steve Pile, and Nigel Thrift, 233–49. London: Sage.

———and Lynn A. Staeheli. 2005. "Permitting Protest: Parsing the Fine Geography of Dissent in America." *International Journal of Urban and Regional Research* 29 (4): 796–813.

Mohrweis, Lawrence C. 2003. "Lessons from the Baptist Foundation Fraud." *CPA Journal*, July. http://www.nysscpa.org/cpajournal/2003/0703/dept/d075003.htm. Accessed December 7, 2014.

Monroe Circuit Court Probation Department. 2008. *Monroe Circuit Court Probation Department Annual Report*. Bloomington, IN: Monroe Circuit Court Probation Department.

Moore, Dawn, and Kelly Hannah-Moffat. 2005. "The Liberal Veil: Revisiting Canadian Penality." In *The New Punitiveness: Trends, Theories, and Perspectives*, edited by John Pratt, et al., 85–100. Portland, OR: Willan.

Moran, Dominique. 2015. *Carceral Geography: Spaces and Practices of Incarceration*. Burlington, VT: Ashgate.

Morin, Sarah. 2003. "PTS Confirms Expansion Plans." *Bloomington Herald-Times*, June 11.

Morris, Ruth. 1995. *Penal Abolition: The Practical Choice*. Toronto, ON: Canadian Scholars' Press.

Muhammad, Khalil Gibran. 2010. *The Condemnation of Blackness: Race, Crime, and the Making of Modern Urban America*. Cambridge, MA: Harvard University Press.

———. 2011. "Where Did All the White Criminals Go? Reconfiguring Race and Crime on the Road to Mass Incarceration." *Souls* 13 (1): 72–90.

Murakawa, Naomi. 2014. *The First Civil Right: How Liberals Built Prison America*. New York: Oxford University Press.

Musto, Jennifer. 2013. "Domestic Minor Sex Trafficking and the Detention to Protection Pipeline." *Dialectical Anthropology* 37 (2):257–76.

———. Forthcoming. *To Control and Protect*. Berkeley: University of California Press.

Myers, Randolph R., and Tim Goddard. 2013. "Community-Driven Youth Justice and the Organizational Consequences of Coercive Governance." *British Journal of Criminology* 53 (2): 215–33.

National Clearinghouse for Criminal Justice Planning and Architecture. 1977. *Technical Assistance Report for Monroe and Owen Counties*. Urbana, IL: National Clearinghouse for Criminal Justice Planning and Architecture.

National Institute of Justice. 2007. "Perspectives on Restorative Justice." Washington: National Institute of Justice. December 3. http://www.nij.gov/nij/topics/courts/restorative-justice/perspectives/welcome.htm. Accessed December 21, 2014.

Neocleous, Mark. 2000. *The Fabrication of Social Order: A Critical Theory of Police Power*. Sterling, VA: Pluto.

———. 2003. *Imagining the State*. Philadelphia, PA: Open University Press.

———. 2008. *Critique of Security*. Montreal: McGill-Queen's University Press.

———. 2011. "'A Brighter and Nice New Life': Security as Pacification." *Social and Legal Studies* 20 (2): 191–208.

Newitz, Annalee, and Matt Wray. 1997. "What Is White Trash? Stereotypes and Economic Conditions of Poor Whites in the United States." In *Whiteness: A Critical Reader*, edited by Mike Hill, 168–84. New York: New York University Press.

Nolan, Bethany. 2008. "Former Inmate's Suit against Jail Filed as Class Action." *Bloomington Herald-Times*, August 27.

———. 2009a. "Monroe Corrections Plan Called 'Bloated,' 'Out of Touch.'" *Bloomington Herald-Times*, May 7.

———. 2009b. "Monroe Jail Remodeling Plans Progressing." *Bloomington Herald-Times*, December 9.

———. 2009c. "Planned Changes to Youth Shelter Raising Concerns." *Bloomington Herald-Times*, October 11.

———. 2009d. "Proposed Corrections Campus Could Cost $85 Million." *Bloomington Herald-Times*, May 5.

———. 2009e. "Tax Increase Considered to Help Youth Services." *Bloomington Herald-Times*, July 6.

——. 2010. "Report Cites 'Dysfunctional, Unhealthy Culture' at Youth Services Bureau." *Bloomington Herald-Times*, January 17.

Nordstrom, Carolyn. 2007. *Global Outlaws: Crime, Money and Power in the Contemporary World*. Berkeley: University of California Press.

Norris, Michelle. 2008. "Indiana Town: From Racist Past to Primary Present." *All Things Considered*. National Public Radio. April 30.

O'Malley, Pat. 1999. "Volatile and Contradictory Punishment." *Theoretical Criminology* 3 (2):175–96.

Paley, Julia. 2004. "Accountable Democracy: Citizens' Impact on Public Decision Making in Post-Dictatorship Chile." *American Ethnologist* 31 (4): 497–513.

Peck, Jamie. 2003. "Geography and Public Policy: Mapping the Penal State." *Progress in Human Geography*, 27 (2): 222–32.

Pepinsky, Harold E. 1991. "The Peacemaking Choice: Peacemaking in Criminology and Criminal Justice." In *Criminology as Peacemaking*, edited by Harold E. Pepinsky and Richard Quinney, 300–24. Bloomington: Indiana University Press.

Petersilia, Joan. 2003. *When Prisoners Come Home: Parole and Prisoner Reentry*. New York: Oxford University Press.

Petteruti, Amanda, and Natassia Walsh. 2008. "Jailing Communities: The Impact of Jail Expansion and Effective Jail Expansion and Public Safety Strategies." Washington: Justice Policy Institute. http://www.justicepolicy.org/research/1946. Accessed December 22, 2014.

Pew Center on the States. 2009. "One in 31: The Long Reach of American Corrections." Washington: Pew Charitable Trusts.

——. 2010. "Prison Count 2010: State Population Declines for the First Time in 38 Years." Washington: Pew Charitable Trusts.

Philly Stands Up. 2015. http://www.phillystandsup.com/home.html. Accessed February 20, 2015.

Piché, Justin, and Kevin Walby. 2010. "Problematizing Carceral Tours." *British Journal of Criminology* 50 (3): 570–81.

Piquero, Alex R., and Paul Mazerolle, eds. 2001. *Life-Course Criminology: Contemporary and Classic Readings*. Belmont, CA: Wadsworth.

Piven, Frances Fox. 2010. "A Response to Wacquant." *Theoretical Criminology* 14 (1): 111–16.

Platt, Anthony M. 2009. *The Child Savers: The Invention of Delinquency*. With an introduction and critical commentaries compiled by Miroslava Chávez-García. Expanded 40th anniversary ed. New Brunswick, NJ: Rutgers University Press.

——, ed. 2014. "Legacies of Radical Criminology in the United States." Fortieth anniversary special issue, *Social Justice* 40 (1–2).

Polletta, Francesca. 2000. "The Structural Context of Novel Rights Claims: Southern Civil Rights Organizing, 1961–1966." *Law and Society Review* 34 (2):367–406.

Potter, Will. 2011. *Green Is the New Red: An Insider's Account of a Social Movement under Siege*. San Francisco: City Lights.

Povinelli, Elizabeth A. 2001. "Radical Worlds: The Anthropology of Incommensurability and Inconceivability." *Annual Review of Anthropology* 30:319–34.

Pranis, Kay, Barry Stuart, and Mark Wedge. 2003. *Peacemaking Circles: From Crime to Community*. St. Paul, MN: Living Justice.

Presser, Lois, and Sveinung Sandberg, eds. 2015. *Narrative Criminology: Understanding Stories of Crime*. New York: New York University Press.

Prisciotta, Alexander W. 1996. *Benevolent Repression: Social Control and the American Reformatory-Prison Movement*. New York: New York University Press.

Prison Culture. 2015. "How the PIC Structures Our World: Resources." http://www.usprisonculture.com/blog/transformative-justice/. Accessed February 20, 2015.

Prison Fellowship International. 2007–8. "RJ City." http://www.rjcity.org/. Accessed February 20, 2015.

Program Administration and Results, Inc. 2009. "Monroe County Justice Complex Master Plan: Executive Summary Project Recommendations, Options and Costs."

Rabuy, Bernadette, and Peter Wagner. 2015. "Screening out Family Time: The For-Profit Video Visitation Industry in Prisons and Jails." Northampton, MA: Prison Policy Initiative.

Rafter, Nicole H. 1990. "The Social Construction of Crime and Crime Control." *Journal of Research in Crime and Delinquency* 27(4):376–89.

"Region Briefs." 1996. *Bloomington Herald-Times*, August 8.

Reiman, Jeffrey, and Paul Leighton. 2009. *The Rich Get Richer and the Poor Get Prison: Ideology, Class, and Criminal Justice*. 9th ed. Boston: Pearson.

Rhodes, Lorna. 2001. "Towards an Anthropology of Prisons." *Annual Review of Anthropology* 30: 65–83.

Richards, Thomas. 1993. *The Imperial Archive: Knowledge and the Fantasy of Empire*. New York: Verso.

Richie, Beth E. 2012. *Arrested Justice: Black Women, Violence and America's Prison Nation*. New York: New York University Press.

———. 2014. "How Anti-Violence Activism Taught Me to Become a Prison Abolitionist." *Feminist Wire*, January 21. http://thefeministwire.com/2014/01/how-anti-violence-activism-taught-me-to-become-a-prison-abolitionist/. Accessed February 23, 2015.

Rigakos, George S., and Richard W. Hadden. 2001. "Crime, Capitalism and the 'Risk Society': Towards the Same Olde Modernity?" *Theoretical Criminology* 5 (1): 61–84.

Right on Crime. 2015. http://www.rightoncrime.com/. Accessed February 20, 2015.

Roberts, David, and Minelle Mahtani. 2010. "Neoliberalizing Race, Racing Neoliberalism: Placing 'Race' in Neoliberal Discourses." *Antipode* 42 (2): 248–57.

Robinson, Gwen. 2008. "Late-Modern Rehabilitation: The Evolution of a Penal Strategy." *Punishment and Society* 10(4): 429–45.

Rodriguez, Dylan. 2001. "The 'Question' of Prison Praxis: Relations of Force, Social Reproduction, Points of Departure." In *The Problems of Resistance*, edited by Steve Martinot and Joy James, 46–68. Amherst, NY: Humanity.

———. 2006a. "(Non)Scenes of Captivity: The Common Sense of Punishment and Death." *Radical History Review* 96:9–32.

———. 2006b. *Forced Passages: Imprisoned Radical Intellectuals and the US Prison Regime*. Minneapolis: University of Minnesota Press.

Rodriguez, Mercedes. 2008. "Biotech Firm to Expand in New, High-Tech Building." *Bloomington Herald-Times*, October 14.

Rose, Nikolas, and Peter Miller. 1992. "Political Power beyond the State: Problematics of Government." *British Journal of Sociology* 43 (2): 173–205.

Rothman, David. 2002. *Conscience and Convenience: The Asylum and Its Alternatives in Progressive America*. New York: Walter de Gruyter.

Rusche, Georg. 1978. "Labor Market and Penal Sanction: Thoughts on the Sociology of Criminal Justice." Translated by Gerda Dinwiddie. *Crime and Social Justice* 10 (fall–winter):2–8.

Said, Edward W. 1979. *Orientalism*. New York: Random House.

Schaffer, Scott. 2004. *Resisting Ethics*. New York: Palgrave Macmillan.

Schenwar, Maya. 2015. "Jail Video Visits Are No Substitute for the Real Thing." Truthout, February 18. http://www.truth-out.org/news/item/29163-jail-video-visits-are-no-substitute-for-the-real-thing. Accessed February 23, 2015.

Scheper-Hughes, Nancy 1992. *Death without Weeping: The Violence of Everyday Life in Brazil*. Berkeley: University of California Press.

———. 1995. "The Primacy of the Ethical: Propositions for a Militant Anthropology." *Current Anthropologist* 36 (3): 409–40.

Schept, Judah. 2014. "(Un)Seeing like a Prison: Counter-Visual Ethnography of the Carceral State." *Theoretical Criminology* 18 (2): 198–223.

———, Tyler Wall, and Avi Brisman. Forthcoming. "Building, Staffing and Insulating: An Architecture of Criminological Complicity in the School-to-Prison Pipeline." *Social Justice*.

Schlosser, Eric. 1998. "The Prison-Industrial Complex." *Atlantic*, December. http://www.theatlantic.com/magazine/archive/1998/12/the-prison-industrial-complex/304669/. Accessed March 20, 2015.

Schwalbe, Michael, et al. 2000. "Generic Processes in the Reproduction of Inequality: An Interactionist Analysis." *Social Forces* 79 (2): 419–52.

Scott, James C. 1985. *Weapons of the Weak: Everyday Forms of Peasant Resistance*. New Haven, CT: Yale University Press.

———. 1990. *Domination and the Arts of Resistance: Hidden Transcripts*. New Haven, CT: Yale University Press.

———. 1998. *Seeing Like a State: How Certain Schemes to Improve the Human Condition Have Failed*. New Haven, CT: Yale University Press.

Shabazz, Rashad. 2010. "Kitchenettes, The Robert Taylor Homes, and the Racial Spatial Order of Chicago: The Carceral Society in an American City." In *Justice et Injustice Spatiales*, edited by Bernard Bret, Philippe Gervay-Lambony, Claire Hancock, and Frédéric Landy, 237–45. Paris: Presses Universitaires de Paris Oeste.

Shaw, Clifford R., and Henry D. McKay. 2011. "Juvenile Delinquency in Urban Areas." In *Criminological Theory: Past to Present: Essential Readings*, edited and selected by Franklin T. Cullen and Robert Agnew, 98–104. 4th ed. New York: Oxford University Press.

Shelden, Randall. 2010. *Our Punitive Society: Race, Class, Gender and Punishment in America*. Long Grove, IL: Waveland.

Simmons, Lizbet. 2009. "End of the Line: Tracing Racial Inequality from School to Prison." *Race/Ethnicity* 2 (2): 215–41.

Simon, Jonathan. 1993. *Poor Discipline: Parole and the Social Control of the Underclass, 1890–1990.* Chicago: University of Chicago Press.

———. 2007. *Governing through Crime: How the War on Crime Transformed American Democracy and Created a Culture of Fear.* New York: Oxford University Press.

———. 2010. "Do These Prisons Make Me Look Fat? Moderating the USA's Consumption of Punishment." *Theoretical Criminology* 14 (3): 257–72.

Sloop, John. 1996. *The Cultural Prison: Discourse, Prisoners, and Prisons.* Tuscaloosa: University of Alabama Press.

Smith, Michael Peter. 2001. *Transnational Urbanism: Locating Globalization.* Malden, MA: Blackwell.

Smith, Neil. 1996. *The New Urban Frontier: Gentrification and the Revanchist City.* New York: Routledge.

———. 2008. *Uneven Development: Nature, Capital and the Production of Space.* 3rd ed. Athens: University of Georgia Press.

Stanley, Eric, and Nat Smith, eds. 2011. *Captive Genders: Trans Embodiment and the Prison Industrial Complex.* Oakland, CA: AK.

Starr, Sonja B. 2014. "Evidence-Based Sentencing and the Scientific Rationalization of Discrimination." *Stanford Law Review* 66 (4): 803–72.

Stein, David. 2014. "Full Employment for the Future." *Lateral* 3. http://lateral.cultural-studiesassociation.org/issue3/theory/stein. Accessed March 18, 2015.

Stewart, Gary. 1998. "Black Codes and Broken Windows: The Legacy of Racial Hegemony in Anti-Gang Civil Injunctions." *Yale Law Journal* 107 (7): 2249–79.

Story, Brett. 2013. "The Prison 'Outside': A Rematerialization of the Prison in the Everyday Life of the Urban 'Million-Dollar Block." Paper presented at the Rethinking Prisons Conference, Nashville, TN, May 3–5.

———, dir. Forthcoming. *The Prison in Twelve Landscapes.* Toronto, ON: Oh Ratface Films.

Stuart, Barry. 2003. "Appendix: Supporting Community Initiatives—Barry's Thoughts on Funding." In Kay Pranis, Barry Stuart, and Mark Wedge, *Peacemaking Circles: From Crime to Community,* 251–55. St. Paul, MN: Living Justice.

Subramanian, Ram, et al. 2015. "Incarceration's Front Door: The Misuse of Jails in America." New York: Vera Institute of Justice.

Sudbury, Julia. ed. 2005. *Global Lockdown: Race, Gender and the Prison-Industrial Complex.* New York: Routledge.

Sullivan, Dennis, and Larry Tifft, eds. 2008. *Handbook of Restorative Justice: A Global Perspective.* New York: Routledge.

Sutherland, Edwin H., and Donald R. Cressey. 2011. "A Theory of Differential Association." In *Criminological Theory: Past to Present: Essential Readings,* edited and selected by Franklin T. Cullen and Robert Agnew, 126–129. 4th ed. New York: Oxford.

Takagi, Paul, and Gregory Shank. 2004. "Critique of Restorative Justice." *Social Justice* 31 (3): 147–63.

Takei, Carl. 2014. "Prisons Are Adopting the Wal-Mart Business Model." *Huffington Post*, September 29. http://www.huffingtonpost.com/carl-takei/prisons-walmart-business-model_b_5900964.html. Accessed February 20, 2015.

Tauri, Juan. 2005. "Indigenous Perspectives and Experience: Maori and the Criminal Justice System." In *Introduction to Criminological Thought*, edited byTrevor Bradley and Reece Walters, 129–45. Auckland, New Zealand: Pearson.

———. 2009. "An Indigenous Commentary on the Standardisation of Restorative Justice." *Indigenous Policy Journal*. https://ipjournal.wordpress.com/2009/12/16/an-indigenous-perspective-on-the-standardisation-of-restorative-justice-in-new-zealand-and-canada/. Accessed February 23, 2015.

———. 2014. "An Indigenous Commentary on the Globalisation of Restorative Justice." *British Journal of Community Justice* 12 (2): 35–55.

Thomas, Jim. 1993. *Doing Critical Ethnography*. Thousand Oaks, CA: Sage.

Thompson, John B. 1984. *Studies in the Theory of Ideology*. Berkeley: University of California Press.

Thousand Kites. n.d. http://thousandkites.org/. Accessed December 18, 2014.

"Torch Lit March through Streets of Bloomington." 2008. *Infoshop News*, June 22. http://www.indybay.org/newsitems/2008/06/23/18510529.php. Accessed February 20, 2015.

Travis, Gregory. 2003a. "The Urban Growth Machine, Part II." *Bloomington Alternative*, February 9.

———. 2003b. "The Urban Growth Machine, Part III." *Bloomington Alternative*, February 16.

———. 2008. "Taking a Different Track." *Bloomington Alternative*, January 27.

Trinder, Liz. 2000. "Introduction: The Context of Evidence-Based Practice." In *Evidence-Based Practice: A Critical Appraisal*, edited by Liz Trinder, 1–16. Malden, MA: Blackwell.

Tyson, Sarah. 2013. "Precarious Safety: Toward Noncarceral Communities." Paper presented at the Rethinking Prisons Conference, Nashville, TN, May 3–5.

———. 2014. "Experiments in Responsibility: Pocket Parks, Radical Anti-Violence Work, and the Social Ontology of Safety." *Radical Philosophy Review* 17 (2): 421–34.

US Census Bureau. n.d. "State & County QuickFacts." http://quickfacts.census.gov/qfd/states. Accessed December 12, 2014.

Valverde, Mariana. 2010 "Comment on Loïc Wacquant's 'Theoretical Coda' to Punishing the Poor." *Theoretical Criminology* 14 (1): 117–20.

Van der Dussen, Kurt. 1998. "New Jail with 'Pod' Design Considered." *Bloomington Herald-Times*, May 9.

———. 2002. "Correctional Facilities Site Purchase Approved." *Bloomington Herald-Times*, March 14.

———. 2003a. "Consultants Propose Jail, Juvenile Facility." *Bloomington Herald-Times*, June 7.

———. 2003b. "Jail Consultant Says Wide Input Vital to Solution." *Bloomington Herald-Times*, June 22.

———. 2003c. "Plans Outlined for Community Corrections Site." *Bloomington Herald-Times*, January 28.

———. 2005. "Secure Detention Costs Key to Decision on Juvenile Facility." *Bloomington Herald-Times*, February 9.

Van Leeuwen, Theo. 2005. *Introducing Social Semiotics*. New York: Routledge.

Viguerie, Richard A. 2013. "A Conservative Case for Prison Reform." *New York Times*, June 9.

Wacquant, Loïc D. 1999. How Penal Common Sense Comes to Europeans: Notes on the Transatlantic Diffusion of Neoliberal Doxa." *European Societies* 1 (3): 319–52.

———. 2001. "Deadly Symbiosis: When Ghetto and Prison Meet and Mesh." *Punishment and Society* 3 (1): 95–133.

———. 2002. "The Curious Eclipse of Prison Ethnography in the Age of Mass Incarceration. *Ethnography* 3 (4):371–97.

———, ed. 2005. *Pierre Bourdieu and Democratic Politics*. Malden, MA: Blackwell.

———. 2009a. *Prisons of Poverty*. Expanded ed. Minneapolis: University of Minnesota Press.

———. 2009b. *Punishing the Poor: The Neoliberal Government of Social Insecurity*. Durham, NC: Duke University Press.

———. 2010. "Crafting the Neoliberal State: Workfare, Prisonfare, and Social Insecurity." *Sociological Forum* 25 (2): 197–220.

Wagner, Peter. 2002. "Importing Constituents: Prisoners and Political Clout in New York." Prison Policy Initiative, May 20. http://www.prisonpolicy.org/importing/importing.html. Accessed March 26, 2015.

Walby, Kevin, and Justin Piché. 2011. "The Polysemy of Punishment Memorialization: Dark Tourism and Ontario's Penal History Museums." *Punishment and Society* 13 (4): 451–72.

Wall, Tyler. 2013. "Unmanning the Police Manhunt: Vertical Security as Pacification." *Socialist Studies* 9 (2): 32–56.

Ward, Geoff. 2009. "The 'Other' Child-Savers: Racial Politics of the Parental State." In Anthony M. Platt, *The Child Savers: The Invention of Delinquency*, with an introduction and critical commentaries compiled by Miroslava Chávez-García, 225–42. Expanded 40th anniversary ed. New Brunswick, NJ: Rutgers University Press.

———. 2012. *The Black Child-Savers: Racial Democracy and Juvenile Justice*. Chicago: University of Chicago Press.

Wehr, Kevin, and Elyshia Aseltine. 2013. *Beyond the Prison Industrial Complex: Crime and Incarceration in the 21st Century*. New York: Routledge.

Welsh-Huggins, Andrew. 1990. "Correction Officials Seek Support for Juvenile Center." *Bloomington Herald-Times*, September 19.

Werth, Brian, 1997. "Thomson Assigns Point Person for Transfer of Plant." *Bloomington Herald-Times*, April 22.

———. 1998a. "Shutdown Cost Non-Thomson Workers Their Jobs as Well." *Bloomington Herald-Times*, March 30.

———. 1998b. "Thomson Loss Part of Economic Shift." *Bloomington Herald-Times,*
January 29.

———. 2001. "New Life for Old Plant." *Bloomington Herald-Times,* March 30.

———. 2004a. "City Enjoys Economic Progress." *Bloomington Herald-Times,* August 6.

———. 2004b. "State and Local Entities Worked on Thomson Site." *Bloomington
Herald-Times,* August 6.

West, Gordon, and Ruth Morris, eds. 2000. *The Case for Penal Abolition.* Toronto, ON:
Canadian Scholars' Press.

Western, Bruce. 2006. *Punishment and Inequality in America.* New York: Russell Sage
Foundation.

———, and Katherine Beckett. 1999. "How Unregulated Is the U.S. Labor Market? The
Penal System as a Labor Market Institution." *American Journal of Sociology* 104 (4):
1030–60.

WFHB. 2010. "Daily Local News." March 31. http://archive.wfhb.org/news/daily-local-
news-march-31–2010. Accessed March 23, 2015.

Wiest, Katherina L., et al. 2007. "Indiana Drug Courts: Monroe County Drug Court
Program Process, Outcome and Cost Evaluation: Final Report." Portland, OR:
Northwest Professional Consortium Research.

Williams, Eric J. 2011. *The Big House in a Small Town: Prisons, Communities, and Eco-
nomics in Rural America.* Santa Barbara, CA: Praeger.

Willrich, Michael. 2003. *City of Courts: Socializing Justice in Progressive Era Chicago.*
New York: Cambridge University Press.

Wilson, James Q., and George L. Kelling. 1982. "Broken Windows: The Police and
Neighborhood Safety." *Atlantic Monthly* 249 (3): 29–38.

Wilson, William Julius. 1997. *When Work Disappears: The World of the New Urban
Poor.* New York: Random House.

Wray, Matt. 2006. *Not Quite White: White Trash and the Boundaries of Whiteness.*
Durham, NC: Duke University Press.

Wright, Erik O. 1973. *The Politics of Punishment: A Critical Analysis of Prisons in
America.* New York: Harper Colophon.

Yates, Peter, dir. 1979. *Breaking Away.* Hollywood, CA: Twentieth Century Fox.

Young, Jock. 2007. *The Vertigo of Late Modernity.* Thousand Oaks, CA: Sage.

———. 2011. *The Criminological Imagination.* Malden, MA: Polity.

Young, Robert J. C. 2001. *Postcolonialism: An Historical Introduction.* Malden, MA:
Blackwell.

Zornick, George. 2014. "Rick Perry at CPAC Panel on Criminal Justice: Shut Prisons
Down. Save that Money." *Nation,* March 7. http://www.thenation.com/blog/178746/
rick-perry-cpac-panel-criminal-justice-shut-prisons-down-save-money. Accessed
March 26, 2015.

ZT [pseud.]. 2006. "The Kreplach Joke." *Divinity Is in the Details* (blog). August 4.
http://divinityisinthedetails.blogspot.com/2006_08_04_archive.html. Accessed
December 19, 2014.

INDEX

abolition: and alternatives to incarceration, 65, 235–238; and carceral habitus, 9, 17, 28, 165, 198; commensurability, 220–222, 231; and Decarcerate Monroe County's identity, 195–196, 213, 227, 232, 274n12; and decarceration, 236–237; geography, 249–251; and global network of resistance, 213–214; and national campaigns, 229–230; neutralization by liberal carceral expansion, 165–166, 177; and scholar activism, 28, 254–255

activist scholarship, 259n21

actuarial justice, 83, 127–129, 134

addiction, 199–200, 248–249; and drug court, 57–60

alternatives to incarceration, 55–62; and carceral expansion, 235–237; and conflict resolution, 238–243; and drug treatment, 246–249; geography of, 249–252; official cooptation of, 176–181

American Civil Liberties Union, 5–6, 176

American Corrections Association, 146

American Jail Association, 146

anarchism: aesthetics of, 232; organizing structure, 223–225; and process, 226–228

antisocial behavior, 77, 92

Baptist Foundation of Arizona, 41–42

Barrett, Allan, 56, 73–74, 76–78, 137–138, 246

Bartholomew County, 101, 110, 141, 154

Begin Again, 71–75, 88, 100, 126; history of, 186–187

"Bike Wheel" organizing model, 223–225, 275n20

Bishop, Helen, 203–204

Bloomington, 2–3; "Bloomington face," 190–191; economic restructuring of, 37–48, 90–91; as exceptional community, 84–85, 113–114; history of jail expansion in, 5–6; methodological decisions regarding, 18–24

Bloomington Alternative, 41

Bloomington Economic Development Corporation, 41–42

Bloomington Flat Tire Brigade, 218–221, 274–275n16; and Decarcerate Monroe County, 218, 221

Bloomington Restorative Practices, 128, 133, 187–189, 239–243

Bourdieu, Pierre, 11–14, 19, 22, 27, 31, 106, 153; on doxa, 197–198, 264n1; and embodied structures, 106; and Foucault's "technicians of behavior," 106; on habitus, 11–12, 71, 185–186; and juvenile justice, 109; on language and power, 121–122, 164–165; on objective structures, 12–13, 109; on perceptions of self, 105–106; on political consciousness, 198; on structuring of dispositions, 264n1

Bourgois, Phillipe, 258–259n18

Breaking Away (film), 90–91

Broken windows policing, 142–144; and economic restructuring, 46

Brown, Michelle, 269n23

Burawoy, Michael, 259n23

ABOUT THE AUTHOR

Judah Schept is Assistant Professor of Justice Studies at Eastern Kentucky University. His work on punishment and the carceral state has been featured in *Radical Criminology, Social Justice,* and *Theoretical Criminology.*

Printed and bound by CPI Group (UK) Ltd, Croydon, CR0 4YY

13/04/2025

14656574-0003